CW00404895

THE WELSH CORGI

POPULAR DOGS' BREED SERIES

THE
WELSH CORGI

CHARLES LISTER-KAYE

and DICKIE ALBIN

POPULAR DOGS
London   Sydney   Auckland   Johannesburg

Popular Dogs Publishing Co. Ltd

An imprint of Random Century Ltd
20 Vauxhall Bridge Road, London SW1V 2SA

Random Century Publishing Group (Australia) Pty Ltd
20 Alfred Street, Milsons Point, Sydney 2061, Australia

Random Century New Zealand Limited
191 Archers Road, PO Box 40–086, Glenfield, Auckland 10

Century Hutchinson Group (SA) Pty Ltd
PO Box 337, Bergvlei 2012, South Africa

First published (as *The Popular Welsh Corgi*) 1954
Revised edition 1956, 1959, 1961, 1965
Revised edition (as *The Welsh Corgi*) 1968
Revised edition 1970, 1974, 1979, 1986, 1990

Copyright © Charles Lister-Kaye 1959, 1961
Revisions copyright © Popular Dogs Publishing Co. Ltd 1965, 1968, 1970,
1974, 1979
Revisions copyright © Dickie Albin 1986, 1990

All rights reserved

Set in Linotron Baskerville by Rowland Phototypesetting Ltd

Printed and bound in Great Britain by
Mackays of Chatham Plc, Chatham, Kent

ISBN 0 09 174485 7

To
Charles *and* Vera
Lister-Kaye

'Nothing like blood, sir,
in hosses, dawgs and men.'
Vanity Fair

REVISER'S NOTES

Charles Lister-Kaye died in August 1965, a few months after the fifth edition of his book, *The Popular Welsh Corgi*, for which he nominated me the reviser, appeared. For that edition Mr Robert Townson, MRCVS, rewrote the chapter on Ailments and First Aid, and some new photographs were included.

For the sixth edition, published as *The Welsh Corgi*, I again made a few minor revisions to the text and brought the appendices up to date. Otherwise the book remained unaltered as the work of a pioneer who, with his wife, contributed over a thirty-year period so much to the development of the breed.

The seventh and eighth editions also required very little revision, the usual updating of appendices and replacement of one or two photographs. However for the ninth edition it was unfortunately necessary to erase our champions from 1946 to 1959. Like so many other facets of our lifestyle today, the old had to make way for the new. Sad but true! Therefore I recommend you, and especially those of you who are keen on keeping records, to retain and cherish your eighth edition of *The Welsh Corgi*. Some newer breeders' names replaced those older breeders who had either died or retired, otherwise the ninth edition remained as it always had been, the 'bible' of the owner and breeder of our beloved companion from Wales.

Between the ninth and this eleventh edition, many changes have occurred. Five years ago Vera Lister-Kaye died and to me was 'willed' this truly dedicated book of *The Welsh Corgi*, both Pembroke and Cardigan. I feel both humble and honoured to be so entrusted.

The main text I have left unaltered, but certain changes I felt should and ought to be made. Some of the practices of the old days no longer ring true and, after consultation with the publishers, I proposed we no longer had a chapter written by a veterinary surgeon. Normally enough copies are printed to allow the book to run on for a year or so, in which time quite a lot of drugs, treatments etc. become obsolete with newer ideas taking their place. I have therefore written a chapter to replace the veterinary one with useful day-to-day suggestions for dog owners and breeders if calamities take place. I in no way advocate d-i-y medicine, but there are various ways in which we can help ourselves and our animals.

I have also replaced some of the very old photographs with more present day ones from both home and overseas. This my seventh revision includes two new pictures – a dog whose achievement was to be the top winning corgi of 1988, and a young bitch I judged in America in 1987, now one of their top winning bitches.

Since my last revision we have a new standard for the Pembroke Welsh Corgi, drawn up by the Kennel Club and providing a standard to which all the Pembroke Clubs in Great Britain must adhere. Also included of course, are the Pembroke and Cardigan champions, up to date at the time of publication.

Charles Lister-Kaye originally dedicated this book to 'His Wife'. As you see, I should like now to dedicate it to Charles and Vera Lister-Kaye, both stalwarts and pioneers of the Pembroke and Cardigan Welsh Corgi. They were two of the kindest and most helpful people any novice such as myself could be fortunate enough to know way back in 'the good old days'.

Dickie Albin
Wiltshire, 1989

CONTENTS

ILLUSTRATIONS

Ch. Finnish, Norwegian and Swedish Hildenmanor Annline Copy
Owned by Mrs A. Sutela

Ch. Mynthurst Carousel of Cellerhof
Owned by Mrs M. Roberts

Ch. Kentwood Fairy Tale
Owned by Mrs E. M. Godden

Sinbad of Wey retrieving a pheasant
Owned by Mrs N. Butler

Two Corgis trained by Mr John Holmes

Between pages 128 and 129

Ch. Gay Dancer of Beecroft
Owned by Mrs Mary Brown

Ch. Hildenmanor Crown Prince
Owned by Mrs D. Albin

Am. Ch. Pennington Gloriand
Owned by Mrs S. Valhaly

Aust. Ch. Dygae Super Spark
Owned by Mrs D. Baillie

Ch. Lees Rhiwelli Blue Ray and puppies
Owned by Miss P. Curties

Ch. Withybrook Caesar
Owned by Mrs A. R. Macdonnell

Ch. Lees Melody and Int. Ch. Lees Symphony
Melody owned by Miss P. L. Curties. Symphony owned by Mrs J. Donald Duncan, USA

Ch. Cordach Golden Plover
Owned by Mrs M. Winsone

Between pages 160 and 161

Typical litter of Pembroke puppies
Bred by Miss E. Gover

Int. Ch. Barngremlin of Braxentra
Owned by Mrs Palmer-Cummings

Ch. Apollinaris Angel Clare
Owned by Mrs V. Higgs

Ch. Lisaye Rebecca of Greenfarm
Owned by Mrs V. Lister-Kaye

Ch. Ringinglow Morys' Treasure
Owned by Miss M. Thomas

Ch. Evancoyd Personality Girl
Owned by Mrs B. J. Thompson

Ch. Hannaford Roy
Owned by Mrs A. E. Abraham

Ch. Olantigh Black Diamond
Owned by Mrs W. Lepper

IN THE TEXT

*The line drawings are by Miss A. J. Arnott
and Miss M. C. McLarty*

CHARLES LISTER-KAYE'S
NOTES TO THE SECOND EDITION

I AM gratified, and not a little suprised, that this book should so soon require a second printing.

This, and the innumerable letters received from Corgi breeders and Corgi lovers from Great Britain to the Antipodes, from which modesty forbids me to quote, have made my labours worth while. To them all I extend my thanks and best wishes.

The opportunity has been taken to repair a few accidental omissions and to bring some of the matter up to date, particularly the treatment of 'Fading' of Puppies.

April 1956

TO THE THIRD EDITION

IT IS satisfactory that I have been able to find very little in the last edition that calls for any radical alteration. At the same time the volume has, I hope, a new look with some fresh photographs and additional matter.

The veterinary chapter has been brought up to date, the use of infra-red lamps fully dealt with, and a list of post-war champions included which should form a useful reference.

C. L.-K.

November 1958

CHAPTER I

EARLY HISTORY

THE origin and early history of the Welsh Corgi is lost in the mists of time; the only thing we can be sure of is that Corgis have existed in south-west Wales for some hundreds of years. It is a common failing with doggy writers to attempt to ascribe breed origins to members of the canine race depicted in drawings on Egyptian tombs. But such efforts are not impressive, for, whatever breed one selects, long or short, prick- or drop-eared, leggy or otherwise, a delineation will be found in some tomb or other which can be seized upon and claimed as the 'father and mother' of the breed under review, which is then credited with a blue-blooded ancestry going back to the days of the Pharaohs, if not earlier. It is not unusual, too, to find allied to such attempts a picture of some peculiar prehistoric animal, with the implication that the origin is involved therewith. Even Mr Clifford Hubbard, one of the most talented and assiduous workers in the field of breed beginnings, is not immune from this temptation. Surely it is better to admit that we know nothing of the Corgi as, and if, it existed a thousand years ago and more? If we can get back a few hundreds we are doing pretty well.

Another difficulty lies in the name 'Corgi' itself, generally agreed to mean 'cur dog', the name, by no means derogatory, applied to a working dog, but claimed by some to mean 'dwarf dog'. I am not convinced that references to 'curres' in Welsh laws of the 10th century AD necessarily denoted the Corgi as we understand it. There is a limitless field for speculation here; to arrive at the truth is another matter and it is better to keep one foot on the ground rather than indulge in flights of fancy. Before going any further it is desirable to state that there are two types of Welsh Corgi – the Pembroke and the Cardigan – which have been recognized as two separate breeds. The differences which distinguish them are fully explained later, but I mention this here as, owing to the Pembroke's (at present) enormously greater numbers, a large proportion of the general public are quite unaware that any other kind exists, and, when they first meet one, ask why he has got a long tail!

The Pembroke was also called 'Ci Sodli', meaning 'to heel', and the Cardigan 'Ci Llathaid', meaning a yard long (the Welsh yard of forty inches). In his books on the breed Mr Hubbard puts forward the theory that the Cardigan belongs to the same group as the Dachshund, the Pembroke being an offshoot formed by crossing with Spitz-type blood, and this latter suggestion receives some support in the points of similarity between the Pembroke and the Swedish Vallhund. But when he flirts with the idea that neolithic man brought the original Corgi 4,500 years ago, then I think it is time to come back to earth! We do at least know that both breeds have occupied a very special place in the pastoral economy of the Welsh counties with which they have had a long and honourable association. On every farm the Corgi was a member of the family, primarily as a herder, driving the cattle to and from the pastures or to market, guarding them against intruders of all sorts, working round and about them, checking the leaders, persuading the sluggards by biting sharply at their heels and avoiding the kick which followed by ducking smartly out of the way, a stratagem which earned for him the description of 'heeler'.

He would accompany the drovers on the long, long trail to the big London markets at Barnet and elsewhere, herding by day and guarding by night. A hard life, calling for stamina, agility and a watchful alertness, qualities in which he excelled and which are inherent in him today. In his spare time he would lie by the door or the kitchen fire, mind the children, guard the house – in fact, do anything except wait at table! A great dog and a great friend. Is it any wonder that he soared into popularity when he eventually emerged from his Welsh fastnesses and made his impact upon the dog-loving public? The Pembroke is now ubiquitous, and the very lovable Cardigan, possessing all of the former's good qualities with the addition of a tail, will undoubtedly follow suit; indeed, there are unmistakable signs and portents that he is already doing so.

The Corgi trait of nipping the heels, so necessary in driving a reluctant steer, was rated a fault when applied to sheep, with whom a biting dog is undesirable. Somewhere about the 1880s farmers in Cardiganshire were having a bad time; many gave up breeding cattle on the hills and took to sheep, for which their favourite 'heeler' was not suitable. This led to crossing with the old Welsh Collie, who was near at hand and who may have been responsible for the blue merles, an attractive colour now well-nigh extinct and extremely difficult to resuscitate, though a few have been reported recently.

The Corgi, Cardigan or Pembroke, is remarkably versatile, as may already have been gathered. A good house dog, a sentry who is always on duty, at the same time he is not averse to a little sport when it comes his way. Ratting and rabbiting are very much in his line, while a number, to my knowledge, have been trained to the gun and have proved excellent gun-dogs. Deprived, as most of them now are, of exercising their natural herding instinct, it is very desirable that they should be given the opportunity, whenever possible, of indulging in sport of all sorts; they will be found equal to almost any occasion. Another field in which they have greatly distinguished themselves is that of Obedience and Working Trials, competing successfully with all breeds in the keenest competition.

The first record of the breed being exhibited was in 1925, though it would appear that they were shown at times before then, often under the description of 'Curs'. In the same year the Welsh Corgi Club was formed, which catered only for the Pembrokes. At its first annual general meeting, held at the Castle Hotel, Haverfordwest, Capt J. H. Howell, MFH, presided, and the Honorary Secretary, Capt. Checkland Williams, reported fifty-nine members already enrolled and a balance in the bank of £5 13s. At this meeting the first official standard for the Pembrokes was evolved, the feet being described as 'like a Collie'; weight 18 to 20 lb; height not exceeding 14 inches at the shoulder. (The Corgi was rather taller in those days.) In 1927 Mrs Victor Higgon, the 'grand old lady' of the breed, alas, no longer with us, judged the breed at Pembroke Dock, the principal winners being Mrs Sid Bowler, Capt. Howell, Capt. Checkland Williams and Mr Merchant Phillips. The Society, which, after several changes in title, is now known as the Cardigan Welsh Corgi Association, was born in 1926, Mr J. J. Jones being its first Chairman and Mrs Partridge the first Honorary Secretary, and is still the only club catering exclusively for the Cardigan Corgi.

Those were early days; the dogs were all shapes and sizes and a complete novelty to the regular showgoers who looked at them askance. When Mrs Higgon took Ted of Sealy to Bath Show, Mr

Walter Glynn gave him first over Caleb, remarking that 'he could
not stand crooked legs either in men or dogs'. Later in the day she
met an all-rounder judge of her acquaintance who said, half
jokingly and half in earnest, 'I don't know that I like being seen
talking to you, leading about that sort of dog.' It reminded her of
the early days of the Sealyham Terrier, when they had a full entry
at Haverfordwest. The great George Raper came down to see this
new breed, which impressed him so little that his only comment
was, 'Drown the lot!' Well, the little Corgi has survived and gone
up to the top among the most popular breeds on the Kennel Club
register.

It must be made clear that at that time the Welsh Corgi was
officially regarded as one breed, divided into two types, Pembroke
and Cardigan. Classes at shows were for 'Welsh Corgis', which
included both types unless they were divided, as I notice was done
at Cruft's in 1927. Adherents of each type competed against each
other, rivalry ran high and competition keen, but a friendly spirit
usually prevailed. Of course the position was very unsatisfactory,
the two types being lumped together in KC registrations, until,
after a long struggle, the two were recognized as separate breeds in
1934. The sorting out was a difficult task, for the two types had
been interbred to some extent, so that there were many Pembrokes containing Cardigan blood and vice versa. For instance,
the noted Cardigan dog, My Rockin Mawer, was sired by Bowhit
Pepper, a Pembroke. However, the separation was duly accomplished, even if some of it was a little rough and ready, and, as a
last resort, in the most difficult cases the owner was invited to say
under which breed he wished the dog to be included. All this is
now in the limbo of the past, and both breeds have been bred pure
long enough for the headaches of that time to cause us no concern
today.

It was only to be expected that a good deal of discussion took
place in those now far-off days as to what a 'show' Corgi should
really look like, and much of this was ventilated in the canine
Press. Mr D. T. Davies, one of the early breed judges, wrote in
1928:

> It must be borne in mind that the Corgi is a working dog,
> must be as hard as nails, with any amount of energy, and must
> be built on strong lines if he is to be capable of undertaking the
> work usually expected of him on the mountainous farms of

Wales. He must be muscular and sturdily built all through. There was a feeling that some of this year's winners were not sufficiently robust, and their size below what is required by the standard of points.

Similar warnings as to size were given when showing was resumed after the Second World War.

Writing in *Our Dogs*, December 1934, the late Mr R. H. Voss, a keen student of the breed, said:

> Although the popularity of the Welsh Corgi has increased by such leaps and bounds during the past two years, yet it must be admitted by the unbiased person, going the rounds of the shows, that there are still many dog lovers, addicted to other breeds, who assert that the Welsh Corgi has a cross-bred and mongrelly appearance. It is the duty of Welsh Corgi breeders, by careful breeding and selection, to so improve both types that such ideas as this, which still have a substratum of truth, shall be knocked on the head once and for all.

It must be said that the Pembroke breeders got off to a very much better start than their Cardigan rivals, and this is shown very clearly in the number of Kennel Club registrations. In 1934, the first year when they were divided, 250 Pembrokes were registered to 59 Cardigans. Three years later the discrepancy had increased to 919 against 96, and the Pembrokes have continued to soar ahead. How is this to be accounted for? I think Mr W. Morgan, writing in the same paper, hit the nail on the head:

> It is the duty of Welsh Corgi breeders to work for the improvement of type by concentrating on an ideal, and by careful breeding and selection. One has to admit that owing to lack of uniformity there has been some ground for the impeachment that Corgis have in the past had a mongrelly appearance. The Pembrokeshires are certainly scoring because they are becoming more uniform and overcoming this objection. Their success and popularity have undoubtedly been due to the energy, enterprise and astuteness of a few enthusiastic breeders who, with a definite goal in view, and with plenty of resources and facilities at their command, have worked assiduously and unitedly on well-defined lines to produce and fix a pleasing type

of Corgi. By the use of two or three well selected stud dogs, that were very similar as regards body and colour, they have certainly succeeded beyond all expectations. A very smart little animal has been evolved which, perhaps owing to the straightness of its legs, has just the suggestion of a terrier about it. I say "evolved" advisedly, for the Pembroke of today – changed and improved in type as compared with the Pembroke of years ago – is the result of careful attention to the breeding.

Turning his attention to the Cardigans, this writer goes on to say:

I feel, like Mr Voss, that the position with regard to Cardigans is not very secure. Although the breeders (who can settle the matter quickly if they are astute enough) are very few, yet they seem so determined that their particular view is correct that it is impossible to foresee who will give way. I cannot understand this stubborn attitude, nor why they do not take a lesson from the experience of the Pembroke breeders, who gave up squabbling about the type years ago and simply got to business – a business which, I guess, they have found very profitable. Frankly, I think that with his pretty "brush" the Cardigan makes a tremendous appeal to the dog lover as a natural dog of very attractive appearance.

It is gratifying to record that the position and future outlook of the Cardigan Corgi is very much better today. Breeders are waking up to the fact that here is a very taking dog, second to none in intelligence and temperament, of a handy size if a shade heavier than the Pembroke, balanced by a fox's shapely brush, with an undoubted appeal to the general public. Many Pembroke breeders are adding the Cardigan to their kennels, others are also taking them up, the scope for breeding operations is being widened, type and quality continually improved. No longer is the 'Cardi' destined to languish in semi-obscurity, and his future is assured.

In theory, and in theory only, the Cardigans are supposed to be born with long tails, the Pembrokes with none. Great stress was at one time laid on getting litters of Pembrokes with no tails, though it happened so rarely as to be an event, and such crossing as took place with the Cardigan made it even more unlikely. Litters contained far more tailed than tail-less, some with half-length appendages, some with just a short stump. The simple remedy was resorted to of docking them at birth. But in July, 1931, the Kennel Club placed a ban on docking Pembrokes – a law which was honoured more in the breach than in the observance and which was rescinded three years later. The position now is that Pembroke puppies are docked if they are born with tails long enough to allow anything to be taken off, and it is unthinkable that the docking ban will ever be reimposed.

CHAPTER II

WELSH CORGIS IN THE SHOW RING

PEMBROKES

CHALLENGE Certificates for Welsh Corgis were first offered at Cardiff in 1928, both types being lumped together. It was not until the Kennel Club Show at the Crystal Palace in 1934, after the two 'types' had been recognized as two 'breeds', with separate classifications, that CCs were offered for each breed. Of course quite a lot of showing was done before then, chiefly by such pillars of the breed as Capt. J. H. Howell, Mrs Victor Higgon, Mr and Mrs Sid Bowler, Mrs F. A. Lewis, Mr Dan James, Messrs D. T. Davies, Symonds, M. A. Phillips, W. R. Morgan, F. Munt, O. Jones, Dai Rees and others. Of the dogs which came to the front in those days one must mention Caleb (sire of Ch. Bowhit Pepper), Shan, dam of Fairmay Fondo, the first dog to win a Challenge Certificate, Ch. Shan Fach and Bonny Gyp. That the early exhibitors had little in the way of pedigrees to help them is shown by the fact that at the three championship shows in 1928 all of the placed exhibits in Limit and Open classes, with the exception of Ch. Bowhit Pepper, were bred from unregistered parents on one or both sides.

In 1929 six pairs of certificates were on offer, the well-known red and white dog Mirador Sensation winning the coveted three to become a champion. He was not, however, outstandingly successful at stud. Mr and Mrs Bowler's Bowhit Bisco, another who scored well, was also a successful brood bitch whose name appears in many pedigrees. The following year saw the entry into the lists of a beautiful sable and white bitch, Ch. Golden Girl, bred by Mr D. Evans and owned by Mr F. Munt of Haverfordwest. She was the dam of Rozavel Golden Eagle, the first Corgi to be acquired by HM King George VI, whose affection for the breed is equalled by that of our greatly loved Queen Elizabeth II.

The early thirties produced a number of Pembroke notabilities, in which we must include Mrs Higgon's Ch. Trier of Sealy, who, mated to Tea Rose of Sealy, sired Chs. Tiffany, Teresa and

Titania. Incidentally, Tea Rose was a lucky buy, for Mrs Higgon dropped across her by chance, paying a Mr Williams of St Davids a pound for her. Mated to Ch. Rozavel Red Dragon, she also produced Am. Ch. Torment of Sealy. Mrs Bowler's Ch. Bowhit Pepper was the outstanding stud force at this time, and it was indeed fortunate that there now appeared another dog, suitable for mating to Pepper bitches, in Ch. Crymmych President. Bred by Mr Oliver Jones, he came into the possession of Miss Thelma Evans (now Mrs Phil Gray) and was responsible for a number of winners, either directly or through his still more famous son, Ch. Rozavel Red Dragon. Mrs Gray answered the description, quoted above, of Mr W. Morgan, in that she knew what she wanted and went all out to get it. The Welsh Corgi was hardly known outside its native counties at that time but the Rozavel expert at once set to work to write its name on the map of England, and there is no doubt that she succeeded. Indeed, those who came after owe much to her pioneer work for the breed. Her enthusiasm inspired others, and I recollect a small band of exhibitors in the Home Counties dashing up to London for an evening show whenever a Corgi class was scheduled, which was not very often, and 'showing the flag' at other shows as opportunity offered. They were happy days, and we were a happy band; now the Pembrokes are so numerous, with many new exhibitors continually coming in, that one hardly knows many of them by sight. Yet the sporting spirit still prevails, and as a Press correspondent I have received many letters from newcomers expressing appreciation of their kindly welcome into the Corgi ranks.

Contemporary with Ch. Crymmych President was Mrs Higgon's Sal o'r Bryn (dam of Ch. Trier of Sealy) who was purchased by Mrs Bruce Fletcher (now Mrs Douglas Redding) to found her 'Wolfox' kennel. Though Mrs Higgon owned the 'Sealys' they were handled in the ring by her daughter Frances, now Mrs Michael Hill, one of the soundest judges of the breed and whom we rejoice to see back again as an exhibitor. Miss Edith Morgan, of the Dingle, Haverfordwest, was another of the old brigade who bred many good Pembrokes, including Vixen and Ch. Cherry Bark. Ch. Clarion of Cwmrhairdr was another dog who did a lot of winning for Capt. Checkland Williams.

We now come to Ch. Rozavel Red Dragon, I suppose the most potent Pembroke stud force the breed has yet known. Bred by Mr Gwyn Jones from Ch. Crymmych President and Felcourt Flame, he passed as a young puppy to Mrs Gray who steered him through a most successful show career. In all he won twelve Challenge Certificates, no mean accomplishment at a time when they were by no means so plentiful as they are now, the first under Mr A. Croxton Smith at the LKA Show at the Crystal Palace in 1934, the last under me at Manchester in 1939. He was a red and white, low to ground, *multum in parvo*, with a wonderful personality and temperament, and a great showman. His bright red coat and foxy appearance were stamped on his progeny and 'Dragon' puppies were easy to pick out. Space does not permit mention of the numerous winners sired by or descended from him; suffice it to say that his impact upon the breed was tremendous and the benefit he conferred incalculable.

The Misses Talmondtt must be included in the early Pembroke exhibitors, their best dog being Ch. Ringbourne Islwyn, bred by Miss E. Morgan. I think two of the best bitches seen in the years preceding the late war were Chs Teresa and Tiffany of Sealy, bred by Mrs Higgon. The former was sold to Mrs Percy Croysdale, the latter to Miss Rosemary Early (now Mrs Donald Lee) who changed her name to Tiffany of Cogges. But on the same high level I would place Mrs Redding's beautiful bitch Ch. Wolfox Garbo. Another who was hitting the high-lights about the same time was Ch. Lisaye Rattle, for whom my wife and I gave a modest 'fiver' at five months old. She was unbeaten at championship shows in this country, subsequently going to Miss E. Loring (now Mrs Davison Power) of the Waseeka kennels in USA, where she soon acquired her International title and was, I believe, the first Corgi to win a Working Group. She came to an untimely end by suffocation in a kennel fire. Mrs Gray wrote of her: 'She is still regarded by many as one of the best bitches of her breed ever seen, and by a few as the best ever. Rattle owned a wonderful straight front, ample bone and body, well-proportioned head and ideal coat and size. She teemed with quality and always showed very well.'

If I were to look for a bitch to compare with Rattle I think I would select Ch. Lyrica Lita, another 'Dragon' from a big bitch with the peculiar name of Crinkle Chestyl, belonging to Mrs M. E. Hutchinson of Carlisle. I well remember her first appearance as a puppy at Birmingham, where I was not the only one who coveted her. I later had the pleasure of awarding her the certificate (her third, if I remember right) at Cheltenham. The last time I saw her was when I judged an open show at Haverfordwest, where she was so heavy in whelp that I asked her handler to take her out! I shall never forget Lyrica Lita.

I wish I could mention all the exhibitors and dogs who held the stage just before World War II, but I am afraid some perforce will be left out: Miss Jessie Fitzwilliams with Chs. Fitzdown Paul and Flash; Mr John Holmes with his brindle and white Nippy of Drumharrow (a great brood and the 'mother' of the Formakin kennels); Mrs Watts-Russell's Ch. Rozavel Actress; Mrs Croysdale's Ch. Aureate of Gays; Miss M. R. Gilbey's Rosario Cymro and Ianto; our own outcross dog, Ch. Bowhit Pompom. Which reminds me: soon after the war started we gave Pompom to a Lancashire ex-police-sergeant living near Horsham. When he had only had him a few days he and his wife went out, leaving him in the kitchen. A dozen miles from home they had a sinking feeling that they had left a box of day-old chicks in the same room, and wondered what scene of carnage would greet them on their return. They need not have worried; they found his lordship lying contentedly with the chicks crawling all over him, one sitting on his head. Moreover, he wanted to know whether they had any right to them before he would surrender his charges. A true Corgi!

But we must get on. Needless to say, Mrs Gray's Rozavel kennel was turning out big winners, such as Ch. R. Scarlet Emperor, Ch. R. Traveller's Joy, and Felcourt Princess. Scarlet Emperor was purchased by Miss E. M. Paton of Renfrewshire, with whom he completed his championship, and was the sire of Traveller's Joy and Miss Early's Ch. Firebird of Cogges. He later, on Miss Paton's marriage, joined the Lisaye kennels. A good Obedience winner himself, he also sired Mrs Kenneth Butler's Sinbad of Wey, TD ex; UD; CD ex. He was a great character, albeit very intolerant of others of his sex; yet he never gave any trouble in Obedience classes. Miss A. G. Biddlecombe's Teekay prefix was also well to the fore with Ch. Teekay's Crawleycrow Hazelnut, bred by Mrs Firbank, but both these kennels scored their greatest triumphs after the war.

The last pre-war championship show was at Harrogate. I hope I shall never see another like it. Had I not promised to take a young dog we had sold to a client I would have stayed at home. I set out from Surrey on the previous day not feeling very hopeful. As I reached Doncaster I saw the news bills 'Germans Bombing Warsaw' and knew the worst, but having got so far decided to go on. I should think three-quarters of the exhibitors or more did not turn up, nor did many judges. The Pembrokes sported two dogs, one bitch and no judge. I went to the Secretary's tent and found Mr Jas. Pye looking a picture of imperturbability and answering 'silly' questions at the rate of several dozen a minute. 'Get yourselves a judge, let me know whom you have got, and carry on,' he said. We managed to get hold of the late Mr George Wallwork, who awarded the Dog Certificate to Stranger Prince of Gays, with Mr W. R. Sampson's Lisaye Rover Reserve Best of Sex; the bitch CC was withheld. I had a Dachshund bitch with me as well, but left before the judging in order to get home before the black-out descended upon us, which I just managed to do. There was no bother about early removals that day!

The Welsh Corgi League celebrated the return to peace conditions by holding a championship show at Buckingham Gate, London, in which they were joined by the Cardigan Welsh Corgi Association – a happy combination which I would like to see in action again. I had the honour of judging both breeds, and, as can be imagined after six years of war, exhibitors turned out in force. A notable dog appeared in Mr J. Holmes's Ch. Formakin Orangeman, who acquired his title in three straight shows, went Best in Show, all breeds, at the Irish KC Ch. Show in Dublin, and was subsequently sold for a big price to go to America. In bitches Miss Biddlecombe held a strong hand, winning Open with Ch. Teekay Foxfire and the CC with Faireyhaze Clever Vixen. The League's second show in the same year was honoured by a visit from Her Majesty the Queen (now HM Queen Elizabeth the Queen Mother) and TRH the Princesses Elizabeth and Margaret Rose. The royal party stayed about two hours and took the keenest interest in everything they saw.

I can mention only a few of the outstanding Pembrokes who have made recent breed history. Of the dogs which cannot be left out are Mrs B. M. Morgan's Ch. Red Pennon of Elsdyle, the Misses Russell and Feeney's Int. Ch. Broom of Ballybentra, Miss Biddlecombe's Ch. Teekay's Felcourt Supremacy, Mr G. L. Mortimer's Ch. Sonec of Rode, Mrs Firbank's Int. Ch. Crawley-crow's Bannow Master Broom (bred in Ireland by Mrs Mervyn Boyse), Mrs Foster's Ch. Knowland Clipper, Miss P. L. Curties's tricolour Ch. Lees Joker and Ch. Lees Symphony (the latter a great loss to this country when he left to grace the Kaydon Kennels of Mrs J. Donald Duncan in USA), Mr & Mrs Lister

Kaye's Ch. Lisaye Disturbance, Mrs Johnson's Ch. Zephyr of Brome and Mrs Thorneycroft's Ch. Maracas Masterpiece.

Two great bitches who gained their titles very soon when showing was resumed after the war were Mrs Gray's Ch. Rozavel Golden Corn and Miss Curties's Ch. Lees Coronet. Miss Biddle-combe had a most successful run with the litter sisters, Chs. Teekay Diadem and Tiara, who were by Supremacy from the wonderful brood bitch, Faireyhaze Empress by Ch. Rozavel Scarlet Emperor. A grand type of bitch who came over from Belfast to gain her title was Dr J. K. L. Pearson's Ch. Ballybentra Daydream. The fickleness of Dame Fortune is illustrated in Ch. Rozavel Rainbow, who was bred by Mrs K. Robinson of Alton. She wanted a dog puppy to fill an order; at the same time Mrs Gray wanted a bitch, so they made an exchange, unseen. When the bitch arrived at the Rozavel kennels Mrs Gray thought her too good to go as a pet and kept her, though her ear carriage at that age was doubtful. Rainbow set the seal on a magnificent show career by winning Best in Show, all breeds, at the City of Birmingham Show in 1950, the first Corgi to gain this honour at a championship show under Kennel Club rules, subsequently being sold to Mrs Andrew Porter of Maryland, USA.

Ch. Lisaye Mariella, a half-sister to Ch. Lisaye Disturbance, cannot be left out of any list of post-war notables. By Ch. Sonec of Rode ex Craythornes Lisaye Good Girl, she has won twelve Challenge Certificates and been nine times Best of Breed at Ch. shows. Miss P. Hewan's Stormerbanks kennel was noted for a nice type of Pembroke, exemplified in the two bitches Ch. S. Dairymaid and Ch. S. Cowbelle. Other well-established kennels are those of Mrs M. Roberts and Mrs M. Banks. Then there are Mrs M. Winsone, Miss S. Taylor, Mrs D. Mason, Mrs M. Parsons, Mrs D. Albin, Mrs P. Gamble, Mrs L. Clarke, Mrs P. Date, Miss J. Fitzwilliams, Mrs M. Johnston, Mr I. Jones and Mr A. Tayler, Mrs W. Lepper, Mr and Mrs S. Magness, and Mrs B. Thompson; all experienced breeders with many successes.

Looking back over the years, there is no gainsaying that the Pembrokes have made great strides. Some of the best dogs in Wales have been acquired by English breeders, and by in-breeding to such as Ch. Crymmych President and Ch. Rozavel Red Dragon the type was improved and to a large extent fixed. While this was going on, the same can hardly be said for the Welsh breeders, and it was not at all unusual to hear references to the so-called 'English' and 'Welsh' types. The Welsh breeders, if they will forgive my saying so, formed far too much of a 'closed shop', mating their bitches to dogs which were resident in that part of the country instead of sending them to the best dogs available, most of which were by now in England. Nor were they willing to buy in fresh blood; having parted with their cream, they made do as best they could. The result was a Pembroke rather short in back, a dead straight front, light bone and by no means always low enough to ground. Fortunately one does not see many of these about today, and even the 'all-rounder' and 'terrier' judges, who once favoured them, now realize that they are not the true and desired type of Pembroke.

The influx of a large number of new breeders after the war cannot be said to have had a beneficial effect on type. The enormous widening of the scope for breeding operations has led many of them, who were not fully aware of the basic principles in breeding livestock, to indiscriminate matings instead of working to a plan of careful line- and in-breeding. Such methods, while throwing up a good one from time to time, are not those best calculated to fix a type which will breed on. However, Pembroke breeders generally have every reason for satisfaction; the breed is in a healthy condition; sales do not flag; exports keep to a high level, with every indication of continuing to do so, and the Pembroke is more firmly established than ever in public popularity.

In Pembrokes we should mention the late Mrs H. Sheldon's Ch. Craythornes Cassia of Cowfold, best of breed at Crufts 1958, and later exported to the USA; Mrs H. Griffith's Ch. Mabinogi Myrddin; Mrs Firbank's three Crawleycrow champions, all from one litter, Chs. Pint, Pineapple and Pincushion; the late Mr M. J. Gray's Ch. Fancy Free of Furstbourne; Miss P. M. Hewan's all-conquering Ch. Stormerbanks Sabreflash; Mrs Montgomerie's Ch. Copshaw Cariad, and Mrs J. Froggatt's Ch. Leonine Sensation.

CARDIGANS

Cardigan Corgi breeders of today owe a debt to the 'old brigade', the band of enthusiasts who blazed the trail in the 1920s – Mr R. W. Jones of Tregaron; Mr J. Jones of Llandarog; Mr Griff Owen of Green Hall, Carmarthen; Mr Dan James of

Llandilo; Mr A. Philips of Carmarthen; Mr D. T. Edwardes; Mr Tom Griffiths of Bronant; Dr J. T. Lloyd; Mrs Partridge; Miss D. F. Wylie of Minsterley, Shropshire; Mr Evan Jones, and no doubt others whose names I have not got. Later there came along Mr and Mrs W. J. Lewis of Fishguard, and Dr F. E. Fox of Brislington, Bristol. To all of these who worked and fought for the Cardigan when the going was indeed hard, both credit and thanks must be given. That there was not quite the co-operation which marked the efforts of their opposite numbers, the Pembroke fanciers, does not matter now; they did their best according to their lights, and Cardigan breeders of today who have taken up the torch are grateful to them, and to their dogs which now lie slumbering under the turf – such famous names as Bob Llwyd, Ch. Golden Arrow, Ch. Brenig Brilliant, Olwen, Tit o'r Bryn, Drudwyn, Ye Brython, Chs. Kicva, Geler Carasser and Glantowy, with many other 'Bussletons' and 'Gelers' from the kennels of Dr Fox and Miss Wylie respectively.

When the Cardigan standard was drawn up it was based on the red and white dog Bob Llwyd, from whom many of the principal winners of those early days are descended. He was bred from unregistered parents, but this did not prevent his having a big influence on the breed. He sired, among others, Mr R. W. Jones's Golden Arrow (the first Cardigan to become a champion), Mr Griff Owen's Ch. Brenig Brilliant, Mr M. Phillips's Tit o'r Bryn and Miss Wylie's Ye Brython; of these Brilliant and Ye Brython had the greatest influence on the breed.

Coming to the championship shows, when Pembrokes and Cardis competed against each other for the Challenge Certificates, we find the former usually getting the upper hand, but at Pwllheli in 1929 Golden Arrow and Nell of Twyn between them kept the Pembrokes out of it, Nell annexing a second CC at Worcester later in the same year. At the four championship shows in 1930 the Pembrokes swept the boards, but in the following year Ch. Golden Arrow (twice), Ch. Brenig Brilliant and Olwen won against hot competition. Drudwyn, Ye Brython and Nell o'Bronant were also conspicuous. My Rockin Mawer, Glantowy, Kicva and Geler Carasser were winning certificates against the Pembrokes in 1933; at Cruft's the next year Glantowy beat Ch. Rozavel Red Dragon for the honour, later acquiring his title at the Kennel Club Show at the Crystal Palace when the two breeds were divided.

Five pairs of CCs were allotted to the Cardigans in 1935, Ch.
My Rockin Mawer, Ch. Geler Carasser, Ch. Kicva and Mr R. W.
Jones's Ch. Red Light scoring well, as did Dr Fox's Bussleton
Mischief and Bussleton Beauty. The year 1936 marked the
appearance of Miss Wylie's black, white and merle dog Geler
Cledwyn, who took the top honours at Cheltenham under Mrs
Bruce Fletcher and repeated the performance at the same show a
year later under me. He was by Geler Coynant, a son of Brenig
Brilliant. Another of Miss Wylie's for whom I had a great
admiration was Geler Coelander, a beautifully turned brindle and
white bitch, going back on her dam's side to Ch. Nell of Twyn.

Mrs Honey's Ch. Dinah of Wilmorton won her first certificate
at Cruft's in 1937; at nearly thirteen years of age she was Reserve
Best of Sex at the CWCA Show held just after the war; a wonderful
laster who never showed her age. Mrs A. R. Macdonell (whose
name, by the way, is accented on the last syllable, not the second
as is frequently done by Cardi folk) took the dog CC at Cardiff in
1939 with Bussleton Chips, bred by Dr Fox. She also acquired
from the same breeder Bussleton Joy and from these two bred, in
1941, the great post-war sire, Ch. Withybrook Brock whose
influence on the breed has been enormous and wholly beneficial.
Naturally enough, and quite rightly, Brock has been used very
extensively, but we are fortunate in having several good-looking
outcross dogs available at stud to prevent too great a saturation,
such as Chs. Marlais Premier and Afonmarlais Prince, the property of Mr J. Williams of Llandebie, and Mr A. J. E Abraham's
Ch. Hannaford Roy. Miss S. H. Godden's beautiful red and
white, Ch. Kentwood Dewin, is another which, though sired by
Brock, introduces other blood on his dam's side. There are also
Mr Oliver Jones's Ginger of Rode and Mrs Honey's Ch. Hannaford Merich, and no doubt there will be more to come.

Like many other breeds, the Cardigans were in pretty low water
at the end of the war. Fortunately they possessed some determined
protagonists: Mrs N. D. Power, Mrs Macdonell, Miss Sonnica
Godden, Mrs B. Lester, Mr J. Williams, Mr Dan James and Mr
E. R. Jenkins. These and others made many sacrifices for the
benefit of the breed, showing their dogs whenever possible,
guaranteeing classes and helping the novice, never losing faith in
the future of their favourites, all without hope or expectation of
immediate reward. They have the satisfaction of knowing that
their efforts have borne fruit and that the healthy position of the

Cardigan today is very largely due to their work and enthusiasm.

In addition to some good dogs, some wonderful brood bitches have played a part in all this, whose names will be writ large in the breed history: Mrs Power's Mari Llwyd Lawen, who produced forty-five puppies without losing one, which have included many winners; Mrs Macdonell's Ch. Teilo Lisa, of Mr Dan James's breeding; Miss Godden's Kentwood Red Petal; Mr and Mrs J. I. Davies's Ch. Hannaford Cora and her daughter, Mrs Lister-Kaye's Ch. Lisaye Rebecca of Greenfarm.

Many breeders have taken up the the fascinating Cardigan in recent years and are breeding on the right lines, including, to mention but a few, the Tonkyns, Miss P. L. Curties, Mr and Mrs S. Bailes, Mr P. Clifton, Miss S. Taylor, Mrs D. Dodd, Mr and Mrs Page, Mrs V. Higgs, Mr and Mrs K. Littlefair and Miss M. Thomas. The breed is in the right hands; sales, both home and export, are good, and wherever the Cardi goes it attracts public interest. Certainly the going is not yet easy for breeders, who have to eliminate two bad faults – gay tails and over-long coats. It is going to take some time to do it and very careful discrimination in breeding operations is called for if they are to correct the one without accentuating the other. It may not infrequently be necessary to use a dog with one fault in order to get some other good point; but to mate two animals with the same fault, or with the same fault behind them, is fatal. I feel sure that both faulty tails and coats will be bred out. When this has been accomplished, and a little more quality and style brought in, the Cardigans will be on top of the world.

Famous Cardigans right at the top included Miss S. H. Godden's Chs Kentwood Cymro, Myfanwy, Nevin and Cydwen; Mr R. T. Eden's Ch. Elkay Mali; Mrs E. M. Roberts's Ch. Gleghornie Blackthorn; Mrs D. Albin's Ch. Hildenmanor Lisaye Rapture; Mrs S. V. Blanchard's Ch. Hildenmanor Oloroso of Veryan; Mr and Mrs J. E. J. Parkinson's Ch. Parmel Cariad; Mr E. R. Hartley's Ch. Edleys Cover Girl, and Mr Arthur Toomer's Ch. Hines of Corfox.

CHAPTER III

MAKING A START

AS I was typing the heading to this Chapter it was borne on me that some well-known breeders and exhibitors never did make a start in the usual sense of the term. They bought a Corgi, perhaps a puppy, as a house pet to which they became very attached. One day some friend came along and remarked, 'That's a nice puppy; why don't you show him?' 'Oh,' was the reply, 'I had never thought of doing so.' The germ of an idea was now planted in the owner's mind. He (more probably she) perhaps hardly realized it at first, but all the time it was growing in his brain; the thought of little Jim going to a real dog show, and of course beating all the 'cracks', kept popping up like a recurring decimal. Jim's owner was now on the slippery slope and it was not very long before Jim was led proudly into the ring at a local show. Did he beat all the 'cracks'? Did he come home loaded with prize cards after receiving the plaudits of the crowd? Not a bit of it; Jim wasn't good enough; but he did not get any blame for that and he remained the happy and spoilt darling of the family, which was all very right and proper.

Jim's owner, however, after recovering from his disappointment at his lowly place in the line-up, found that he had enjoyed himself; he had seen others enjoying themselves, and their dogs having red prize cards placed over their benches. Moreover, he had met and talked to several Corgi exhibitors and found them pleasant; told him, not too brutally, just where Jim failed as a show specimen, and gave him encouragement. He is all afire now to get a good one, and – well, to cut a long story short, he is in the dog game up to his neck.

Sir Jocelyn Lucas in one of his books gave this advice to the would-be exhibitor who finds difficulty in deciding what breed to go in for. Go to a big show, walk round all the rings, then take up the breed which has the nicest lot of exhibitors! Though I read this many years ago, and though I did not actually take the advice, I have been fortunate in this respect in both the breeds in which I have been interested, one of which is the Welsh Corgi (Pembroke and Cardigan), and I would not swop them for any others in the world. Good sportsmanship, good fellowship; that is the order of the day; win if you can by fair means and pull no punches; then, when all is over and the smoke of battle has cleared, winner and loser can be seen making their way to the bar for a friendly drink and a talk. So we go along, enjoying ourselves in the company of fellow breeders and exhibitors, all talking the same language, then going home to the company of our dogs.

In taking up dog breeding there are many considerations to be examined, ways and means to be sized up, much preliminary thought to be expended. Are you living in the country or in a town? Have you to make do with the premises and land you have got, or are you free to go where you like? What scale of operations do you contemplate: just a couple of brood bitches or a dozen or more? Have you the capital to spare for the venture and to keep you going until financial returns begin to come in? Do you expect to make money at it? If you do, you will probably be disappointed. Very few are richer by virtue of their doggy activities; if you can make your kennel pay its way you can consider you are doing pretty well, and it will take you all your time to do that if you have to pay labour. But if you can rub along, then you will get a tremendous lot of interest and enjoyment. You must consider, also, what provision can be made for feeding and care of the dogs when you are away at shows, etc. A responsible person of some sort is needed for this, which can seldom be left to a young, inexperienced girl. All these factors have to be taken into account with many others which will occur to you in your own particular circumstances.

Whether you decide to start where you happen to be living, or to look for a new place, here is a timely word of warning. Make sure, if dogs have not been kennelled there before, that you will not have complaints from the neighbours. In some parts of the country the local council, on representations from householders, will promptly place a ban on your operations. If you are well out in the country, visit any neighbours who may be not more than a few hundred yards away, tell them what you have in mind, assure them that your dogs will be properly controlled and not noisy, and you will probably find that they will have no objection. In other cases it is advisable to enquire of the local authority; with their blessing you will be in a strong position.

We will assume that you are going to start from scratch, with

everything to buy, including the house and land, and that you are
not tied to any circumscribed district. Within a radius of twenty
miles or so of a large town is favourable for selling puppies.
However high-class your stock is you will have many to weed out,
and a handy pet market for their early disposal is an advantage.
Prospective purchasers never mind a run out in the car at the
week-end to see a litter, and one satisfied customer brings others.
You will also want to be within reasonable distance of the main
championship shows, at least a few of them, otherwise your
expenses in travelling will be greatly increased. These shows are
the shop window for pedigree stuff and you will find you cannot do
without them.

How much land will you require? If dogs could talk they would
say they cannot have enough of a good thing, and there is no doubt
that the more room they have, in reason, the better. Suppose you
aim at a kennel of a dozen or so adults; then there will be some
young stock coming along, litters of puppies, perhaps one or two
stud dogs and visiting bitches. If, on top of this, you contemplate
taking a few boarders to bring grist to the mill – and these are
definitely a paying proposition, though they can be a nuisance at
times – then they must be catered for too. An acre is only seventy
yards by seventy, and you will need this for what one might call
the kennel 'compound'; that is, to accommodate the housing, dog
kitchen, isolation block, puppy kennels, in-season bitches, the
hard runs adjoining the kennels, some grass runs for puppies, and
so on. Many breeders manage with this because they have to; but
more land is better – just a few acres for one or two grass paddocks.
In these you can let the dogs have a real gallop round; and what a
lot of good it does them. You can plant some trees in the paddock,
in whose shade the dogs will lie gratefully in the hot weather, and
there you can sit with them sometimes, and smoke your pipe, and
talk to them, and you will all be happy. Wherever you go, do try to
get enough land to include a good paddock.

It will make quite a difference to the comfort of your job, and the
welfare of the dogs, if you have suitable soil. A gravelly or light
loam is the best as it dries up quickly after rain. A cold clay is to be
avoided if possible; during winter the grass runs will be almost
unusable; where the dogs pad up and down the wire will be a
quagmire, and on coming in from exercise they will be plastered
with wet mud, requiring washing, towelling and drying before
they can be put away. If, with a choice in the matter, you veer

towards a property on clay soil, I can only quote Mr Punch's famous advice to those about to marry – Don't!

An approximately southern aspect is obviously desirable, especially in winter when advantage should be taken of all the sunshine possible. But in summer kennels can get uncomfortably hot, calling for some ingenuity in providing shade without depriving them of sunlight at other times of the year. This difficulty can be got over to a large extent by planting deciduous trees in the runs in front of the kennels. These will give shade in summer and, losing their leaves in winter, will admit the sun when most needed. They should not be allowed to get too big; therefore cut them well back when necessary even if you have to spoil their beauty. The chief drawback to trees is that there will be a lot of leaves to sweep up in autumn. In grass runs or paddocks a lime is excellent, being one of the few trees which permit grass to grow under them.

Now as to runs. A hard run attached to each kennel or corridor range I regard as a necessity; how it is to be surfaced is a point on which opinions differ. Many favour concrete, some prefer asphalt or gravel, others bricks. I have never liked concrete; it is very cold and does not dry so quickly after rain as bricks. The latter are expensive nowadays, but it is sometimes possible to get throwouts, such as overburnt bricks, at a fairly reasonable price. Bricks are warm, and dry quickly. They may be a bit rough and less easy to sweep down, and are said to be less hygienic for this reason, but it is a simple matter to wash them down periodically with a strong disinfectant. The best way to lay brick runs is first to take off the turf and level the ground, then apply sand to a depth of several inches. Now lay the bricks carefully, cementing between the joints. An easy way of doing this, though I hardly think it is the best, is to lay the bricks on the sand, then, first making sure they are thoroughly dry, throw dry cement down and brush it all over the surface till all the gaps between the bricks are filled up. Then brush off any surplus and give a good watering from a garden can and rose. I have had quite satisfactory results with this treatment.

Housing

If you own or buy a property embracing some outbuildings, such as stables, an old barn or anything of that sort which can be made use of, these will save you much money in the purchase of kennels. The flooring must be made good if necessary, partitions of wood, asbestos sheeting or other suitable material erected, and possibly some windows put in on the south side. Even with these you are sure to require some bought kennels. There are reliable makers of excellent wooden kennels whose catalogues will provide you with an almost embarrassing choice, but very careful selection is advisable before committing yourself. A kennel must not only be strong, weather-resisting and draught-proof; it must also be convenient and labour-saving to work in; the windows should be capable of being opened without letting in a gale of wind, and it should be possible to let the inmates out into the runs and get them in again, even the recalcitrant ones, without a lot of hard swearing. This applies particularly to the corridor type.

Personally, I favour corridor kennels; they make for rapidity in cleaning out and feeding; you can have a lobby at one end with a table on which to put the feeding-dishes, to put dogs on for grooming or attention in other ways, while in wet weather a lot of work can be done under cover. I had a corridor type built to my own specification by a local man and very satisfactory it has been – except for one or two mistakes on my part. One was to save money by not being sufficiently generous over height; had I realized how many thousand times I should bang my head I would have spent the few extra pounds without any regrets. The most convenient type, in my opinion, has a feeding passage on the north side with a door to each compartment, which should be large enough to take two adults, each having a tea chest to sleep in. The chest is raised off the floor and the front boarded up for six inches to keep the litter in. (Mine have generally shared a bench, but sometimes one will not let the other on; separate boxes are better.) On the south side each compartment has a door, with a built-in pophole, giving access to the run. A separate run to each compartment. Or there can be a pophole only, which can be opened or shut from inside or outside.

A similar type of corridor kennel can be conveniently used for growing puppies; also, if the numbers justify it, for in-season and visiting bitches, these being sited as far away as possible from the male element. An isolation kennel for dogs returning from shows, or 'suspects', is a desirable adjunct, and a few single kennels with runs will frequently be found useful for one purpose or another.

All kennel runs should have strong gates with extra-safe fasteners; an additional hook and staple costs nothing and makes assurance doubly sure. I like a sheet of corrugated iron to provide the first couple of feet or so of the surround, with three feet heavy-gauge wire netting above. This gives five feet in all, which I have found sufficient for all Corgis except real climbers; these, and in-season bitches, require different treatment, using chain-link in place of the netting, and preferably wire netting to cover the whole of the top of the run. One so often takes a chance; but when an unfortunate and avoidable accident occurs one is sorry.

Puppy and whelping kennels are most conveniently placed near home; the nearer the better for one's comfort in going out with the ten o'clock last feed, or nightly visits to a whelping bitch.

The dog kitchen, if not in the house, should be provided with running water, have a cement floor and some means of quickly heating up and boiling food. After putting up for years with an oil heater I bought a Calor gas outfit with a two-ring burner which has proved extremely satisfactory.

BEDDING

I have no doubt there are some people who still use good clean straw, but be particularly careful that straw is not contaminated with rat urine.

Woodwool is another satisfactory and popular bedding. Equally popular now in these modern times is a manufactured bedding, available in various registered names: Vetbed, Snugbed etc. It is easily washable, comes out of the washing machine as good as new, and is wonderfully cosy for tiny puppies.

KENNEL FLOORS

These should be treated to render them impervious to water and urine. Linseed oil, ship's varnish or wood preservative are recommended. We have used the latter, giving two applications on new floors, but dogs should be kept out of them till all danger of fumes has passed. Dry pine sawdust from imported timber is generally preferable to English.

Wooden kennels should be lined with plywood in order to keep them warm and draughtproof, and be raised off the ground on brick piers. (*See* chapter on General Management.) Puppy kennels need a ramp from the popholes or doors, so that the occupants can run up and down instead of jumping. This is extremely important if they are not to shake their shoulders out. Similarly, benches or boxes in which puppies sleep must have a ramp to the floor. To permit young puppies to take a flying leap, with a six-inch drop to the ground, constitutes to my mind one of the silliest crimes a dog breeder can commit.

Hygiene

Dirty dogs in dirty kennels! Not a common sight among pedigree breeders, yet perhaps not so rare as it should be. It is a matter of degree; where these conditions do obtain to any serious extent they are often due more to a lack of observation than to any sinning against the light. No kennel or dog should have a doggy smell; yet one does sometimes come across one. Clean dogs, both internally and externally, should be insisted upon. This satisfactory state of affairs is quite easily ensured by a regular routine, which takes up no appreciable amount of extra time. When cleaning out in the morning, shake up every bed; straw which looks too clean to need attention may be found to be wet underneath. Make sure that no droppings are left covered up in the sawdust; some dogs will do this in a laudable attempt at cat-like cleanliness. Pine disinfectant (which, though not a powerful germ-killer, is excellent for general use in kennels) can be sprayed lightly over the floors and the whole kennel left sweet and clean.

Look over your dogs' coats and skins frequently, and don't forget the (oft-neglected) grooming. Have a set order in which you do all these jobs and you will be surprised how quickly you will get through them. Whether you have an incinerator or just a dump, place it away on its own, if necessary protected by wire netting, and burn whenever you can. Be generous in disinfectant on the runs.

CHAPTER IV

FOUNDING A KENNEL

LEARNING THE BREED

SOMEBODY once said that the best way to learn a breed is to buy a dog of that breed, take it into the ring and show it. There is a good deal of common sense in this; certainly you will quickly learn the imperfections of that particular dog, and you will probably learn more besides which will be useful to you in the future. At least you will discover some things to avoid. I am not necessarily disparaging such a course so long as it is combined with a sense of perspective; that is to say that you do not buy this dog to found your kennel. It may be good enough for that purpose, but more probably not. If not, and you let yourself get so attached to it that you could not possibly sell it, then you will be landed with a 'passenger' at the start; and, as many of us know, it is easy enough to saddle oneself with passengers without going out of one's way to buy them. By the same token, never buy a second-rater if you can avoid it; you can breed plenty of these, and will do so in any case.

Before buying anything, apart from the little excursion mentioned above which you may or may not indulge in, it is most essential that you should acquire the most comprehensive knowledge of the breed that you possibly can. If you happen to have a natural eye for a dog you will get along much quicker; but my advice in approaching the serious task of founding a kennel is to make haste slowly, resist temptation to throw away money before you know what you are at, and, above all, not to imagine yourself pretty knowledgeable while you are really still very much at the novice stage. I have frequently overheard ringside comments, discussing the merits or demerits of exhibits, or criticizing the judge, which have revealed only a profundity of ignorance. It were better to cultivate a sense of humility; when you have been in the game a dozen years or more you will know that you have still not finished learning. Everybody dislikes the 'know-all' type; and there are generally a few of them about.

It may be that you are already 'in dogs', or that you have previously kept another breed or breeds, in which case many of the remarks that follow will not be applicable; in fact, you are already half-way there, for you will only need to add to your knowledge of the general principles the essential points of the breed, Cardigan or Pembroke, which you are taking up, and the various respects in which they differ from your old love. I am assuming, however, for the purposes of this Chapter that you have had no previous experience. How does one start? Well, I suppose the first thing to do is to study the standard; but it is as well not to pay too much attention to it until you have the opportunity of applying the printed word to the living animal. There are no short cuts; and though much is written nowadays about helping the novice, 'judging' classes, lectures and what not (many of them useful enough no doubt), experience ever remains the best, if the hardest, school. We will try to get it without paying too high a price.

If you can manage it, and can afford it (everything comes back to this terrible question of money), I would strongly advise going to a good kennel as a pupil for six months or so. It is far better to pay than to be paid; in the latter case you will be expected to justify your remuneration by doing all the dull work of the kennels at least six days a week; in the former it will be understood that you are there to learn all you can, to go to a show or visit other kennels whenever you want to, to be present at whelpings, matings and the veterinary surgeon's visits. By all means throw yourself into every kennel activity and take the rough with the smooth; that is the way to learn. But do not allow yourself to be exploited as cheap labour; I cannot think of any Welsh Corgi kennel where this would happen – but you never know. Time your stay to begin in the early months of the year if you can, then you will be likely to have the busiest and most interesting spell in front you, for this is usually the time when many puppies are born, the stud dogs are getting plenty of work, and the days are longer. If you don't like the place, or the owner, pack up and try another.

Place an order for one or both of the weekly dog papers; read the breed news, articles on general topics, and the advertisements of forthcoming shows. The latter will tell you when and where the shows are to be held; you should make a point of attending as many as you can, but confine your visits to championship or big open shows where the best specimens of the breed are to be seen, so that you will get the right sort in your eye. Arrive in good time, buy a catalogue and get a ringside seat before judging begins. Now you can try applying the standard to the dog. Don't be despondent if at first you find yourself thoroughly fogged and feel like giving up. Most of the 'experts' whom you see in the ring handling their dogs and carrying off prizes were themselves novices like you when they started and no doubt had the same hopeless feeling. Persevere and you will find yourself beginning to get the hang of it. If the judge puts down what appears to you to be the outstanding exhibit in a class, it is possible that you are both right; for the judge is in a position to see a good deal more than is evident from the ringside and may have spotted a serious fault which does not disclose itself to the spectators. This is one reason why reports written by the judge are usually more reliable than those composed by others. One can report only what one sees – and the judge sees most.

When the judging is over you can go round the benches. You will not see much of the dogs when they are on their benches but you will see some of the exhibitors, and if you show that you are interested in the breed and are keen to learn many of them will be glad to help you. Thus you will pick up sundry bits of knowledge, all of which will be useful to you. If you drop a quiet hint that later on you are likely to be in the market for some foundation stock you may find some of them falling over you, but on the principle of making haste slowly do not commit yourself at this stage to making any purchases. You will need a very much wider look round first, and early impressions do not always turn out to be the best. Do not, however, miss any opportunity, or decline any invitation, to visit other kennels. One can pick up all sorts of tips in other breeders' kennels; there are very few systems of management which are not susceptible of improvement in one way or another, and even the most experienced of us are never too old – and should not be too proud – to learn.

As you go along, and see more and more dogs at the shows and elsewhere, you will begin to discover which dogs and which kennels are doing the winning. A good dog will not win every time, nor will the 'crack' kennels always have a good day, but on balance the best will come to the top. Now is the time to study pedigrees and strains, and begin to form in your mind where you propose to go for your foundation stock. Do not make hasty decisions. A dog which is worthy of the title of champion will assuredly become one; unfortunately there are always a few champions which have got there by lucky or devious routes and which are kept strictly at home when they have gained their title. You cannot be expected to know which these are, but you will find out in due course. This is not to say that only champions, or so-called 'champion-bred' animals, are good enough for you; there will be a number which have never quite managed to reach the heights but which, on their breeding and conformation, may be extremely useful to you, and such should on no account be ignored. Not a few breeders who ought to know better have spoilt any breeding plans they may have made – they have probably not made any – by chasing after the latest champion dog as a mate for their bitches. If he really is the dog for them they should have been able to recognize this fact sooner; if he is not, the conferment of the title does not make him a better dog than he was before. Some people never seem able to make up their minds for themselves; or is it that they lack faith in their own convictions?

WHAT TO BUY

You want to get into a strain or family which has a habit of producing winners, or, to put it in another way, which 'breeds on'. This is not easy as they will be very much in demand and you may have to wait a long time in the queue. (I waited for years in one queue; eventually got a really beautiful bitch puppy, then lost her from hard-pad! Such cruel blows of fate must be taken philosophically; they come to all of us at one time or another.) Moreover, the owner will be loath to part with his best, while he will ask a stiff price, and get it, for any he has to sell. If you were lucky enough to be born a 'John D. Rockefeller' all this does not matter; you can put the money down and buy practically anything you like – except good health. But I am assuming that means are a consideration.

If you can buy a good bitch or two from a winning strain, not necessarily champions, there is no better way of starting. Sometimes older bitches are offered for sale to make room for youngsters coming on, and if you get only one or two litters from them they will be worth buying. Failing this, buy a few bitch puppies. One advantage of buying 'weaners' is that you know pretty well as much as the owner does about how they will turn out. The best of a litter at eight weeks is not always the best at six or twelve months. If the puppy has the breeding you want, with no apparent faults such as bad shoulders or head, she is just as likely to breed something good as her more spectacular sister, and will cost you less money. Half a dozen puppies can usually be got for the price of one good adult bitch, but you must be prepared to sell off a proportion of them at pet prices if they do not turn out as you hoped. On no account whatever buy a dog, whether puppy or adult, which is shy or a bad 'doer'. I have always maintained that a dog which won't eat when given good food, or which will not show when taken into the ring, is only worth shooting. (I have had some like that, but could never afford the treatment here prescribed!) The point I want to emphasize is that temperament is of the greatest importance; anything in the way of shyness, nervousness or lack of a robust appetite should be avoided like the plague. I am well aware that these failings can sometimes be cured; the puppy may be shy for the sole reason that it has never been allowed to see the sights, or has not been sufficiently handled; a poor appetite may be due to some cause which can be removed by suitable treatment. But unless you are sure, it is better to leave them alone. The ideal is a kennel of dogs who will eat what they are given and ask for more; who will go into the ring with assurance but not pugnacity; in a word, who are good mixers, prepared to enjoy themselves wherever they may be. A counsel of perfection? Yes; but well worth striving for.

Buying a Puppy

Selecting a puppy from a litter at eight weeks old is something in the nature of a lottery, but not altogether so. There are various points to look out for, and a *modus operandi* which is greatly to be recommended and which I personally have found fairly successful. It is quite impossible to pick a puppy from a squirming, wriggling mass; make up your mind that you will not attempt to do so and insist on taking your time over the job. Your first glance at the litter will give you an idea as to whether they look healthy, if their coats shine, and if there is quality there. If they answer these questions satisfactorily you may proceed to the next step, which is to sit down with them and let them climb all over you. Ignore them completely and they will soon decide that you are not worth making advances to, and will begin to play about in a natural way, when you will be able to observe individuals standing, sitting, going away and coming towards you. Now pick out those which you are clearly not interested in, one at a time. These will have some fairly obvious faults such as light bone, narrow heads, bad, clumsy movement, flat sides, long legs, or doubtful fronts and feet.

Now you are left with perhaps two or three and can really get down to business. A good puppy at this age should have a substantial body with 'a leg at each corner'; he should be low – but not exaggeratedly low – to ground, and have good bone; but ultra-heavy bone is a fault from which he may grow coarse. He should be a sprightly mover with true action fore and aft, and bold withal, not backing away when you go to pick him up. Turn him on his back to make sure he is wide between the ears, which should be set at the correct angle, neither too long nor too short. See that he is not apple-headed, has the right amount of stop, and is fine enough in fore-face. A puppy which appears a bit thick in the snout will generally fine down; one that is already too fine is likely to remain so. Examine his mouth, with the teeth closed; if the lower front teeth are a fraction behind the upper ones he will be all right when he gets his second set. But if he has a pincer bite now he may grow undershot, which puts him out of court. Avoid an eye which is appreciably lighter than those of his litter mates.

BUYING AN ADULT

I am dealing here only with bitches, for it is with these alone you should be concerned at this stage. Many novices make the mistake of buying a dog as well; they think it would be nice to mate him to their own bitches. Put the idea right out of your head. All the best dogs in the country are available to you at reasonable stud fees, and it will cost you more to keep the dog for twelve months than anything you are likely to spend in fees. Furthermore, you will not be tempted to use your own dog just because he happens to be on the place. There is only one consideration to take into account: that is, choose the dog, no matter where he resides, which you believe to be most suitable to mate to your bitch. The strength of a kennel lies in its bitches. Concentrate your resources on them for the time being; you may breed or acquire a good dog later on.

The bitch you buy need not necessarily be a big winner, provided she is bred right. But do not make the not uncommon mistake of thinking that any faults she has will be rectified in the progeny by the stud dog she will be mated to. I assume you are buying her for a brood, not for show particularly. You can by all means show her if she is good enough, and if you can pick up a few prizes with her, all the better. You will get a lot of satisfaction thereby. The ideal brood bitch should be free from outstanding faults and should pretty well pass muster in all points of the standard as explained in this book. If she has already bred and reared a litter, well and good. But enquire what has happened to them all. Have any been sold to exhibitors? Have they been shown, and with what success? Have they all gone as pets? All these questions are important as the answers may give you some idea of the quality of the puppies she has produced so far. If she is a maiden, ask if she has ever been mated; she may have been once or twice and missed, which is the reason for her being sold, or she may have bred and proved to be a bad mother. Get all the information you can and deal only with reliable and well-known breeders who have reputations to lose. They may charge you a stiff price, but at least you will get a square deal and they will often help you when you have puppies to sell, as they always get more enquiries than they can supply from their own kennels. Like buying a pair of shoes, or a suit of clothes, it generally pays to give a little more money for the best.

As her principal role in life will be to breed, it is desirable that she be strong, robust, healthy and roomy. If, by the standard, she is a little on the big side, I would have no objection to that; I have known many big bitches who have produced plenty of winners and hardly any oversized progeny. On the other hand, I would not recommend a light-weight or one inclined to shelliness, short back, flat sides, light bone, or one lacking the equable temperament and kind eye which are so desirable. You will also enquire when she is next due in season. If she has recently reared a litter it would not be advisable to mate her again next time, which means waiting a year or more before you get any return on your money.

All these things have to be considered. 'The buyer has need of a thousand eyes, the seller of but one.'

Line- and In-breeding

Before buying a bitch you will, as I have suggested, have made up your mind from which strain you want her; or it may be you have given yourself an alternative. Stick to that decision and do not be lured from your chosen path by any specious arguments; you are planning for the future which should ever be in your mind. Let us suppose a well-known dog, Ch. Runnymede. He comes of a winning family, is a big winner himself, and – even more important – is seen to be siring winners. You may have some difficulty in buying a bitch by him; everybody is after them. But some other breeder may have a bitch which has been mated to a son of Runnymede and will sell you a puppy from her. We will christen your bitch Elegance and will mate her to her grandsire; then the pedigree of the resulting litter may read something like this:

	Ch. Rataplan	Ch. Riprap
		Doris
Ch. Runnymede		
	Bangle	Ch. Red Ensign
		Doris
	Ch. Royalist	Ch. Runnymede
		Rosebay
Elegance		
	Emblem	Persimmon
		Evergreen

There is some confusion in these terms, which are not always used in the same way. Some writers regard 'in-breeding' as such a close blood mating as brother to sister, or half-brother to half-sister; 'line-breeding' as the mating of two animals of similar blood lines but less closely related. Others, while agreeing with the above definition of in-breeding, regard line-breeding as unions

Diane Pearce

Ch. Blands Solomon of Bardrigg

Sally Anne Thompson

Ch. Wey Blackmint

Thomas Fall

Ch. Evancoyd Audacious

Thomas Fall

Ch. Kentwood Cymro

Sally Anne Thompson

Ch. Blands Limited Edition of Belroyd

Sally Anne Thompson

Ch. Lees Blue Rose of Bymil

Mabinogi Masquerade (top) and Ch. Mabinogi Maori

Am. Ch. Renefield Rockhopper

of father to daughter or grand-daughter. I take the latter view. It does not matter, so long as we are quite clear as to what we are talking about.

In the example above Elegance has been mated to her grand-sire, to whom her puppies are said to be line-bred; while Runny-mede is himself in-bred, by a half-brother and half-sister mating, to Doris. I call it 'vertical' and 'horizontal' breeding, but the terms are only my own invention as far as I know. Elegance's daughters should be mated to a dog who also carries Runnymede blood; thus you will standardize type. Never go far away from your successful line, but keep going back to it. A violent outcross is liable to throw a spanner into the works, producing all sorts of types and sizes. Nor is there any necessity for it, as a rule.

One frequently hears that too much in-breeding tends to weaken the stock physically and mentally. Yet many animals in the wild state interbreed to an enormous extent without any apparent harm being done. There is the point, however, that in nature the weakest go to the wall; it is a case of the survival of the fittest. To close breeding we must therefore add 'selection', which means that we must be ruthless in our weeding out, retaining for breeding purposes only those which are robust in every way and show no undesirable qualities. We must also be careful never to mate two animals carrying the same fault. If the bitch fails in some particular point, then she should be mated to a dog which excels in that respect; better still if his immediate forbears also excel. Do not try to make extremes meet by mating a short-headed bitch, for instance, to a very long-headed dog, but to one with a correct head and, if possible, with correct heads behind him.

Certain it is that close breeding is absolutely necessary if we are to build up a kennel conforming to type instead of just a collection of Corgis. Type has been described as a 'model of the ideal', and a 'typical dog' as 'a living model of, or approximating to, the ideal set up by the standard of points of the breed'. The differences between different strains constitute variations in type, though all represent in some degree the original idea. A famous breeder and exhibitor, the late Sir Everett Millais, a keen student of breeding problems, affirmed:

A pedigree dog is not only an animal which has a pedigree (for a mongrel may have a pedigree), but which, by his pedigree, shows that he has been in-bred enormously, but without any deterioration in quality. The value of such a pedigree dog lies in the fact that, in comparison with a dog not in-bred, he has the power of impressing on his progeny his own form and external characteristics, which no dog has to such an extent if not bred on these lines.

VITALITY IN THE SIRE

That there can be exceptions to the rule quoted above is shown in the case of the Pembroke dog Ch. Rozavel Red Dragon. He was by Ch. Crymmych President; his dam, Felcourt Flame, was bred from two unregistered parents; so he was by no means in-bred. Moreover, the same union never produced another even remotely approaching his excellence. Yet he proved to be one of the most prepotent sires there has ever been, stamping his type and quality on his progeny to an extent that has not yet been equalled, and doing an immense amount of good for the breed just at a time when it was most wanted. He was an exceptionally virile dog, bursting with vitality even in comparatively old age, always on his toes and ready for anything, while his showmanship was superb.

I seldom think of him but my mind recalls the day when, as a small boy, I was privileged to see St Simon, one of the greatest racehorses and sires of all time. (How excited I was when my father told me we were going to see the great St Simon!) He was an old horse then, well over twenty I should say, living at Welbeck in honourable retirement. The scene as the groom led him out of his box remains photographed in my memory. He seemed to move on electric wires, his head and tail so proudly carried, snorting as he sniffed the air. To my youthful mind the whole atmosphere became charged with the brimming vitality which emanated from him.

Just as St Simon impressed himself on the generations to follow, so did the progeny of Red Dragon 'breed on', and I cannot but think that a dog possessing this wonderful vital force must have a more powerful influence for good than some of the inert creatures one too often sees in the ring today.

CHAPTER V

STANDARDS OF POINTS

THE Kennel Club has now assumed responsibility for the drawing up of standards in all breeds. From now on alterations to the standard can only be made with Kennel Club sanction and the approval of the breed clubs.

Until 1949 the drawing up of the standard of points for a breed was the responsibility of the breed clubs. There was nothing particularly official about it and in some breeds one had the rather anomalous position of different clubs adopting slightly different standards.

Happily in Pembrokes, the breed clubs have always worked together, and our previous standards were drawn up by joint meetings of the then existing clubs, the first one in 1925, by the Welsh Corgi Club; the second by a joint meeting of delegates from the Club and the Welsh Corgi League.

The third standard (detailed on pages 53–6, 64–7) was drawn up and published by the Kennel Club in consultation with the four breed clubs then in existence.

There is now on the drawing board at the Kennel Club a newer standard being considered. To my knowledge all the breed clubs have co-operated and the new standard will be available in 1986.

I therefore suggest that breeders and buyers apply to the Kennel Club for a copy of the revised standards for both Pembroke and Cardigan.

It is a common complaint of novice breeders that the standards are not sufficiently detailed to enable them to appreciate what exactly is meant by such terms as 'medium length', 'fairly long', etc. The answer to this is: it is beyond the wit of man to devise any standard, however detailed and however lengthy, which could forthwith be applied to the living dog without further study. If every measurement possible of the ideal dog were inserted in the standard precisely the same difficulties would arise, and judicial decisions would show no less variation than they do now. Nor would judges invariably agree on the accuracy of the measurements themselves. One cannot judge a dog, or any other animal, with a measuring tape and a pair of callipers.

A study of the standard presupposes some knowledge of the structure of a four-footed animal and the manner in which its limbs should function. I have long been of the opinion that the trouble with many who so enthusiastically take up dog breeding is that they have never kept animals before, or perhaps only a pet dog or two with whose show points, if any, they have never had occasion to concern themselves. Thus they find themselves up against difficulties they had not expected, for which they blame the standard or its creators. To learn a breed for the first time it is necessary to attend shows – and championship shows at that, for here is where the best specimens are likely to be seen, i.e. those conforming most closely to the standard – to make the acquaintance of breeders and exhibitors, to ask questions, and then to ask more questions. The earnest novice seldom fails to get a helpful response from Welsh Corgi folk; indeed, this good fellowship is by no means the smallest attraction of the two breeds, the Pembroke and the Cardigan Corgi.

It has been said that judges are born and not made. That may be, but it is certain that some people appear to have 'an eye' for a dog and will very quickly get the hang of a new breed, whereas others experience considerable difficulty in improving themselves in this respect. A few, judging by the exhibits they bring into the ring after some years at the game, seem that they can never learn. But let not the budding breeders and exhibitors be deterred on this account from taking up this fascinating hobby; even if they can never aspire to judge at Cruft's they will get immense pleasure out of their dogs, and by conducting their operations with common sense, and not being too proud to take the best advice they can get, they will have a lot of fun.

Recruits to the ranks of dog breeders are frequently non-plussed by the varying decisions of different judges. They see a dog awarded a Challenge Certificate, and not unnaturally assume that he is the best dog of all those present. The following week, under another judge, he is placed below several dogs whom he has previously beaten, and they cannot understand why, with the same dogs and the same standard, this should happen. It is perfectly true, in theory at least, that, other things being equal, all the exhibits in the same condition and the same 'form', they should finish up at any rate in pretty nearly the same order. That this does not always happen may be due to a variety of reasons. The first is that judging a living animal is not an exact science like mathematics; the standard of points is a guide with niceties not always interpreted in the same way; this in itself is sufficient to account for 'in and out' judging. Then, again, judges can differ as to the amount of stress to be placed on the various points. Dog A is a bit out at elbow; dog B is well made in shoulder and elbow but falls down on some other point; which will the judge put up? Nobody knows the answer to that question; they know only that he will put up the one which, *in his opinion*, most nearly conforms to the standard. In other words, dogs are not shown with the object of having them placed in their 'correct order', for there is no such thing, but to get the opinion of that particular judge.

There are other reasons for exhibits beating each other. For instance, a dog can vary to an alarming extent in condition and coat from one show to another. He can also give of his best today yet refuse to do so next week. It may be that for some reason or other he is not feeling on top of his form (we all have days like that ourselves), or perhaps something has upset him. With a dozen really good ones in the ring any judge has difficulty in deciding which to leave out, but with a ringful of moderate animals he has an even more unenviable task, for whatever he puts up he cannot feel satisfied. The judge's lot, like the policeman's, is not a happy one!

This is not to say that everything in the garden is lovely; it would be wrong to give that impression or to gloss over the fact that one sees cases of what can be described only as rank bad judging; so bad, indeed, that there can be no two opinions about it in the minds of knowledgeable folk. The best thing to do when we meet it is to forget it as soon as possible, with the mental reservation to stay away the next time that particular judge is officiating.

STANDARD OF POINTS OF THE WELSH CORGI (PEMBROKE)

Reproduced by permission of the Kennel Club – as at 1987

GENERAL APPEARANCE

Low set, strong, sturdily built, alert and active, giving impression of substance and stamina in small space.

CHARACTERISTICS

Bold in outlook, workmanlike.

TEMPERAMENT

Outgoing and friendly, never nervous or aggressive.

HEAD & SKULL

Head foxy in shape and appearance, with alert, intelligent expression, skull fairly wide and flat between ears, moderate amount of stop. Length of foreface to be in proportion to skull 3 to 5. Muzzle slightly tapering. Nose black.

EYES

Well set, round, medium size, brown, blending with colour of coat.

EARS

Pricked, medium sized, slightly rounded. Line drawn from tip of nose through eye should, if extended, pass through, or close to tip of ear.

MOUTH

Jaws strong with perfect, regular and complete scissor bite, i.e. Upper teeth closely overlapping the lower teeth and set square to the jaws.

NECK

Fairly long.

FOREQUARTERS

Lower legs short and as straight as possible, upper arm moulded round chest. Ample bone, carried right down to feet. Elbows fitting closely to sides, neither loose nor tied. Shoulders well laid, and angulated at 90 degrees to the upper arm.

BODY

Medium length, well sprung ribs, not short coupled, slightly tapering, when viewed from above. Level topline. Chest broad and deep, well let down between forelegs.

HINDQUARTERS

Strong and flexible, well angulated stifle. Legs short. Ample bone carried right down to feet. Hocks straight when viewed from behind.

FEET

Oval, toes strong, well arched, and tight, two centre toes slightly advance of two outer, pads strong and well arched. Nails short.

TAIL

Short, preferably natural.

GAIT/MOVEMENT

Free and active, neither loose nor tied. Forelegs move well forward, without too much lift, in unison with thrusting action of hindlegs.

COAT

Medium length, straight with dense undercoat, never soft, wavy or wiry.

COLOUR

Self colours in Red, Sable, Fawn, Black and Tan, with or without white markings on legs, brisket and neck. Some white on head and foreface permissible.

SIZE

Height: approximately 25.4-30.5 cms (10-12 ins) at shoulder. Weight: Dogs 10-12 kgs (22-26 lbs); Bitches 10-11 kgs (20-24 lbs).

FAULTS

Any departure from the foregoing points should be considered a fault and the seriousness with which the fault should be regarded should be in exact proportion to its degree.

NOTE: Male animals should have two apparently normal testicles fully descended into the scrotum.

Let us now attempt to clothe the bare bones of the Pembroke standard with some amplification of the various points in the hope that it may be of assistance to the novice in pursuit of knowledge.

GENERAL APPEARANCE

(Fig. 1.) This clause is an innovation to the original standard, to which, in my opinion, it forms a valuable addition. The first sentence hardly calls for any comment; it gives an admirable description of the first impression a Pembroke should make upon the beholder. The remainder deals with the very important matter of movement, which is dealt with later.

FIG. 1
Correct Pembroke Type

HEAD, SKULL AND EARS

Fig. 2 gives an excellent picture of the correct Pembroke head viewed from the front, the diagonal dotted lines showing the relative positions of tip of nose, eye and tip of ear. The horizontal line emphasizes the wide and flat top of the skull, completing the triangle which the learner should carry in his eye when viewing the head from this angle. In front of the eyes the foreface should be nicely chiselled out to the slightly tapered muzzle; fullness below the eyes gives a very untypical effect.

EYES

(Fig. 2.) 'Medium size' of course conveys nothing to a complete novice, who can learn this point only in practice and from more experienced breeders. But having once got the correct size in his mind he will quickly recognize a too small or too large eye. A small 'button' eye is the worst as it gives a meanness to the expression which the large eye, however objectionable, does not.

FIG. 2
Correct Pembroke head

The word 'hazel' admits of some latitude, ranging from light, through medium, to dark. But the phrase 'blending with colour of coat', which was incorporated in the revised standard, simplifies matters a good deal. An eye that would look light in a black and tan may not cause any misgivings in a light-coloured dog. A black eye is not correct, nor is a really light eye which obviously shows up. A kind, yet alert, expression is a most desirable characteristic in a Welsh Corgi.

Mouth

As has been seen from the standard, the Pembroke's bite must be the scissors type; this is the more common and to my mind is preferable. A badly over- or under-shot mouth amounts to an unforgiveable fault in the show ring. The adult dog has forty-two teeth, which are set out in the table below, the top figures denoting one half of those in the upper jaw, the lower figures one half of those in the lower jaw.

$$\frac{Incisor \quad Canine \quad Premolar \quad Molar}{3 \qquad \quad I \qquad \quad 4 \qquad \quad 3} = 21 \times 2 = 42$$

Fig. 3
Correct Pembroke
front

NECK

Too long a neck is much less common than a too-short one; the latter gives a stuffy appearance and often goes with straight shoulders. The Pembroke should be fairly reachy or rangy in neck, which should be slightly arched in the nape, giving a nice set-on of head and sloping gracefully into the shoulders (Fig. 1).

FOREQUARTERS

Chest oval shaped, broad and deep, giving plenty of depth through the heart. The forearm should conform to the line of the chest; then, from what is commonly called the knee, but is more accurately the wrist, the line of the leg should be vertical, the feet pointing straight to the front or not more than very slightly turned outwards (Fig. 3). A Pembroke with the due width of chest and terrier-straight legs from the elbow down will stand and move wide in front (Fig. 4).

The angulation of the bones of the fore-limb is considered under 'Movement'.

FIG. 4
'Terrier' front – incorrect

BODY

(Fig. 1.) 'Medium length' is not a very positive description, yet it is difficult to see how it could be improved upon. To relate length of body to height at shoulder looks tempting on paper but is not so satisfactory when translated into practice, if only for the reason that no two persons will measure a dog the same length. The late Mr R. H. Voss computed that the length of body of a Pembroke, measured from the centre of the shoulder blade to the set-on of tail, should exceed the height at shoulder by as nearly as possible one-fifth, or 20 per cent. Thus a low-to-ground dog, standing only 10 inches at shoulder, should measure at least 12 inches in length of body. A Cardigan's length should be one-quarter more than the height at shoulder, or 25 per cent.

However, it is generally better to leave out arithmetic in assessing an animal's merits and rely upon the eye. If we take it that we mean longer than a terrier, but not so long as a Dachshund, I think that is about as far as we can go, and a novice should not really have any difficulty in acquiring an eye for the right length, bearing in mind that it is a relative term; a big dog will obviously be longer in actual inches than a small one, provided that both are built in the correct proportions.

'Level top-line' does not mean as flat as a billiard table. There are no straight lines in nature, and in practically any dog there can be detected some slight depression at the shoulders and arch over the loins. The important thing is that the dog should not stand higher at the rump than at the shoulders. Equally, sloping quarters, as in the Alsatian, are a fault.

HINDQUARTERS

Slightly tapering as viewed from above. The pelvic bone should be long and moderately sloping, the thigh bone being set at approximately a right angle to it. When standing correctly the point of the hock should be slightly in rear of the pin bone of the pelvis (Fig. 1). Fig. 5 shows a short pelvis, the thigh bone set at an obtuse angle to it. The formation produces 'straight hocks' and bad angulation which hampers the free-going, smooth action.

Fig. 6 shows the very bad fault of 'sickle hocks'; the pelvic bone is set at too steep a slope, with low set-on of tail. This is a very weak conformation.

Viewed from behind, the hind legs should be set well apart and be exactly vertical, the hocks neither turned inward (cow hocks) nor outward (barrel hocks), and should show no deviation when moving.

FIG. 5
Faulty hind angulation; bad top-line

FEET

The old standard described the Pembroke as 'inclined to be hare-footed'. Unfortunately many read into this that he should have a hare foot, which of course was not intended. The revised wording, which prescribes oval feet, is an improvement; a round, Foxhound foot is wrong.

FIG. 6
Sickle hocks; a very weak conformation

Tail

I don't know why the words 'preferably natural' were retained in
the standard; they have no meaning for the present-day exhibitor.
It is said that tail carriage does not matter, but who has not seen a
Pembroke in the ring with a couple of inches of tail stuck up
proudly, completely spoiling his outline? Tails should be removed
at the first joint to ensure that this cannot happen.

Coat

The coat should be dense and hard, but not wiry, with a good
undercoat. Here, again, personal inspection will be required of the
learner before he can rightly interpret the term 'medium length'.
Similarly, the 'feel' of a correct coat can be recognized only by
handling various dogs; it cannot be learnt from a book. Too short
or too thin a coat is a fault; a long, soft coat is an abomination.

Colour

There is little doubt that the most popular colour at the present
time – fashions can change – is the bright red with white socks. A
sharply, alert, free-moving Pembroke thus arrayed is one of the
most attractive of all dogs, while pet puppies in this garb practically sell themselves. Black and tans are not so easy of disposal,
though helped if they sport some white (particularly on the feet),
when they are known as Tricolors. A deep, chestnut red is a good
colour, but light reds and fawns are not greatly favoured. A sable,
with dark pencilling on a red background, is generally popular.

The above remarks apply, of course, to the 'pet' market; all the
colours specified are equally correct in the show ring, and no judge
should allow himself to be influenced by any personal preferences
in the matter of colour.

Weight and Size

While I have very seldom taken the trouble to weigh a dog –
perhaps I should have done so more frequently – the novice is
recommended to get some idea of what his dogs do in fact weigh
and try to keep his kennel within the limits laid down.

MOVEMENT

There is probably no point in which so many of the breed fail as in movement; one hears the same tale in many other breeds, if it comes to that. Nor, I believe, is there any point on which so many judges fall down. It is a surprising thing that so little progress has been made during the last twenty years in improving movement; the breeders cannot congratulate themselves on their efforts in this direction. It is true that they have frequently had no guidance from the judges; too often we have seen two dogs run down for a final decision, the worse mover of the two put up, then reported as a good mover.

Perhaps the first requisite in a good mover is the ability to stride out freely in front, and this depends primarily on the angle of the shoulder blade, which should slope well in a backward direction, the upper arm being set approximately at right angles to it (Fig. 1). Now the articulation of these two bones enables the upper arm to widen this angle to a limited degree; it stands to reason, therefore, that if the shoulder blade is set more uprightly, making already a wider angle with the upper arm (Fig. 7), then the latter is

FIG. 7
Too straight shoulder

allowed less play, giving the dog a shorter stride; and we want a long, low, easy stride by which he can cover the ground in smooth, effortless fashion. A very straight shoulder is liable to throw the elbows out and to cause the forelegs to knuckle over.

How do we recognize a straight-shouldered dog? By having him run past us we can see whether he has a long, easy stride or a short, 'proppy' one. If he is standing: with the hand, palm downwards, find the seat of the withers – the point at which the shoulder blades nearly meet at the top. Now place the hand directly behind the withers; this is the place where the saddle sits on a horse. If he has a good, sloping shoulder there will be plenty of room between the hand and the dog's neck; what the horseman calls 'plenty of room in front of you', or a 'good long rein'. The rider finds himself sitting well back, and not, as with a straight-shouldered horse, sitting 'on the neck'.

The two forelegs should move in parallel planes, like the piston rods of a locomotive; any deviation from this, such as plaiting (the leading leg crossing the line of the other) or dishing (flinging the feet outwards), is a fault. Hind movement should be similarly true and free. If the angulation is correct, as in Fig. 1, then the dog will flex his hocks and will get them well under him when galloping, the whole construction enabling him to give a powerful thrust from the muscular second thighs, which, combined with the free-striding forelimbs, gives that liberty of action which makes for easy travel.

Standard of Points of the Welsh Corgi (Cardigan) 1978

Reproduced by permission of the Kennel Club

January 1978

Characteristics

Alert, active and intelligent, with steady temperament.

General Appearance

Sturdy, mobile and capable of endurance. Overall silhouette long in proportion to height, terminating in a fox-like brush, set in line with the body. Alert expression.

Head and Skull

Head foxy in shape and appearance, skull wide and flat between the ears tapering towards the eyes above which it should be slightly domed. Moderate amount of stop. Length of foreface in proportion to skull as 3 is to 5, tapering moderately towards the nose, which should be black, slightly projecting and in no sense blunt. Underjaw clean cut, strong but without prominence.

Eyes

Medium size, clear, giving a kindly alert but watchful expression. Rather widely set with corners clearly defined. Eyes preferably dark, or to blend with the coat, rims dark. One or both eyes pale blue, blue or blue flecked, permissible only in blue merles.

Ears

Erect, proportionately rather large to the size of the dog. Tips slightly rounded, moderately wide at the base and set about 9 cm (3½ inches) apart. Carried so that the tips are slightly wide of a straight line drawn from the tip of the nose through the centre of the eyes. Set well back so that they can be laid flat along the neck.

Mouth

Teeth strong, with a perfect, regular and complete scissor bite, i.e. the upper teeth closely overlapping the lower teeth and set square to the jaw. Pincer bite permissible. The teeth should be evenly arranged and not crowded in relation one to another.

Neck

Muscular, well developed and in proportion to the dog's build, fitting into well sloped shoulders.

Forequarters

Shoulders well laid and angulated at approximately 90 degrees to the upper arm; muscular, elbows close to sides. Strong bone carried down to feet. Legs short but body well clear of the ground, forearms slightly bowed to mould round the chest, feet turned only slightly outwards.

BODY

Chest moderately broad with prominent breastbone. Body fairly long and strong with deep brisket, well sprung ribs and clearly defined waist. Topline level.

HINDQUARTERS

Strong, well angulated and aligned with muscular thighs and second thighs, strong bone carried down to the feet, legs short; when standing hocks should be vertical viewed from the side and rear.

FEET

Round, tight, rather large and well padded. All dewclaws should be removed.

GAIT

Free and active, elbows fitting closely to sides, neither loose nor tied. Forelegs should reach well forward without too much lift, in unison with thrusting action of hindlegs.

TAIL

Like a fox's brush set in line with the body and moderately long (to touch or nearly touch the ground). Carried low when standing but may be lifted little above the body when moving, but not curled over the back.

COAT

Short or medium of hard texture. Weatherproof with good under-coat. Preferably straight.

COLOUR

Any colour, with or without white markings, but white should not predominate.

WEIGHT AND SIZE

Height as near as possible 30 cm (12 inches) at the shoulder. Weight in proportion to size with overall balance as prime consideration.

FAULTS

Any departure from the foregoing points should be considered a fault and the seriousness with which the fault is regarded should be in exact proportion to its degree.

NOTE

Male animals should have two apparently normal testicles fully descended into the scrotum.

FIG. 8
Correct Cardigan type

In very many respects the comments I have made on the Pembroke standard are equally applicable to the Cardigan and it is not necessary to repeat them here. I will therefore ask my Cardigan readers kindly to refer back, and will content myself with reporting and emphasizing those points in which the two breeds differ.

A Cardigan is not a Pembroke with a long tail. It should be unnecessary to mention this but for the fact that judges have been known to put up exhibits answering this description, wherein they have been very, very wrong. The differences between the two are plain for all to see; any tendency to merge the types would be hotly and rightly resented by the devotees of either breed. The Cardigan Corgi (Fig. 8) is a longer, heavier dog than the Pembroke, with larger and more rounded ears, heavier bone and having a distinct crook to the forelegs. But there are other distinctions, as will appear.

HEAD AND SKULL

While the skull and foreface proportions (5 to 3) are similar to the Pembroke, it is generally agreed that the Cardigan should be rather less fine in foreface, though retaining a foxy appearance.

MOUTH

If the standard admits both pincer and scissor bites, it does not make it clear. I would not fault a pincer bite, though I prefer the other, which I should say predominates in the breed.

FOREQUARTERS

The slightly bowed front, with distinct crook, is an essential characteristic of the Cardigan Corgi which breeders should never forsake and which does not imply unsoundness in any way. The elbows should lie close to the sides, below properly angulated shoulders and upper arm as in the Pembroke, the lower arm conforming to the wall of the chest, the large, round and well-padded feet being turned slightly outwards (Fig. 9).

FIG. 9
Correct Cardigan front

TAIL

A very important item which can completely mar the dog's appearance. It should be set in line with the body and have a low, graceful carriage. Though most long-tailed breeds will cock their sterns up when excited, the Cardigan's tail should not ordinarily be carried above the line of the back. In this connection the set-on of the tail is involved, a high-set tail being much more likely to result in faulty carriage than a correctly set one. When the dog is standing the tail should sweep downwards as shown in Fig. 8, which, I think, indicates a tail of 'moderate length', and a typical fox brush.

A 'whip' tail is bad, as is a 'flag' tail like that of a long-haired Dachshund; the latter usually goes with too full a coat.

COAT

The coat is described as 'short or medium', as against the 'medium' of the Pembroke. One may read into this that the

Cardigan's coat should be somewhat shorter than the Pembroke's, albeit not so short as a Bull Terrier's. Like the Pembroke's, it should be dense and weather-resisting. Over-long coats are frequently accompanied by fluffiness at the base of the ears, and there are too many of them in the breed. But we cannot do everything at once, and some breeders are putting up with them for the time being while they fix the correct tail carriage, a policy which I, for one, would not quarrel with. Both these faults – long coats and gay tails – will be bred out, but it cannot be done in a day.

COLOUR

The Cardigan appears in some beautiful colours, but none of them is even mentioned in the standard. Black and white, red, red and white, brindle, brindle and white, tri-colour and the attractive blue merle – all of these are favoured.

The Blue Merle Cardigan Welsh Corgi, once rare almost to extinction, is no longer so. Mr Jones of Taxicar prefix bred a blue merle dog Samswn Bach from a tri-colour bitch to a wall-eyed red dog. Samswn Bach was not an especially good Cardi, being rather on the leg and small and pointed in ear. To offset this he had a perfect coat and a good-shaped, triangular head. He was the first blue merle to be shown in this country since Miss Wylie's Ch. Geler Caressa and Ch. Geler Cledwyn. After several attempts on the part of Mrs Gray she finally produced a well-marked dog, Rozavel Blue at Last, from which all present-day merles in this country have come. And to Mrs Gray goes the distinction of having bred the first post-war Blue Merle Champion, Rozavel Blue Rosette.

BODY

Please refer to my comments under Pembroke regarding length of body.

MOVEMENT

On this subject I have nothing to add to my remarks under Pembrokes. Precisely the same considerations apply, so I will refer my Cardigan readers thereto, adding the (I hope) unnecessary exhortation never to forget that a working dog is useless if he cannot move. I have experienced few greater pleasures than watching a well-constructed Cardigan moving at speed, using fore- and hind-limbs to the fullest extent, the brush flying out behind level with the back, the whole *ensemble* giving an impression of smooth, machine-like precision. It is a beautiful sight and I wish I had a dozen of them to look at every day.

CHAPTER VI

THE WHELPING BITCH

I SUPPOSE nothing causes more apprehension in the mind of the novice breeder than his first whelping case. It is a very natural anxiety, for he is undertaking something which he has never done, and probably never seen, before. The advice which he may have received from doggy friends will vary from assurances that there is nothing whatever to worry about, to predictions of possible calamities which will throw him into the depths of gloom. I have read discourses on the subject, reciting all the difficulties which can possibly crop up, calculated to frighten the novice away from dog breeding for good and all! There is no need to be unduly alarmed; bad whelpings can and do happen, but they are not the rule, less so in some breeds than others. Both the Cardigan and Pembroke Corgi are usually easy whelpers, requiring no assistance beyond common-sense supervision and precautions, and wanting, more than anything, not to be fussed. If you have an experienced friend nearby, he or she will gladly give you assistance, while the mere fact that they are within call will take a deal of weight off your mind. Failing this, it is recommended that you contact your veterinary surgeon and warn him that you may require his services.

The average period of gestation is sixty-three days, but parturition frequently takes place several days earlier. If the bitch goes two days over her time, let the VS examine her. With a large litter an early whelping is a blessing; the pups will be smaller, making for an easier time, and they will by now have become a burden on the dam from which she will be glad to be relieved.

The first symptoms you will notice, if the bitch is in whelp, is that her teats will stand out more prominently; at six weeks she will look more rotund, especially after a meal, and she will be less inclined to dash about. A maiden bitch is generally more difficult to diagnose than one which has had a litter or two. My advice is: don't worry. Some breeders have an uncontrollable desire to find out whether a bitch is in whelp, and how many puppies she has on board, at the earliest possible moment. As nothing they can do will alter the situation, and it is a matter in which the cleverest veterinary practitioners are frequently proved wrong, it would seem to me that she is best left alone. If you really want to know the truth, have her X-rayed, which will disclose not only the number of pups but also how they are lying. In the case of a valuable bitch there is much to be said for this practice, which is becoming increasingly common. The picture may cause your VS to recommend a caesarian operation and thereby save a lot of trouble. If, on the other hand, it indicates a perfectly normal whelping, so much the better and you will feel happier in your mind. This is not to say that I recommend an X-ray every time; in my own kennels I have never had recourse to it; there may have been one or two occasions when it might have been of advantage, but I am not sure about that. Caesarian section is a straightforward operation which is seldom attended by any untoward results.

If you have a room to spare in the house, or an outhouse adjoining, this is probably the most satisfactory place for the whelping bitch. Here you can give her more frequent supervision without having to trail out to a kennel, perhaps on a cold winter's night. It is absolutely essential that it be quiet and not subject to interruptions from other dogs or humans. The temperature of the room must be capable of control and a thermometer should be hung low down on the wall. In cold weather some heat must be given to bring the temperature to that of a fairly warm living-room.

The bitch must be provided with a box or bench in which to give birth to and nurse her litter. A suitable box for a Pembroke is illustrated in Fig. 10. It is 30 inches square, three of the sides being 14 inches high, and having a rail fixed at a height of three inches from the floor, with a two-inch space between the rail and the side. This prevents a clumsy mother accidentally overlying a puppy or crushing it against the wall. The fourth side has a flap, five inches high, hinged to the floor and falling outwards. This can be kept closed at first, being lowered later when the pups are old enough to come out. An additional removable board, five inches deep and sliding into grooves, can be inserted on top of the flap. The whole front should be open till whelping takes place, when the flap should be closed. The top board is slid into place later, and prevents the bitch, when jumping out of the box, carrying a puppy with her on a teat. This happens sometimes, but the jump causes the puppy to release its hold. For a big, roomy Cardigan, the floor

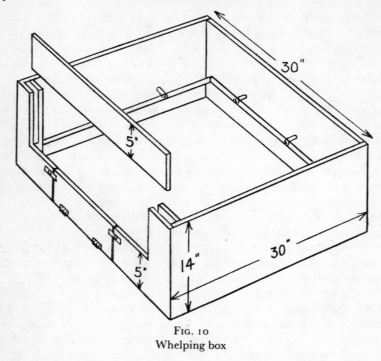

FIG. 10
Whelping box

area can be given slightly more ample dimensions, allowing sufficient room for her to stretch out comfortably.

I like to introduce my in-whelp bitch to the whelping box and its situation about a week before she is due to produce her puppies. The kind of bedding to be used is often a personal choice. In the initial period of 'waiting' I use layers and layers of newspapers, on top of which I give my bitch a blanket for her comfort. When she shows signs of starting to whelp I remove the blanket and leave her on the newspapers. These I find are an excellent medium on which to whelp a litter. They are absorbent, can be replaced easily as the whelps are produced and then, when all is finished, can be completely removed and the bitch given fresh bedding of blankets for the underneath warmth she and her babies require.

Today modern science has given us a synthetic material known, among other things, as Vetbed or Snug Bed, which is quite incredible. I know many breeders who whelp their bitches on Vetbed and its like. It is easily washable, dries rapidly and gives the puppies a soft surface beneath them which helps them to get a foothold to 'mum'. It is advertised as being 'soft as down, warm as wool and tough as leather'.

Later on, when the puppies are up on their feet and becoming active, they can be put on woodwool which, when soiled, can be replaced with fresh bedding and the dirty bedding burned.

Now your bitch is getting ready for what you hope will be a normal whelping, and you must have to hand everything you are likely to require. If we listen to some of the experts, this means half a chemist's shop, but I am going to suggest that the following are all that is necessary:

Cotton wool; a pair of sharp scissors; a few pieces of soft cloth or towel; a solution of Dettol; some brandy; a box containing a soft blanket and a covered hot-water bottle, large enough to take three or four newly born pups; and a small bucket half full of strong disinfectant; to which I might add a comfortable chair – but not so comfortable that you will go to sleep in it – in which you can sit and read the paper if you have to stay with her for some time, as you probably will.

Bitches vary greatly in their behaviour immediately prior to whelping. Some take it almost as a matter of course, though this is seldom the case with the first litter, whereas others will make rather heavy weather of it. The most common mistake made by novice breeders is to be impatient, mistakenly expecting that something has gone wrong or is about to do. A maiden bitch will often exhibit restlessness as much as twelve to twenty-four hours in advance. As the time approaches she will become very uneasy and show great activity in the nest, continually pushing the bedding about, sitting up, lying down, and curling round in circles. At intervals she will appear to settle down and will lie quite peacefully for a time. She will pant, turn her head round towards her hinder parts, and lick herself. There will be a mucous discharge from the vulva.

It is not generally known that there will be a rapid and steep fall in temperature (below 100 degrees) a few hours before labour pains begin. When the pains start they may quickly result in the birth of a puppy; if not, there may be a delay of an hour or more. Do not worry her or interfere in any way at this stage. In the case of a young bitch you can help her best just by being present, the sound of your voice being a comfort to her. Each foetus is enclosed in a membranous envelope which is likely to be the first sign that a puppy is about to be born.

In the normal course of events, the puppy having been ejected from the vagina, the dam will tear open the bag with her teeth and sever the umbilical cord by which the body is attached to the placenta, or afterbirth. If she does not, it must be done for her. Tear the membranes away from the puppy's head quickly (it cannot breathe till this is done), passing the little finger into the mouth to ensure all is clear; then cut the cord about an inch from the puppy. It is commonly recommended first to tie the cord tightly with surgical thread, then cut it on the side away from the puppy. I can only say that I have never done it and have never had any ill results from the omission. The afterbirth is removed and dropped into the disinfectant. It is advised by some that the bitch be allowed to eat the afterbirth, which she would do in a state of nature. Personally, I am against it, in which opinion I am fortified by some good veterinary advice.

I have assumed that the first puppy has arrived in good time. If it has not, and the bitch seems to be exhausting herself by continued straining, expert assistance should be called in without delay. The normal presentation of the foetus is with the head lying between the forelegs. If the head appears, but gets no further, take a piece of cloth, grasp the head and exert a very steady downward pull in time with the bitch's straining; the rest should follow without difficulty.

If a puppy comes in what is called a 'Breach' presentation, that is, hindlegs first, it must be dealt with promptly; if allowed to remain in the passage it will die. As soon as you can grasp the feet, exert a downward pull as described above. A long continued straining without result may indicate a bad presentation, the puppy being sideways on, or both forelegs being back instead of coming with the head, or the head being bent back, so that parturition is impossible without manipulation. For the inexperienced breeder these are cases for the veterinary surgeon, who may have to use instruments to deliver it dead or alive. A bitch who sits about a lot, instead of getting on with the job, may have a dead puppy.

After the birth of two or three pups the bitch will be glad of a drink of warm milk and glucose. If very exhausted, give her a small teaspoonful of brandy in a dessertspoonful of warm water and a little glucose. Spirits should not be given with milk, and all drinks should be warm. As each pup is born the dam will clean it thoroughly, pushing it about with her nose, and it will very soon make its way to a teat. If she is having a large litter, or is inclined to be clumsy, it is often wise to make use of the box and hot-water bottle, slipping one or two pups away from her for a time; but one must use discretion about this, as it may worry her and do more harm than good. If she knows you well and trusts you, she will generally raise no objection; but you must watch her reactions and give her one or more back if she gets worried.

A puppy which has had a rough passage into the world may appear lifeless at first; but do not accept defeat too readily; it can often be resuscitated in a surprising manner. Open its mouth and blow vigorously into it three or four times. Take it in your two hands in a rough towel and jostle it about briskly. Now, still holding it in the hands, head downmost, jerk it sharply towards the floor several times. As a last resort put a drop of brandy on the tongue. If and when life appears, place the pup in a the box along with the hot-water bottle. When thoroughly dried and warmed it can be given to its mother. Remember that warmth is the most important factor. When the whelping is all over, the bitch will lie comfortably with her puppies; but before she settles down give her another warm drink, then take her out on a lead for a few minutes to relieve herself. Before putting her back you must do some tidying up; remove all wet and soiled bedding, giving her and her puppies a fresh, warm bed on which to settle down.

Docking and Removal of Dewclaws

At three days old the pups should have all their dewclaws removed, Pembroke tails being docked at the same time. Though I would recommend the novice to see these operations done once before undertaking them himself, they are both very simple.

The dewclaws are easily dealt with by means of a strong pair of curved nail scissors. With someone to hold the puppy for you, place the open scissors with a blade on each side of, and close up to, the claw. Then, while exerting a strong downward pressure of the scissors against the limb, snip the claw smartly off. Make the cut firmly and quickly. Staunch the bleeding with a piece of cotton wool soaked in Friar's Balsam (or dry permanganate of potash can be applied). Very occasionally a claw will continue to bleed for some time and must have further attention. Take another piece of cotton wool, soak it well with the balsam, and hold it on the wound. On no account dab it, nor remove it to see how it is getting on; keep the wool firmly pressed on, now and then pouring a little more on it. If these instructions are followed there need be no fear of any dire consequences.

Nearly all Pembroke kennels have now adopted the rubber-band method of docking. It would probably be incorrect to say that the Corgi people introduced it, but it is certainly true that many owners of other breeds, and not a few veterinary surgeons, have taken their cue from the Corgis and substituted the rubber band for the knife or shears. It is clean, effective and causes less discomfort to the puppy and less distraction to the bitch.

The ideal time in my opinion is when the puppies are 24 to 36 hours old. The bands should be strong and natural coloured (NOT coloured bands). I use bands one sixteenth of an inch wide. Cut the band to open the circle. A helper is useful to hold the puppy, back up and rear end facing operator. The helper holds the tail upright while the operator places the middle of the rubber band just exactly above the lip of the rectum and brings the ends firmly around each side of the tail over the back. The helper lowers the tail firmly to hold band in place. The operator then makes the first knot, but before tying the knot make sure the band is pulled tightly. The second knot is then made and the ends cut off to about a quarter of an inch. Always check your band hasn't slipped and the lip of the rectum is clear away from the rubber band. Nothing further is required and the tails shrivel and drop off within three to five days.

There are only two points to watch. One is that the tail sometimes comes off with the band, or it may be hanging by a small piece of dried skin; a snip with the scissors will put this right. The other point is that there may be a slight amount of suppuration which in hot weather will attract flies. Though it rarely happens, keep a look-out for this and dab on a little Dettol.

In surgical docking the skin of the tail should be drawn backwards towards the body and a firm cut made with the knife or docking shears; the skin will then cover the wound. Styptics should be applied as for dewclaws. I have found it easier to get a really short dock with the rubber band than by the other method.

The use of infra-red lamps has now become widespread and by all accounts they have proved very satisfactory. There is nothing forcing about this form of heating; its great advantage over others lies in the fact that it directs the heat where it is wanted instead of dissipating it in the air near the ceiling, as is the case with the conventional methods. The dull-emitter type is recommended, with a small pilot light and a metal shade; this does not give a bright light. The lamp is suspended above the whelping or puppy box, the intensity of heat being regulated by lowering or raising it as required.

The makers will give the best height to start with, but a good guide is to be able to feel a gentle heat on the back of the hand laid on the bedding.

Puppies should be lying happily in the nest; if scattered round the outsides they are too hot, when the lamp should be raised. They will ask for more warmth by crowding on top of each other directly under the lamp, which should then be lowered.

In practically all things connected with animals it is necessary to use common sense rather than stick rigidly to rules in a book. It is the person on the spot who is responsible for their well-being and who should keep close observation – and act upon it.

On the mistaken principle that one can never have too much of a good thing, heating is sometimes kept on longer than is necessary or desirable. Keep them happy, and dispense with the lamp as soon as you can safely do so.

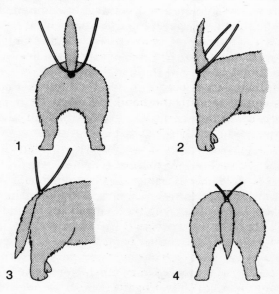

FIG. 11
Tail docking

CHAPTER VII

REARING CORGI PUPPIES

'DO 'em well when they're young,' was the advice given to me in my youth by an old cattle breeder, and how very sound it was. No young stock will ever grow into the animals they should be if they are not well reared, nor will they be a credit and profit to their owner. A promising puppy can be made or marred by the treatment it receives in early life. Bad management, faulty feeding and wrong treatment in various ways can do an immense amount of harm, resulting in poor physique, bad temperament and susceptibility to disease. Both the Cardigan and the Pembroke are hardy breeds, a fact which is sometimes made an excuse for bringing them up tough. No one suggests that they should be coddled – far from it – but a good puppy is worth taking care of, and time and trouble spent on it will be amply repaid.

It is necessary to exercise a good deal of common sense with puppies as with children, keeping them growing and developing in body and mind, being neither too hard on them nor killing them by kindness. It must ever be remembered – a point which many pet owners forget or do not think of – that puppies *are* children; their young bones are soft and pliable, their muscles easily tired, and they require much more rest and sleep than grown-ups. Parents who would not dream of allowing their small son to play all day with boys twice his age will quite cheerfully expect a puppy to keep his end up with adult dogs. Nor is it always the pet owners who sin in this way; I have seen breeders who ought to know better doing the same, and it has always exasperated me. When little Georgie comes in with his feet wet he is made to change his shoes and stockings, but I have seen small puppies sitting out in the rain and mud till I have wanted to take them in and dry and warm them.

All this sort of thing can do a puppy no good, and may do infinite harm, just as wrong and foolish treatment will ruin his temperament. If children are badly behaved we rightly blame the parents. Similarly, an ill-behaved dog reflects the errors of those who have been responsible for its upbringing; there is no getting

Thomas Fall

Ch. Belroyd Lovebird

Sally Anne Thompson

Ch. Wyeford Roberto of Wey and Ch. Georgette of Wey

Ch. Caswell Duskie Knight

Finnish, Norwegian and Swedish Ch. Hildenmanor Annline Copy

C. M. Cooke

Ch. Mynthurst Carousel of Cellerhof

Ch. Kentwood Fairy Tale

Sydney Francis

Sinbad of Wey, T.D. ex; U.D.; C.D. ex, retrieving a pheasant

A. P. Fyffe

Two Corgis trained by Mr. John Holmes jumping together to retrieve dumb-bells. Royal Horticultural Hall, Westminster, June 1951

away from it. Many a nice puppy, well reared in kennels, has gone to a kind home and yet had its temperament ruined by the most stupid and ignorant – albeit well-meant – treatment, and its digestion thoroughly upset by wrong feeding. I stress all this because I feel very strongly about it, and my breeder friends will know that it is true.

EARLY DAYS

The feeding of puppies does not begin when they are born, but while they are *in utero*, for they are being fed then through the dam, a subject dealt with in another Chapter. We start now, then, with day-olds and will assume that the mother has plenty of milk to keep them going satisfactorily and without any supplementary assistance for at least the first three or four weeks. We shall probably be helping her, and beginning the weaning process, before this time expires; and certainly so if, as may happen, her milk begins to go off. The pups should be contented, just feeding and sleeping, the bitch equally contented. If they are not, there is something amiss. We used to hear a lot about acid milk, too high an acidity causing digestive disturbance in the whelps, and advised to test it with blue litmus paper. I never found this test satisfactory, but if in any doubt the bitch may be given a few doses of milk of magnesia, and the puppies a drop or two apiece as well.

It is impossible to lay down any hard and fast rule as to the number of whelps a Corgi bitch should be asked to rear. A big, strong, mature matron can obviously rear more than a small one, while a young bitch with her first litter should be given a lighter task. Another consideration is her breeding history; how much has been taken out of her in previous litters and the time which has elapsed since her last. As a rough guide shall we say four or five for a first litter, six to seven afterwards? But discretion must be used in each individual case. The slightly larger Cardigan will generally manage one or two more than a Pembroke. It is better to err on the side of two few than too many; dogs are not machines, though one might think so from the way a few of them are treated.

When a bitch produces more puppies than you consider she can cope with, the question of what to do with the surplus arises. You may be lucky – if you can call it lucky – to have a weakling, or a 'whiteley' (i.e., with too much white coloration) which you can dispose of right away. A small one which has been given the benefit of the doubt has before now grown remarkably well and caught up with its brothers and sisters, finishing up as good as any of them. This is only one of the glorious uncertainties of dog breeding. Doubtful cases can well be given a week or two for further consideration, as the strain on the bitch is not great during this period. With a large and valuable litter it pays to put half of them on a foster mother.

Puppies in the nest should not be exposed to strong light before their eyes are opened, which will be at about twelve days, and then should be accustomed to it gradually. If any are a bit late in opening their eyes they may be encouraged by very gentle massage with the tips of the fingers lightly smeared with vaseline.

Between three and four weeks the weaning process may be begun, though mother and family will not finally part company for another month. But before this the pups should have their nails cut. Nail cutting at a very early age is essential. For one thing, the sharp nails will irritate the dam, even causing a reluctance to suckle her whelps; for another, neglect of this precaution allows the quicks to grow so that the nails can never be shortened to a suitable length later in life. They are easily snipped off with a pair of strong nail scissors, being careful not to draw blood if possible. Whatever kind of whelping box you use you should provide a bench, box or something of the sort on to which the bitch can jump away from her puppies. When they get older they will pester the life out of her and give her no rest so that any but an extremely patient bitch may resort to turning on them – and who can blame her?

LEARNING TO FEED

Whether the first introduction to supplementary food should be by way of milky food or meat is a matter on which opinions differ, but I think the majority of breeders would plump for the latter. During the war, when good meat was difficult or impossible to get, I deferred meat feeding till four weeks, having previously got them on to milk food. We used the best bits of the knacker's meat, chopped or minced very fine, with quite satisfactory results. In using meat at three weeks it is advisable to buy the best you can and scrape it so as to omit the more indigestible sinews. Each pup must have individual tuition, the best way being to place a small quantity of the scraped meat on the finger and encourage him on to find out what it is all about. He will soon discover that he is 'on a good thing', though, of course, some take longer than others. It does not matter how little they take for the first time or two; you have got them started and they will soon be emulating Oliver Twist in asking for more. A small teaspoonful is quite enough at this stage; within a few days they can be getting two meat feeds daily. Always feed puppies after the dam has been away from them for some time and just before she returns.

You can now start them on milk food. Any of the proprietary puppy foods are suitable; or you can use a good baby food mixed with milk, fed fairly warm, so that at six weeks they will be having four feeds a day, two of meat (to which may be added a little cod liver oil or a few drops of halibut oil), some calcium lactate or gluconate, and a few drops of orange juice or rose-hip syrup. All this in addition to the dam, who will be increasingly away from them during the day. At seven or eight weeks the mother will be spending only the night with them, or finishing with them altogether, the pups now getting four feeds and a 'nightcap'.

WORMING OF PUPPIES

At this stage it is as well to deal with the essential task of treating for worms. It can be taken as an axiom that all puppies have round worms, the symptoms of which are thin necks, distended abdomens (particularly after feeding) and staring coats. But in many cases these symptoms are by no means apparent, yet worms will be present just the same. Make up your mind to worm your puppies at six weeks, symptoms or no symptoms, or earlier if they show signs of needing it; four weeks is not too early for a bad infestation. Wormy puppies cannot possibly thrive or grow properly until relieved of the presence of these parasites.

Worming these days is painless and effective, and your vet is the best person to approach for a suitable medicament to use. These are usually based on the weight of the puppy and modern science has given us preparations that do not require starving the puppy prior to its use.

MENU FOR CORGI PUPPIES

Here, then, is the menu for eight-week puppies, divided into four feeds and a 'nightcap'. I never feed by weight; the eye is a better guide than the scales and individuals vary in the amounts of food required. The aim is to keep them growing and doing well, never over-feeding to blow them out after a meal, yet retaining their puppy fat. If they get diarrhoea they are being over-fed. A puppy should feel weighty, firm and solid, not light or flabby.

7 *a.m.* Stale wholemeal bread or rusks, or puppy meal, soaked in milk or gravy. Oatmeal or porridge with milk, or raw eggs beaten up in milk. Ring the changes on these, adding a little honey and calcium gluconate.

12 *noon.* Raw meat cut very small or minced; cooked paunch or tripe; cooked rabbit or fish (no bones!). Add cod liver oil or halibut oil, and orange juice.

3 *p.m.* As for 7 a.m.

7 *p.m.* As for noon feed.

10.30 *p.m.* The 'nightcap', which may consist of any easily prepared milky food; an egg and milk is as good as any.

Some orange juice and dried brewer's yeast should be supplied daily right from the start of solid feeding, but the former may well be dropped at three months. The yeast can be given as tablets crushed into the food. At three months the feeds can be reduced to three and a nightcap, and at six months to two feeds daily. A hard biscuit daily is very desirable. The ration must be increased as the pups grow, keeping them nicely bodied and solid without being fat; if allowed to get top-heavy their fronts are liable to go. Care must be taken at all times to ensure that each gets its share and is not crowded out by the more voracious members of the litter. I never like to feed more than two at one dish, then one can see fair play. A dish to each puppy is the ideal – but how far short of the ideal we often fall!

Fresh Air, Sunshine and Exercise

At three weeks the pups will be pretty lively and now the front flap of the whelping box can be let down so that they can come out and play on the floor of the kennel, care being taken for the first time or two to see that they all find their way back. Then the flap can be left down during the daytime and they will exercise themselves when they feel like it, retiring to their box to rest and sleep. They should now get all the sunshine possible, while being able to lie in shade if it gets too hot. Windows should be open as much as weather permits; if the kennel has a removable bottom board with

wire netting behind it this can be taken out to admit direct
sunlight on to the floor. There is no better arrangement than this;
they are out of cold winds and draughts while getting exercise,
fresh air and the sun.

On no account must young puppies be given opportunity to
jump down, even from a height of a few inches, a golden rule which
should be observed until they are several months old. Even up to
six months any jump should be small. Their young bones and
joints are soft and pliable, any jar on the shoulders tending to
throw out their elbows and weaken their pasterns. A snug whelping box, with a four- or six-inch board to keep the straw in, looks
very nice and comfy; but the pups will take a delight in diving
overboard, than which nothing could be worse. In the case of
Cardigans, which are more heavily bodied than the Pembrokes
and have a crook to the foreleg, these considerations are even more
essential.

At about four weeks or a little less they will be ready to explore
the outside world, though only to the extent of the kennel run. This
should have a hard floor; bricks are best, but any hard surface
which does not get cold or damp will do. A gentle slope should be
formed from the kennel to the run, and a wide board (raised an
inch off the ground) provided for them to rest or sleep on in the
run. Again, on their first time out make sure they can find their
way back. If at first they show a reluctance to leave their kennel
they can be put out, provided the weather is good, but not left long
enough to get cold. A corner of the run should be provided with
shade and their board placed under it in hot weather. If there is no
natural shade, some canvas or a few sacks stretched over wooden
uprights will serve very well.

Sorting Them Out

As the puppies play about in their run you will have ample
opportunities of observing them. You will note how they are
doing, whether any are falling behind the others in physical
development, which are the bold and which the shy ones (if any),
and sizing them up generally. Time spent sitting in the pen with a
litter is never wasted provided you exercise your powers of
observation. It may be that one which you have previously fancied
does not look now quite so good as you thought; it appears to lack
the body of the others, shows rather more daylight under it and

seems to be outgrowing its strength. More often than not this wayward growth occurs in the dog rather than the bitch. But do not be in too much of a hurry in passing judgment; if soundly constructed in frame it may be a slow developer which may, with time and care, turn out as good as any, if not the best of the lot.

An 'eye' for a puppy at this age is often a great help in making a judicious purchase, for you will see possibilities which may not be apparent to the seller, and may one day be in a position to congratulate yourself on your astuteness. When I buy a puppy which turns out well I pat myself on the back for my good judgment; when the reverse happens I call it bad luck! However, an eye for a puppy is a quality to cultivate; at least it will help you to decide which of your own to part with. But it cannot be acquired in a day. At the other end of the scale is the puppy which looks 'made up' at an early age; it has a very good body, perhaps a trifle short, is a real smart one, perhaps not growing quite so fast as the others but very taking to the eye, and you feel sure you have got a winner. But by the time it is six to eight months old it begins to look stuffy and, though it may do some winning in the early puppy classes, to your great disappointment it will slip further down the line as the shows go on. You wish you had parted with it, but it is not so easy to sell now.

We all make these mistakes sooner or later; the important thing is not to do it too often.

Temperament in a Puppy

I suppose dogs, like humans, are born with the kind of temperament they are going to have; but this is not to say that a bad temperament cannot be improved to some extent, nor that a good one cannot be ruined. We have a big responsibility in the care we take of our dogs' temperaments during their formative age. If a nervous bitch, and there are a few in every breed, is mated it is reasonable to expect a fair proportion of her progeny to take after her, even though a bold dog be chosen for her. How many times have I been approached by the owner of a pet bitch whom she (for it is often a lady owner who asks me) wants mated? The owner then volunteers the information that 'She is very nervous,' and to my query 'Why mate her?' the reply is that a friend, or her vet, or somebody, has said a litter will do her good. I dare say, but I doubt if it will improve her temperament to any appreciable extent. If, after all the discouragement I can give her, she persists, then I say 'Bring her along,' on the principle that I might as well have the stud fee as let someone else have it. But I am strongly opposed to perpetuating nervous strains in this way, for they do the breed an immense amount of harm and we have a responsibility for its future.

The time to start on temperaments is before the puppies get their eyes open; pass your hand over them as they lie in the nest so that they will imperceptibly become accustomed to the touch and smell of human hands. Do this every day. Later on you can pick them up one at a time, being very quiet and deliberate, talking to them and nuzzling them against your cheek. But before this, while they are lying sightless in the nest, get them used to noises by banging the cleaning things about, dropping the shovel, and so on. Small puppies like to be cuddled and made a fuss of. When they are getting about sit with them in the kennel and encourage them to come to you; always be handling and talking to them, turning them upside down on their backs, rolling them gently over – in fact anything you like that teaches them to repose in you complete confidence. What happy puppies; they have no fear!

But there is a lot more to their early education besides this. They must have confidence, not only in you but in every human being. So let other members of the household talk to them in the same way, and your friends, too, including children. But children should never be allowed to pick one up in case they drop it. Let other inmates of your kennel talk to them through the wire so that they will not be overawed when they meet other dogs. Tuck one under each arm when somebody arrives in a car and let them hear the engine running, strangers talking, the house dogs barking, all the sights and sounds which they will have to meet in the world. Put a few in the car for a short drive. Take them with you into the town, but only to stay in the car if they have not been inoculated. The more they can get about and see the world, get used to traffic, trains, people, crowds and other dogs, so much the better.

Be careful not to ask too much of a young puppy and let him get frightened; this will undo much or all of the good you have done. If you have a puppy-run near the house they will see the tradesmen and other callers who will often stop and talk to them.

TEETHING

At 3½ to 4 months puppies begin to exchange their temporary teeth for permanent ones and this process should be carefully watched. The gums will become swollen and tender and teething fits may occur, though I am bound to say that I have never experienced this. Large, meaty bones which they can pull at and gnaw, or a hard biscuit to crunch, will help the teething period to be got through easily.

As a rule the milk teeth will fall out or be pushed out by the permanent teeth, but not infrequently one of the latter will grow up alongside a milk tooth which will then have to be drawn before a faulty mouth is caused. Teething is generally all complete by five months.

REARING PUPPIES BY HAND

There are rare occasions – if you are unlucky enough to lose your bitch at the whelping, or if the bitch has no milk or, in very rare instances, rejects her puppies – when it becomes necessary to rear a litter by hand. Let me say at once that unless you are extremely fond of work and do not mind getting up frequently in the night, and unless you are prepared to make a full-time job of it, it is better to try to get a foster mother as soon as you can. Your best bet is to consult your vet. He may know of someone whose bitch has either lost her entire litter or has whelped only one or two puppies, and this owner might be willing to help you. In a large kennel there may be another bitch who has whelped a small litter at about the same time, or a breeder friend may have one to help you out so that a few at least can be transferred. The secretaries of the breed clubs or the mixed canine clubs might also know of someone who would be willing to come to your aid. It is always well worth a telephone call. A good cat will rear two or three Corgi pups very well, but one feels safer with a bitch.

While you are waiting for a foster, or exploring other possibilities, the pups must be kept going, and this is where hand rearing comes in. Of course many good litters of puppies have been reared entirely by hand, and there is no reason for despair. But you must make up your mind to devote your whole attention to them, day and night, for at least three weeks. By that time you will be able to take the middle hours of the night off, and by four weeks a very late and very early feed will further relieve you of work. If you have someone to share the duties with you, so much the better.

I would not recommend rearing a large litter by hand; the fewer the number the more individual attention you can give them. If any are weakly or mismarked, or in any way unsatisfactory prospects, they may be put down. If there is a preponderance of one sex, or of a sex which you are not particular about, that is the direction in which to look for any to put out of the way. You will probably find that four or five are as many as you want if you are to do them properly, but this must be left to your discretion; larger numbers have been successfully reared. Here are the paraphernalia you will require to have at hand before you begin operations: saucepan, cup, teaspoon, small dish, vaseline, cotton wool, dropper or (needleless) plastic syringe, thick apron, and a Glaxo premature baby bottle – it may be necessary slightly to enlarge the hole in the teat. You will also need a box big enough to accommodate all the pups, in which you can put some soft bedding such as very fine woodwool or an old blanket, and a hot-water bottle. The latter must be well and securely covered to prevent any possibility of a puppy burning itself. It is a good idea to duplicate the box and hot-water bottle for reasons which will be seen later.

Now as to the actual feeding, starting with a satisfactory mixture for the first few days:

> one pint milk (boiled)
> one tablespoon lime water
> one ditto glucose
> one ditto dried milk

Warm the feed milk by standing a cupful in boiling water in the saucepan, thus keeping it at the desired heat for each puppy, and measure it out into the bottle. Now sit down and pick up the first puppy, holding it firmly by the body and placing it on the apron on your knees. Ruck up the apron so that it can push against it with its hind feet. Moisten the teat with a little of the milk, move it about the puppy's mouth and try and persuade it to take hold. (A lot of patience is required for this.) If not successful bring the plastic syringe into action, squirting a very little into the mouth. Within a very few feeds the pup will be taking food from the bottle, and the sooner they are all on it the better, as the act of sucking is a natural essential to their well-being.

The bottle must be used with considerable discretion. Keep tilting it back so that the milk mixture does not flow too freely, and make them work for their grub as they would do on the mother. 'Little and slowly' should be the watchword; you will soon get the hang of it and know how much to let them have. After a few days you can introduce a little proprietary puppy milk food into the mixture. To avoid the mistake of feeding a puppy twice, while another goes without, transfer each one as it is fed to the duplicate box. So much for the feeding, the rest of which can be left to my readers' common sense. But there is a lot more to it than this.

In the first place extreme hygiene must be practised with all feeding utensils, which should be scalded immediately after each meal, thereafter being kept in water to which a little bicarbonate of soda has been added. The dam, rearing her puppies naturally, will frequently clean them, licking them all over with her tongue, pushing them about with her nose, cleaning up their abdomens and under their tails. Hand-reared puppies should be wiped over twice a day with a piece of damp cotton wool, but not to make them wet. After each meal – and this is of the utmost importance – each must be massaged over the rectum with damp wool to encourage evacuation. If water is not passed at the same time, gently massage the sheath of a dog puppy or the vagina of a bitch. If there is any sign of serious constipation recourse may be had to the soap stick. Wet a small piece of soap and mould one end into a stick; this is gently inserted into the rectum and held there for a minute or so. During the first week, when the puppies are being fed every two hours, a bowel movement every three feeds is sufficient.

Docking and removal of dewclaws may well be deferred to a week old in the case of hand-reared puppies. If the eyes are very slow to open they can be massaged as described earlier in this Chapter, or bathed with warm, weak boracic lotion, using a fresh piece of cotton wool for each eye. The interval between feeds can be lengthened gradually until at four weeks they are being fed by day only, the last feed being given as late as possible. If you are a late 'bedder' that will suit the pups very well.

If they go on in the right way, and there is no reason why they should not, they will be lapping in a very short time, which saves a lot of trouble, and solid food is introduced as with puppies on their dam. Remember that they have no mother to keep them warm and look after them; this is your responsibility.

The 'Pet' Puppy

I hope the kind-hearted people who are wise enough to choose a Corgi (Pembroke or Cardigan) for a family pet will, if they read these words, not take amiss what I say here. It does not apply to all of them by any means – probably to only a few – but for those few it needs saying, not as a criticism but as a help.

The puppy you have bought to take back to town is very young, perhaps has only recently left his mother, still more recently his brothers and sisters whose companionship he has happily shared. Though he has got about a bit he confesses to being a country bumpkin. Not for him the sights and noises of the town, the roar of traffic, the bustle of the crowds. These things have not existed for him, and nobody has been able to tell him; he is in for a rude awakening if he but knew it. Now let me tell you what happened to a puppy of mine – and has happened to thousands more in all probability. He was a nice, sensible puppy with a perfect temperament, and enjoyed life. His purchaser, with a flat in London, fell for him at once and he was clearly destined for a good home. On arrival, the two children, who had been promised a puppy, were overjoyed to see him and dashed at him with cries of delight. Thoroughly alarmed at this lavish display of what he did not realize was affection, the unfortunate youngster bolted precipitately under the sofa, from which he was extricated with some difficulty. A bad start you will think.

Next morning he was put on the lead for a nice walk. Within a few seconds he learned what London traffic was like and it nearly scared the wits out of him. A daily woman came in the mornings; a very worthy creature no doubt, but not very fond of dogs, still less of a puppy which had a habit of getting under her feet as she went about her work. Sometimes in her impatience she would give a surreptitious kick when no one was looking. To cut the story short, the puppy was eventually brought back to me. 'He is so nervous, we can do nothing with him.' How do I know all this? It would not take a Sherlock Holmes to deduce it from what I was told. As for the surreptitious kick, it is a curious fact that the moment our own 'daily' donned her white apron he ran for his life!

Fortunately this episode had a happy sequel, for the puppy, after many months of careful treatment, forgot his unpleasant experiences, eventually going to South Africa where he now bears the proud official title of Champion. I do beg all inexperienced dog lovers who take a Corgi puppy home: first, to get all details of feeding from his breeder and, secondly, to get inside the puppy's young mind, realizing that this is a tremendous upheaval for him, and to treat him tenderly and quietly as a child, accustoming him gradually to his new surroundings and all the strange sights and sounds which he has not met before. Your care and patience will be repaid a hundredfold. He will do many things wrong, but never, never slap him; just take him gently by the loose skin of the cheek, put your face down to his and scold him. You will be surprised how quickly he will learn and how soon he will look to you for everything and become your devoted friend and companion.

Lead Training a Puppy

I never put a collar and lead on my puppies before they are getting on for four months old, and then only to let them get accustomed to the feel of it, postponing any further instruction for another three or four weeks. Some qualification must be made for puppies in towns or built-up areas who have to exercise on the roads; these can be lead trained at three months and will take to it quite happily if patience is used. I need hardly add that their walks must be extremely short at first; two or three ten-minute outings are better than one long one which can tire them more than is desirable. Do, please, remember that the puppy is very small and very young; what to you is but a few steps seems a long way to him. If you have a garden, however small, in which he can exercise himself, let him do so until he has been inoculated; public roads spell danger in more ways than one.

I have seldom found a Corgi puppy require more than three lessons (or shall I say three days?) to train properly to the lead. The first reactions to this form of education are invariably far from promising; he will either lie flat on his tummy, or possibly on his back, and refuse to budge. Alternatively, he will jump about like a hooked fish, threatening to break his neck or tie himself in knots. Some patience is needed for the first couple of lessons, allied to much kindness to instil confidence. The sulky beggar must be encouraged to get up on his legs, then to move a few steps – it does not matter in what direction. When he hangs back on the end of the lead kneel down and get him to come to you, making a fuss of him when he does, then tempting him again to move a little way with you. Spend only a few minutes on the first lesson; he will do better at the next, which you can make a little longer.

As a small boy I used to tie my puppies to a tree, an unyielding object from which they made frantic efforts to get away. This was their first introduction to the lead – and a very bad one; I know better now. The 'hooked fish' type must be given time to settle down, playing him on the lead as though you really had a big fish on light tackle. As soon as the lesson is over, sit down and have a game with him; give him a tit-bit if you like, just to show there is no ill feeling.

When you have got him going well with you, train him to walk by your side on a loose lead, without pulling or holding back. Put the puppy on your left side, with the end of the lead in your right hand. In your left hand hold a folded newspaper or a leafy switch cut from a hedge. Now walk forward and every time the puppy goes ahead tap him back on the nose, at the same time saying 'Heel' or 'Come in'; it doesn't matter what you say as long as you always use the same word. Having got him perfect at this, you can now teach him to sit. Take him by the collar, say 'Sit', and with the other hand along his back push him down into a sitting position. With a few lessons every day it will not be long before he learns what is expected of him. Do not ask him to sit for more than a minute or so at first, lengthening the time by degrees and always rewarding good progress by a few words of praise or, occasionally, a tit-bit.

House Training

I believe it to be a fact that Welsh Corgi puppies learn clean house habits more quickly than most breeds; it is only a matter of taking some trouble over them for the first week or so and sticking religiously to the 'drill'. Please remember that the puppy, when you take him from kennels at about eight weeks old, knows nothing at all of what is expected of him. Start him off in the way you want him to go on, and make up your mind to forgo visits to the cinema or elsewhere, the luxury of going to bed early or getting up late; you will find it is well worth it and will save you much trouble later on. If you have a garden, or even a small backyard (preferably with some grass in it), your task will be lightened, for you can turn him out there and he will soon learn that he is to go outside. Failing this, provide him with a wide, shallow tray covered with earth, sand or sawdust, and teach him to use it.

A young puppy cannot go for long periods without relieving himself; therefore put him out at frequent intervals. Always put him out, or on his tray, last things at night and the moment you get up in the morning, immediately after every meal, and whenever he wakes up from sleep. Always stay with him until he has done what is expected of him, even if you have to shiver in the cold for ten minutes, then praise him when you bring him in. If he should make a mistake in the house, show it to him, scold him as I have described, and put him outside. Wipe over the scene of the crime with a strong disinfectant, otherwise he may be tempted to repeat the offence on the same spot.

Do not be surprised or annoyed if the puppy cries the first night; children starting a term at boarding school tend to behave in the same way. Here is your first opportunity to be understanding, so do not scold him for doing something he cannot help. Make him as comfortable as you can, with a nice snug box to sleep in, a bowl of water nearby, in a room which is warm enough, and *leave him to it*. On no account make a fuss of him nor go down to comfort him; he will only cry the more as soon as you leave him. He will tire of it in time and you will all get a good night's sleep.

INOCULATION

It is very necessary that puppies should be inoculated against distemper, hard pad, parvovirus, hepatitis and leptospirosis. This is given in two injections, the first at twelve weeks, the second two weeks later. Puppies should not be taken into public places until two weeks after the last injection. Great strides have been made in prophylactic treatment for these diseases, and you should consult your veterinary surgeon as soon as the puppy is twelve weeks old, so that he can be inoculated against them.

CHAPTER VIII

MANAGEMENT OF THE BROOD BITCH AND STUD DOG

COMING IN SEASON

A BITCH will come in season for the first time usually between eight and ten months, but this varies in individuals. A precocious youngster may come in at seven months, another may go to twelve or fourteen. One must be careful and watchful, particularly if the bitches are to be mated, as it is important to know the exact day they started. If you have a dog on the place he will generally give warning in good time before the bitch shows colour, then lose interest until her condition becomes interesting. House bitches frequently keep themselves very clean and may be in quite an advanced stage before anything is noticed.

The first outward sign of season is a red discharge from the vulva; this is reckoned the first day. Generally about the tenth or eleventh day the now pinker discharge almost or quite ceases, when the bitch will be ready to mate and will remain matable for several days. The eleventh or twelfth day is considered the most suitable. Let me make the reservation here, however, that not all bitches are obliging enough to conform to the rules. Occasionally one will conceive only if mated within the first week, yet I have had one which was mated on the sixteenth day, continued in full colour for a week after, and produced a satisfactory litter. I knew a Dachshund bitch years ago who would be in season only for a few days, and then matable only for a few hours; the owner had to buy a dog specially for her, who practically lived with her. But such cases are rare and we need not concern ourselves with them here.

CONCEPTION

Conception takes place when a male spermatozoon unites with an ovum, or egg cell, of the bitch. The ova are not all released from the ovaries together, but singly, usually beginning about the seventh day of season. If the mating takes place early there will be only a few ova released and ready to unite with the spermatozoa, resulting in a small litter, though this is offset to some extent by the fact that some of the male cells may remain active for several days after mating and thus be capable of fertilization. It is for this reason that the later the mating takes place – provided the bitch has not gone off – the more likelihood there is of a decent-sized litter. Nature has bestowed great prodigality on the male in the matter of sex cells, many thousands, if not millions, more than are ever required to fertilize all the ova, a physiological phenomenon which man has taken advantage of in the artificial insemination of cattle, one ejaculation from the bull being sufficient to fertilize a large number of cows in different herds. The ova of the female, however, present themselves in strictly limited numbers, the size of the litter thus depending on the bitch and not on the dog. Should a bitch be mated by two dogs in the same season one cannot say with any certainty which dog is responsible for the puppies. It is a Kennel Club regulation that both dogs must be included in the pedigree. It is also possible, if several days elapse between the matings, that the litter will include whelps by both dogs. It is better to avoid such complications if you can.

AGE TO MATE

The age at which it is prudent to let a bitch have her first mating depends upon several factors. She should not be too young as she will still be growing and will not yet have reached full physical development, a natural process which may be seriously retarded by the extra demands made upon her. On the other hand, if the event is postponed too long the pelvic bones will have become set and she may have difficulty in whelping. The second season is generally considered best, though there is no objection to the first if she is over twelve months old. It may happen that you are showing her, perhaps trying to make her a champion, and do not want to retire her to maternal duties just yet; in such case there is no harm in waiting till she is over two years old, but it is as well that she has her first litter by the time she is three.

Another good reason for early mating exists in the case of a bitch who is lacking in body and depth, showing too much daylight under her. A litter will often improve her to a remarkable extent and make a great difference to her chances in the show ring. While nature provides for the bitch to come in season, or 'heat', twice a year, it is inadvisable to let her have more than three litters in two years; most certainly a twelve-month interval should elapse after the first litter. A highly fecund bitch who produces a large family every time should always have a year's rest so as not to wear her out. To deny her this, for the sake of sordid gain, not only wears her out before her time but, to my mind, constitutes a form of cruelty which might very well be dispensed with. Nor do I approve of expecting them to go on for ever; a bitch who has presented her owner with half a dozen or so good litters has surely earned some consideration in the autumn of her days, and should be allowed to spend them pottering about and enjoying herself in a quiet way, without being turned into a sausage machine.

No special feeding is called for at this stage, but I refer my readers to the Chapter on feeding.

You will already have decided what dog she is to be mated to, and booked the service. (I am assuming that on this occasion you are sending her away, and not using a dog of your own.) The dog's owner should be notified as soon as she begins her season, so that he will know when to expect her and can reserve the dog for her. If you can take her yourself, by car or otherwise, so much the better. A young maiden bitch will benefit by your presence; she is going on an unknown adventure, a stranger in a strange land, and you will be a comfort to her.

THE MAIDEN BITCH

Every maiden bitch should be given a manual examination before mating. You can do this yourself, ask your veterinary surgeon to do so, or leave it to the (probably experienced) dog's owner to do it for you. The method is to pass a greased middle finger, the nail being well pared, into the vagina as far as it will go. If a tight fit, work it about a little to make sure no obstruction is present and to ease the way. She may have a stricture, rendering her difficult or even impossible to mate, a disability which is by no means so rare as might be thought, and which can usually be broken down with instruments by a VS. If you make the examination yourself you will need an assistant to hold the bitch for you, and it may be necessary to 'tape' her. This is done by passing a broad, strong tape round the jaws, tying it at the top; then passing it round again and tying underneath. The two ends should now be taken up and tightly tied on top of the head behind the ears. She is now safe to handle, even if, through fear or excitement, she tries to snap. Many stud owners tape all bitches as a matter of course, a not unwise precaution from the point of view of both dog and handler.

Sending by Rail

In sending a bitch by rail, first find out from your local station the best time to send her and by what route. Use a properly ventilated travelling box allowing her plenty of room to turn round, stand or lie down, and give her a comfortable bed of straw. If she has not been boxed before it is just as well to pop her in it for a few minutes beforehand once or twice, to get her accustomed to it. Be sure to make telephone inquiries with British Rail in advance, as some destinations will not be open to receive dogs on certain days. Other things being equal, I like them to travel by night if the trains fit in, as then they are only doing what they would be doing at home – sleeping. Attach two strong, clearly addressed labels, including the consignee's telephone number; give the latter the time despatched and the time to expect her. Send her on the tenth day; this will give her twenty-four hours' rest before mating.

Stud fees are payable in advance – in theory at least. In practice payment is usually made at the time of, or immediately after, mating, and you will be expected to pay the return carriage. If you wish her to be given two matings – often desirable in the case of a maiden bitch – this must be clearly arranged in advance. Sometimes a puppy from the resultant litter will be accepted in lieu of a stud fee. It is better to pay the fee and have the pick of the puppies yourself, otherwise you may lose the best one. There are occasions, however, when such an arrangement is advantageous to both parties.

Whatever is decided upon should be clearly stated in writing, thus avoiding any possibility of doubt. Practically all stud dog owners will give a free service next time if the bitch does not prove in whelp; but this, again, should be clearly stipulated beforehand.

Treating for Worms

Three weeks after service the in-whelp bitch should be treated for worms. It is not advisable to leave it later than that.

EXERCISE

This should be perfectly normal for at least a month or five weeks but after that it is advisable to ease up a bit, and during the last three weeks exercise should be restricted. On no account allow a pregnant bitch to run up and down steep stairs, to jump off chairs, or go hunting with other dogs. She can have gentle exercise practically up to the time of whelping. Common sense must be used according to the size of litter she is carrying.

THE STUD DOG

One of the best paying propositions in a kennel is a really good stud dog, but let not the novice infer from this that it is an easy way of picking up shekels; first find (or breed) your dog! I have not infrequently had letters from correspondents saying they have a young dog they would like to 'use at stud'. With child-like simplicity they imagine he has only to be mentioned to conjure up a whole horde of bitches waiting in the queue for the honour of his services. Enquiry has almost invariably elicited the information that he has never been shown (and probably would not win if he were), has never mated a bitch, with no certainty that he ever will, and possesses none of the qualifications which would enable him to make a start, let alone make a successful sire. I have had to point out to them that there is already plenty of competition in this line, that the entry into the lists of a completely unknown and unproved dog would not stir a single ripple in the pond, and that they had better take him to a show first and see how he gets on. The plain, unvarnished truth must be stated, and that is: an aspirant to stud work has to prove himself in more ways than one before he can be expected to attract the attention of breeders.

Stud dogs range from the locally known who may get a few bitches from private owners at a low fee, and the cost of whose keep out-balances the returns, through the moderate animal who has done a little winning and is reasonably well bred, to the high-class dog to whose name are attached the magic letters 'Ch.', or who at least has a Challenge Certificate or two and has shown himself capable of winning in top company. This latter is the only sort which the serious breeder should have in mind, and is by a long way the most profitable. But the winning of no matter how many prizes is not enough in itself to put him among the select few. First of all, his pedigree must be such as will attract the attention of discriminating breeders, and he should not be an unpopular colour. He must have a good temperament, comporting himself with assurance and dignity, slow to anger, for these qualities, with others, will be passed on to his progeny. A sire, however, good in other respects, who is quarrelsome, sour or timid, can do the breed a great deal of harm and one should think a very long time before using him.

On top of all this he must be capable of performing the functions expected of him, and this is where the small breeder, with only a very few bitches of his own, is placed in some difficulty. Breeders are naturally chary of sending a bitch to an untried dog whose clumsy efforts may not be attended by success, by which time it is perhaps too late to send her anywhere else. This can often be got over by advertising a free service for the first bitch sent him, but it should be stipulated that she is a reliable matron who will not play him up; it is always advisable that at least one of the parties to the union should have the 'know-how'. If he has distinguished himself in the show ring, and possesses the other qualifications outlined, there need be little fear that this free offer will not be taken advantage of.

Starting the Young Stud

Dogs vary greatly in the way they approach their first bitch, though most of them are very little trouble. As I have said, choose a bitch who will not make herself awkward; some of them can be extremely so. Make sure she is really ready, which she will show by standing with her posterior to the dog and cocking her tail to one side. She should be controlled with collar and lead. If the dog shows no inclination to get on with the job, take him away for ten minutes, then try again. If still unsuccessful, shut him in where he can see the bitch but cannot get to her. If nothing happens at the next attempt, give up for the time being and repeat the tactics later in the day, or next morning, when in all probability the desired result will be obtained. Every breeder heaves a sigh of relief when a promising young dog has proved himself.

At what age should a young dog be expected to start stud duties? One cannot lay down the law about this; it really depends upon the dog, and individuals vary. One will show a strong inclination as early as eight or nine months, another not till some months later. I consider ten months early enough, with an interval of a couple of months between his first and second bitches. Thereafter he should be used very sparingly for the next six months, being allowed not more than three or four during this time. Many a good dog's stud career has been ruined by too early or too frequent use.

If he evinces little or no interest in the opposite sex till over twelve months, do not worry and do not try to hurry him; nature takes her course and he will come to it in time. By the time a Corgi is two years old he can be in full work; but, if you want him to last, it is better to turn bitches away rather than overdo him. During the busy season two a week, or three at a pinch if the others have been easy matings, will be all right; but when he has had several in quick succession he should be rested for a fortnight. By not being too greedy you will prolong the working life of your dog, at the same time giving your clients – who are doing the paying – a fair deal. It is a crime to take stud fees for a dog which is being grossly overworked.

Visiting Bitches

We will say you now have your own stud dog. He is a good one, as shown by his winning record, breeding and temperament, and you may reasonably expect that he will be patronized by other breeders. Those who are not too far away will generally bring their bitch by car, which is all to the good from your point of view as a novice, for their practical knowledge will make up for any lack of experience you may still suffer from, and you will often learn something from them to add to what you have already learnt when taking your own bitches to other dogs. An ounce of practical demonstration is worth a ton of theory or anything you can read in books.

Where no car is available, bitches will be sent by rail. You will have to collect them from the station, bring them home, take care of them while there, and return them duly mated. Any dog belonging to someone else is a big responsibility; an in-season bitch is the biggest responsibility of all. Do not on any account release her from the travelling box until you are in some kennel or enclosure from which she cannot possibly escape. It is astonishing how quick some of them can be, perhaps when you are least expecting it. If she gets away it is highly improbable that you will ever catch her, then the fat is in the fire with a vengeance. Put on

her a very secure collar and lead, and let her have a run on some
grass; if enclosed by high enough wire let her off the lead to relieve
herself, then feed her and put her in her kennel. Make sure that she
cannot jump or bite her way out.

It is advisable, particularly if you are inexperienced, to get a
doggy friend to help you with the mating. The bitch may be
awkward and need to be taped, and he can hold her while you
superintend the dog's end of the business; he can also hold the
bitch during the 'tie' to ensure that she does not struggle with
possible injury to the dog. I always like to mate bitches on a table;
it saves a lot of backache and enables everything to be more easily
controlled, but it should not be attempted without an assistant.
The table, which should be covered with some non-slip and
washable material (a clean sack will do), is placed in the corner of
the room or shed; the bitch facing the open end and being held by
the assistant, while the dog has a wall behind him so that he
cannot fall overboard. If the dog is not accustomed to a table the
mating can take place on the ground. Occasionally a dog who is
used to a table will show a rooted disinclination to mate a
particular bitch there, but will at once do so on the floor. There is
no accounting for these things.

One more word about mating. Do not be in a hurry; let them
run round together to make each other's acquaintance. Have the
bitch on a lead at first, in case she resents the dog's attentions, but
if she is all right let them both be loose. Then, when both give
indication of a desire to mate, either leave them to get a natural
union or put them on the table as described above. After mating,
the bitch should be shut in her kennel for a time, given a light feed,
and returned to her owner next day.

Monorchids and Cryptorchids

The male testes, or testicles, are developed in a position behind the
kidneys, from which they gradually descend into the scrotum. It
sometimes happens that one fails to descend, when the dog is
known as a monorchid. If neither descends, he is a cryptorchid.
To what extent this is hereditary is a debatable point. While a
testis retained in the body cavity degenerates and does not
produce spermatozoa, a monorchid is quite capable of siring
puppies. Whether it is desirable to use him at stud is a matter on
which breeders disagree.

Monorchidism and cryptorchidism is a show fault in this country and to my knowledge every other country in the world. Any male being exported must have a certificate of entirety from a Veterinary Surgeon before the Kennel Club will issue an Export Certificate.

CHAPTER IX

COMPOSITION OF FOODS

THE animal body is made up of a number of substances, all of which must be supplied in the food; they cannot be obtained in any other way. Some of these substances, e.g. Proteins, are necessary for the building up and repair of the body tissues. Some, Carbohydrates and Fats, furnish heat to maintain the body temperature and energy for muscular activity. Others, again, the Minerals and Vitamins, are necessary for the regulation of the body processes. It will give us a good foundation to work upon if we take the various components of foods one at a time, and see what they are and what their functions are.

PROTEINS

A protein is a complex substance made up of a number of elements known as amino-acids. There are at least twenty amino-acids, all or any of which may be combined in different proportions to form different proteins. A protein which contains all the amino-acids which are necessary to the body is a 'complete' protein, and is found in eggs, meat and milk. The protein in maize lacks certain amino-acids; thus maize can never be a complete food. It is quite feasible, however, to combine two or more incomplete protein foods so that between them they will supply all the necessary amino-acids. We then get the protein complete.

All amino-acids contain Nitrogen, the factor that enables proteins to perform their essential work. It is necessary to realize that the animal body is continually undergoing a process of breaking down and rebuilding; even in an animal at rest some destruction of the tissue cells is always taking place. In the growing animal not only must ordinary wear and tear be provided for; new cells are being built up all the time, therefore the young animal requires more protein in proportion to its body weight than the adult. In starting puppies on raw, lean meat at three or four weeks old we are helping the protein part of their ration.

In addition to its primary functions of building and repairing tissue, protein can to some extent supply heat and energy; it is more economical, however, to utilize other substances for this purpose. Furthermore, there is some risk in feeding too much protein, in that an excess throws a strain upon the kidneys. (A reliable test for impaired functioning of the kidneys is assessment of the proportion of protein in the urine.) The best protein diet is a mixed diet. Though proteins do not primarily produce energy, the more work (especially fast work) the animal does, the more protein is required.

Another point to bear in mind is that animal proteins are better for growth and maintenance than those from plants, and have a higher absorbability. A serious insufficiency of protein can cause an effusion of fluids into the tissues (dropsy). In the process of digestion the proteins are broken up into their amino-acids, in which form they are absorbed into the body where they are rebuilt into animal proteins.

CARBOHYDRATES

These comprise all the starches, sugars and glycogen providing the fuel for the body; they take no part in building or repairing tissue. Wholemeal foods, bread, cereals and potatoes are rich in carbohydrates; flaked maize is a good food for dogs. The Fibre of plants and the Cellulose of bones are also included here. Cellulose undergoes no chemical change in digestion and is not absorbed into the body; but it acts, like fibre, as an aid to peristalsis – the muscular movements of the bowel in eliminating waste products from the digestive tract.

Such of the carbohydrates as are not needed immediately can be stored in the body, some as glycogen in the liver, the rest being changed to fat and stored as fatty tissue, acting as a reserve of energy. Fats can replace carbohydrates only to a certain extent, being less readily digested and absorbed.

Glucose is the most important of all the carbohydrates and the most easily assimilated of all the sugars. It can pass directly into the circulation without having to undergo any catabolic processes, this rendering it most valuable in emergency cases such as shock after whelping or extreme weakness from any cause.

FATS

Fats are composed of the same elements as the carbohydrates – carbon, hydrogen and oxygen – though not in the same proportion. They may be in solid form (butter, lard or suet) or as oils (olive, linseed or cod liver oil etc.), the main difference being the temperature at which they liquefy. The mineral oils (paraffin and vaseline) come in another, and inedible, category. All fats and oils are insoluble in water, but are dispersed in water if certain substances known as colloids are dissolved in the water.

Fats are oxidized in the body to produce heat to keep up the body temperature, and are the richest source of energy. Stored in the body they provide a reserve supply of fuel; incorporated in the tissues they help to protect muscles, nerves and vital organs, while a layer of fat under the skin helps to conserve body heat. They cannot make muscle or repair tissues.

Fat meat, fat fish and beef suet are good sources of fat. But they should not be over-used, as they tend to slow down the digestive processes and large amounts are not tolerated by the body, causing nausea and loss of appetite. As with humans, dogs vary greatly in their likes and dislikes where fat is concerned. Fatty foods remain longer in the stomach and are thus more satisfying to the appetite, delaying the return of hunger after a meal. The fatty content of a food will form a coating over the particles of protein and starch, preventing digestion until the intestines are reached, where the film of fat is broken down by the intestinal digestive juices.

MINERALS

The principal minerals comprise: Calcium, Phosphorus, Sodium, Potassium, Sulphur, Magnesium, Iron, Chlorine and Iodine. All are present in the body in measurable quantities.

There are also the 'trace' elements: Manganese, Copper, Aluminium, Zinc, Silicon, Fluorine and Cobalt. These are present in such small amounts that they cannot be measured, though it should be said that the modern chemist, armed with a spectroscope, is capable of a degree of detection and measurement far greater than was formerly the case.

Though a great deal could be written about the various functions of minerals in the animal body, I have confined my treatment to those aspects of the subject which are likely to be of some practical interest to my readers. All the principal minerals named above enter into the cells and fluids of the body, or are essential for the carrying out of their functions. On the other hand, the trace elements (if essential, and not all of them are, according to present knowledge) act as Catalysts only; that is to say, they stimulate the activities of other substances without undergoing any change themselves.

The absorption and circulation of food nutrients are very much tied up with the mineral content, as also is the excretion of carbon-dioxide from the lungs. The breaking down of tissues causes loss of minerals in the excreta, while the building up of new tissue by the growing or pregnant animal, and secretion of milk, all call for a continuous supply of minerals in the food. How much it is necessary to supply is not known, but the point is not of supreme importance as the body is able to maintain a proper balance in the fluids and tissues, excreting any excess via the kidneys and intestines, and temporarily making good any deficiency by drawing on reserves in the skeleton. This last thought indicates that it is best to be on the safe side where mineral feeding is concerned, though here caution must be exercised as serious deficiencies or excesses of minerals in the diet can be a cause of disease, especially in the young animal.

CALCIUM AND PHOSPHORUS

It will be convenient to deal with these together, their functions being inextricably bound up with each other and with Vitamin D.

Calcium may be regarded as the most important of all the minerals, not only because the body contains more of it than any of the others but also for what it does. In conjunction with phosphorus and Vitamin D, calcium is responsible for the building up, sound formation and repair of the bones and teeth; it is necessary for the proper functioning of many muscles and nerves and is present in all the cells of the body. The demand for calcium and phosphorus is at its greatest during growth, pregnancy and lactation, while both these minerals are actively concerned in many of the metabolic processes.

The amount of calcium in the blood stream is regulated by the parathyroid gland. If the supply is insufficient the body draws on the stores of calcium in the bones, which may thus become fragile and porous.

Phosphorus is present in every cell nucleus and is particularly important to the brain and nervous tissues. Absorption of both calcium and phosphorus takes place from the small intestine. Let it be made quite clear that calcium cannot do its work unless accompanied by phosphorus in correct balance. Fortunately most foods which supply calcium also contain phosphorus, though the reverse does not apply.

For the formation of sound bones and teeth the presence of Vitamin D is also necessary; any serious upset in the balance of these three factors may result in Rickets in the growing puppy, or Osteomalacia (the adult form of the same deficiency disease) in the adult, the bones losing their lime salts, becoming soft and liable to bend. Osteomalacia can be an unseen and unsuspected condition in dogs. Calcium and phosphorus are found together in whole milk and cheese; phosphorus (but little calcium) in eggs, white fish and ox liver.

Sodium and Chlorine

Both occur in the body and are found in most foods combined as sodium-chloride (common salt). Chlorine is necessary for the production of hydrochloric acid in the stomach. Eggs, meat, milk and vegetables are good sources, meat being particularly high in salt. Vegetables contain more potassium than sodium and, as the body needs a balance of these two substances, it is usual to add salt to vegetables. When primitive man turned from hunting to agriculture he found the need for salt. Herbivorous animals often have a craving for salt, and in the wild state will travel miles to salt-licks. As a flesh eater the dog gets all the salt he requires.

Potassium

Occurs in the blood cells but not in the cell contents (plasma). It bears a close relationship to sodium.

Sulphur

This is absorbed into the body in the form of amino-acids and is a part of the protein metabolism. Contained in many foods, it is most unlikely that there will be any deficiency, and the same goes for potassium. Sulphur is often used, of course, for external treatment of skin troubles, either as ointment, in solution, or as a fumigant, frequently with most satisfactory results.

MAGNESIUM

A deficiency of magnesium need not be feared in a complete diet. It is closely connected in the body with calcium and phosphorus, and is mostly found in the bones and teeth.

IRON AND COPPER

Iron must be treated at somewhat greater length in order to get a full understanding of its importance as an essential of *Haemoglobin* (the red pigment of the blood). Haemoglobin carries oxygen to all parts of the body, where the fuel constituents of the food are burned. There being little storage of iron in the body, the daily intake must be sufficient, any serious drop resulting in *nutritional anaemia*. Generally speaking, where there is iron there is also the trace element, *Copper*, which appears to have a definite function in assisting the work of the former. For our purpose here we can talk about iron with the words 'plus copper' understood.

The most vital period for iron is during pregnancy, the mother passing large supplies to the foetus. There is, however, little iron in milk, so puppies during the suckling period are dependent upon iron stored in their livers during ante-natal feeding, which should tide them over until they begin to receive solid food. It was found that the livers of puppies just after birth contained 400 to 500 per cent more iron than those of adult dogs.

Experiments made in America with young rats fed on milk have shown a similar anaemia, which has been cured by iron and copper. In this country sty-reared pigs not infrequently develop anaemia at two to three weeks. It is cured or prevented by administration of iron salts or by providing them with grass turves in their run.

Iron is definitely a factor to watch in our breeding operations. It is present in lean meat, but in the form of haemoglobin which is not very digestible; it is, however, improved by cooking. Cooked liver is a good source, as are eggs. Whole wheatmeal and oatmeal are fairly good, and some iron can be got from green vegetables (except spinach). Milk, as we have seen, is useless for supplying iron. Parrish's Food is an excellent iron tonic.

Iodine

Iodine is present in the animal body in minute quantity only but plays an extremely important part in the whole metabolism of the body and is, of course, associated with the thyroid gland in the formation of thyroxin. (The Thyroid has been described as the first line of defence against infections. Removal of the thyroid in dogs causes death within a few days.) Iodine deficiency in humans is the cause of Goitre, the gland becoming greatly enlarged, a condition frequently obtaining in certain well-defined parts of the world, and indeed in this country. Limestone soils have long been known to be responsible for iodine deficiency both in plants and water; in Derbyshire the disease is known as 'Derbyshire neck'.

Iodine and thyroxin deficiency can bring about cretinism in humans (Cretin: an ugly, half-witted dwarf), but this can be cured by treatment, if started early enough, with thyroid gland extract. A form of goitre can affect practically all animals and fish. Salmon and trout hatcheries, if overcrowded and the water not frequently changed, have been found to benefit from the addition of iodine to the water.

The thyroid gets its iodine from the circulation, stores it as thyroxin and distributes it to the body via the blood stream and lymphatic system. Fed to lactating mothers, it increases the iodine content of the milk and stimulates the growth and development of the young. Iodine penetrates to the hair follicles, a significant point for dog breeders in treating for loss of hair and kindred complaints.

The sea, and practically every living thing therein, is rich in iodine, and it is noteworthy that goitre seldom occurs in coastal districts. Sea foods of any kind, including cod liver oil, herrings and seaweed powder, are good sources for dogs. Excessive doses of iodine can give rise to toxic symptoms.

The Trace Elements

These are mentioned briefly here, though the functions of some of them are not as yet clearly defined, nor is their significance, if any, in canine nutrition. They act as catalysts only.

Cobalt is contained in Vitamin B.12 and is thought to be essential for cattle and sheep, particularly in the cure of pernicious anaemia. *Copper* has already been mentioned along with iron. *Fluorine* is known to be a component of the enamel of teeth.

Experimental work with *Manganese* has been carried out on rats. The feeding of a manganese-free diet was found to have a disastrous effect upon the reproductive system, the males becoming sterile through testicular degeneration, the females producing their young but refusing to suckle them, abnormalities which have been corrected by addition to the diet of minute traces of manganese.

It is probable that we need not concern ourselves with the trace elements if we feed a varied diet.

WATER

A well-known professional boxer – I forget his name now – gave, as his prescription for keeping young, plenty of sleep and a lot of water to drink. However that may be – there is probably some truth in it – it is certain that water plays an enormously important part in the physiology of the body, of which it constitutes about two thirds by weight.

Water enters into all the cells and tissues, and is necessary to the processes of digestion and absorption. As a constituent of blood and lymph it assists in carrying food nutrients to all parts of the body. It gives elasticity to the cells, enabling them to withstand shocks, and helps in lubricating the joints. The digestive juices and enzymes which break down the food in the alimentary canal are carried in aqueous solutions, while water also enters greatly into the processes of excretion.

Next to air, water is the most important necessity for life; an animal can live a long time without food but will quickly die if deprived of water. The young animal has a higher water content than the adult.

Dogs taking much exercise, with a corresponding increase in respiration, need more water than others. For growing puppies and whelping bitches plenty of water is essential. It sounds elementary to say that a dog should have constant access to fresh, clean water, yet in how many cases is this requirement really fulfilled? A dog will drink any sort of water when thirsty, not that such is always good for him. I have frequently seen a dog turn from a dust-coated bowl, yet drink freely when it was replaced clean and fresh. If I had to assess the value of a kennelman on one point alone I would take a look at his water bowls; a man who takes the trouble to keep these all correct is unlikely to be slack in other ways.

CHAPTER X

THE VITAMINS

WE have seen that the animal organism requires for its normal nutrition proteins, carbohydrates, fats, minerals and water. But if these were all the animal would die. As far back as the seventeenth century it was found that certain foods prevented or cured the disease of scurvy, though the reason was not known. It was therefore assumed, quite correctly, that such foods contained some substance or factor, which for long remained a mystery, possessing the power to protect the subject from this disease. It was Vitamin C, contained in oranges, lemons, fresh fruit and vegetables. All the foods supplying essential vitamins are now designated 'protective foods', and the vitamins themselves 'accessory food factors'.

Beri-beri was another disease which was cured by a change of diet from polished rice to a food which contained the bran in addition. Similarly, the substitution of wholemeal for white bread proved an effective preventive. This vitamin turned out to be what is now called B.1, which, as beri-beri is a disease of the nerves, is known as the 'anti-neuritic' vitamin. By the same token the scurvy-preventing Vitamin C is called 'antiscorbutic'. The history of vitamin research to the present day makes a fascinating story but would be out of place here. It will be sufficient for our purpose to set forth those which are, or may be found in the future to be, of direct interest in the feeding of dogs, and to give readers a broad picture and, I hope, a greater understanding of the whys and wherefores of canine nutrition.

First, here are a few general observations. All the (so far) known vitamins – and their number runs into the twenties – are present in minute traces. Some have been isolated and given a chemical name and formula. Generally speaking, they have to be supplied in the food, though in certain cases they can be synthesized in the body, and are catalytic in action. Adrenalin, secreted by the adrenal glands, and thyroxin, secreted by the thyroid, are examples of hormones or body-made catalysts; the vitamins, however, must be fed, either in ready-made form or as precursors from which the vitamin can be produced.

A particular vitamin may be essential for one kind of animal but not for another, either because it does not require it or because it is able to synthesize it in its own body. For instance, Vitamin C is necessary to man, monkeys and guinea-pigs, but not to dogs, rabbits, cats, birds and rats. (But in regard to dogs we shall have something to say later on.) Each vitamin is associated with one deficiency disease and is of no use as a cure for any other. This has led to some being known by the name of the disease, such as: Vitamin A (anti-infective or anti-ophthalmic); Vitamin C for scurvy (anti-scorbutic); Vitamin D for rickets (anti-rachitic). Others are known not by letters but by their chemical names, such as Folic Acid, and it seems likely that as more are isolated their nomenclature will tend more to chemical than alphabetical description. The activities of vitamins can be measured, expressed as so many International Units (IU), and these values will be noticed printed on the bottles of vitamin preparations.

The diseases resulting from absence or inadequate supply of the necessary vitamins are known as 'Deficiency Diseases', though the description is equally applicable to states of ill-health resulting from lack of minerals, or, indeed, of any of the other food nutritives. Anaemia, for instance, is a deficiency disease for iron, goitre for iodine. Just plain starvation could fairly be described as a deficiency disease – deficient in practically everything! There is a border line, arbitrary though it be, between good and bad health, across which disease may have advanced a long way before visible symptoms appear. They may never appear, yet the dog may be suffering from a deficiency, or latent deficiency, which keeps it below optimum health. We must never assume, therefore, that all is well just because we cannot actually see anything wrong, but must take all steps, so far as humanly possible, to ensure that our dogs are properly supplied with everything needed to keep them 100 per cent fit.

Vitamin A (Axerophthol)

Anti-infective or anti-ophthalmic. Vitamin A is necessary for growth and health, deficiency manifesting itself in various ways:

Conjunctivitis, leading to *Night-blindness*, axerophthol being required to combine with the visual purple in the retina of the eye. (This is not to be confused with the hereditary form.)

Xerophthalmia: absence of the vitamin causes degeneration of the mucous membranes, rendering the subject more liable to infections of all sorts; the eyes and eyelids become dry and inflamed.

Infections: these can affect many parts of the body. Professor Mellanby found that puppies fed on an A-deficient diet developed broncho-pneumonia; the addition of cod liver oil to the diet ensured good bone and freedom from this disease. No doubt the lack of other vitamins tends to lower resistance to infections, but not so directly as lack of Vitamin A.

Pro-vitamins are present in many plants, the most common being carotene, and can be converted into Vitamin A in the body, ability to convert varying in different species. Not being vegetarians, it is doubtful to what extent dogs can perform the conversion, but we are on safe ground in supplying them with the vitamin in the form of cod or halibut liver oil. It can also be fed in the form of milk, ox liver and egg yolk. CLO and halibut liver oil should be stored in the dark.

All Vitamin A emanates from plant life, whether in the liver of the ox which has consumed green grass, or in cod liver oil. In the latter case the vitamin is formed by minute marine organisms (algae) which are devoured by molluscs, which are in turn eaten by the cod, halibut or other fish. By far the greater proportion of the reserve Vitamin A in the animal body is contained in the liver; there is comparatively little in the muscles. It can be supplied from the mother to the foetus, and through the milk to the young.

VITAMIN B (Anti-neuritic)

Known as *Aneurine* in Britain and as *Thiamine* in America, it comprises a complex group of vitamins not all of which we need concern ourselves with here.

Vitamin B.1

Known as the cure for beri-beri in humans, which can cause wasting of the muscles, severe damage to the nervous system, leading in advanced cases to paralysis of the legs, mental depression, fearfulness, lack of appetite, oedema, gastro-intestinal derangements and other symptoms.

Some of the earliest experiments on B.1 deficiency were made in connection with the disease of Polyneuritis in pigeons over half a century ago. Fed on a B-free diet, the birds were collapsed and helpless, showing a peculiar retraction of the head which was bent back over the body. Administration of the vitamin effected a complete cure in a matter of hours.

A dietary consisting largely of polished rice or white bread, from which the husks have been removed, tends to create B.1 deficiency. It is easily administered in concentrated form as dried brewer's yeast. Wheat germ is another good source and, to a lesser degree, wholemeal bread, oatmeal and egg yolk.

I have on several occasions treated nervous dogs to a prolonged course of B.1 and noted decidedly beneficial results. The daily dose for a Welsh Corgi is two tablets of Benerva Vit. B.1 (Roche), obtainable from any chemist. They can be given in the food and the treatment continued for at least several months.

Vitamin B.1 is known to be a factor for normal growth and is needed more during this period than in maturity. The body's needs for it are immeasurably greater during pregnancy, parturition and lactation. It is also believed to play a part in the carbohydrate metabolism. Capacity for storage in the body is very limited, so that massive doses, in the hope that they will act over a long period, are useless; it must be fed more or less continuously. Its keeping qualities in a cool place are pretty good and it is not affected by atmospheric oxygen.

Vitamin B.2

A complex in itself, though once thought to consist of one vitamin only, called the 'anti-dermatitis factor'. It must be borne in mind that experiments on one class of animal may not prove anything for another. It is usual to select for experimentation such convenient subjects as rats and guinea-pigs, which mature and reproduce with great rapidity and can be carefully bred over many generations to ensure typical results. Quite a lot of work has of course been done on dogs, the results of which we can accept without question (insofar as present knowledge goes, that is to say), but in other cases we can only make a reasonable assumption and decide to be on the safe side by providing the appropriate vitamin in optimal amount. Science never stands still, knowledge ever grows, and the 'facts' of today may be stultified by fresh knowledge in the future. Many a nutritional discovery is hailed by a credulous public as a panacea for all ills, and is promptly exploited to the profit of the unscrupulous. The scientists cannot be blamed for this.

P.P. Factor (*Nicotinic acid, or Niacin*), which prevents the disease known as pellagra in man and black-tongue in dogs. Treatment is usually given in the form of nicotinamide. Foods containing comparatively good amounts are dried yeast or yeast extract, meat juice, meat extract and Marmite.

Riboflavin has been found to be essential for the growth of animals, including dogs, and cannot be stored in the body. A deficiency is known as aflavinosis.

Pyridoxin (*Vitamin B.6*); a deficiency has been shown to be responsible for a skin disease in rats, but I cannot find that any work has been done on dogs.

Pantothenic Acid was found to prevent a disease in poultry somewhat similar to human pellagra, and is said to be essential to dogs.

Choline is concerned with the movement of fat in the body and has been shown to be necessary to dogs, a deficiency causing fatty liver, occasionally cirrhosis (degeneration of the fibrous tissue) and paralysis.

Biotin, Inositol, Folic Acid, Vitamin B.12 (containing cobalt) are others that are possibly required by dogs, but I can trace no direct evidence for the first three. (See further note on *Vitamin B.12*, page 121.)

As a general proposition, foods which contain one B vitamin will be good for most of the others, though there may be occasions (see Vit. B.1 above) when special administration is indicated. In the ordinary way, however, only minute quantities are required, and if the changes are rung on wheat germ, oatmeal, wholemeal cereal, liver and eggs, supplemented by dried yeast, there need be little fear that our dogs will go short of any of these factors.

VITAMIN C (Ascorbic acid)

The anti-scorbutic vitamin which prevents scurvy, the scourge of seamen in the long voyages of the old sailing-ship days before it was discovered that fresh lemons and oranges were a certain preventive and cure. Symptoms of scurvy are: roughness of the skin, swollen and painful gums, loosening of the teeth, pains in the

joints, weakness and lassitude. Gastric and duodenal ulcers are
believed to be often associated with lack of the vitamin. There may
be haemorrhages causing oedema, and osteomalacia or fragility of
the bones.

Man, monkeys and guinea-pigs are subject to scurvy; dogs,
rats, birds, rabbits and cats are not. As we are concerned here only
with dogs it might be thought that this dismisses the subject,
particularly as the scientists, having failed to induce the disease in
dogs, draw the conclusion that they do not require ascorbic acid,
or, alternatively, that they can synthesize it in their own bodies.
This is a conclusion which I, for one, and I believe many others,
cannot accept, and there are many breeders who regularly make
use of orange juice in the feeding of whelping bitches and young
puppies with, as they believe, beneficial results. No doubt some
of my readers will have had puppies in the nest coming out with
what I call, for want of a suitable scientific term, 'scabby backs',
which clear up within a few days on administration of a few
drops of orange juice. I have known cases of dogs continually
licking the woodwork of their kennels, or legs of tables and chairs,
as though intuitively seeking something needed but lacking in
their diet. This habit has been completely cured with orange
juice.

For once I am prepared to disregard the findings of the scientists, and a recommendation to use Vitamin C will be found in the
Chapter on feeding. Orange juice and rose-hip syrup are concentrated and convenient sources of ascorbic acid. Fresh, green
vegetables are good, though by no means so rich, the best being
Brussels sprouts, cauliflower and spinach. The vitamin is un-
stable to heat and oxygen, therefore being largely destroyed by
cooking. Modern canning methods frequently ensure little loss;
but as a source of Vitamin C we can well afford to dispense with
the tin opener and rely on the well-tried substances mentioned
above.

Vitamin D (Calciferol)

The 'anti-rachitic' vitamin which prevents rickets and helps to
build up sound bones and teeth. An enormous amount of work has
been done on Vitamin D, much of it, especially in the early stages,
directly on dogs by Professor and Mrs Mellanby. The symptoms
of rickets are fairly well known to most of us; it is not necessary to

go into them here and I refer my readers to my notes on calcium and phosphorus.

It must be remembered that bone is not an unchangeable structure but is living tissue like many others, and constant changes are going on with substances in the circulating fluids. In the newly born the bones start as cartilage which, as growth proceeds, becomes calcified. The rate of growth of a puppy is about thirteen times that of a child, calling for very rapid deposition of calcium and phosphorus. Furthermore, there is often a shortage of calcium during pregnancy and old age, the body then drawing upon the supply in the bones, resulting in porosity and fragility (osteomalacia).

Vitamin D can be supplied ready formed, or through the pro-vitamin, ergosterol, a substance residing in the skin. The ergosterol must first be irradiated with ultra-violet light, either from the sun or a mercury-vapour lamp. We are therefore faced with the simple choice of supplying Vitamin D to our dogs by feeding it directly in the form of cod or halibut liver oil (the two richest sources available), or indirectly by exposure to sunlight. CLO is very satisfactory but is not always tolerated; it is then advisable to use halibut oil, a few drops of which will give results equal to a teaspoonful of the other.

Making use of the sun for supplying ultra-violet is not always practicable. Even when it shines there are several factors affecting its potency for our purpose. In polluted atmospheres near towns a great deal of the value of the UV is dissipated before reaching the earth. In the winter months, from October to April, it is only during the two hours around mid-day that sunshine contains any significant anti-rachitic radiations. They are all practically absorbed by ordinary window glass. A special glass (vita-glass) which admits the UV rays, is now used to a fairly large extent in office and industrial buildings, but one must not expect too much from it. In the first place it admits only from one quarter to one third of the radiation. Secondly, the windows must be kept scrupulously clean; the finest layer of dust is sufficient to bar admission of the rays. Lastly, the person or animal at the receiving end needs to be directly irradiated, there being little benefit conferred by scattered light. I cannot recommend dog breeders ever to go to the expense of installing special glass; it is far better to have kennel windows which can be taken out in suitable weather, leaving wire netting to admit the sunshine.

Cereals and oatmeal have an anti-calcifying effect, which can, however, be neutralized by supplying Vitamin D in adequate amount. Egg yolk is a good source, while summer milk and cream contain appreciable quantities. Mellanby, in his experiments with dogs, found that when the dam had been adequately supplied during pregnancy and lactation it was difficult to induce rickets in her puppies, and the influence of the maternal feeding lasted for a considerable time in the life of the offspring.

There is evidence indicating that comparatively heavy and continual administration of CLO may produce toxic effects, nausea and anorexia (loss of appetite) and fatty degeneration of the muscles of the heart. These experiments were made on animals on synthetic diets, and it is at least doubtful whether such a degree of toxicity would be found in CLO fed along with natural, well-balanced diets. They do, however, provide an argument in favour of the use of the alternative, halibut oil.

Lack of exercise has been said to influence the onset of rickets, but it is more probable that it is the sunshine obtained during the taking of the exercise, and the diet, that prevent it.

I hope sufficient has been said to indicate the importance of a generous supply of Vitamin D to pregnant and lactating bitches, growing puppies and, especially during winter, to other dogs of all ages.

Vitamin E

This is the anti-sterility vitamin, experimental work on which has mostly been carried out on rats, the results being very striking. To what extent it is required by other animals or humans is problematical, though effects have been obtained both in cattle and women which would appear to demonstrate its value. I have personally seen results in dogs which could be attributed, rightly or wrongly, to administration of the E Vitamin. A great deal more research will need to be done before any positive assertions can be made as to its value for dogs.

Briefly, female rats fed an E-free diet show normal generative processes, but the foetuses die *in utero* and are resorbed. In the male, sterility is caused by degeneration of the testes. Curative treatment with Vitamin E elicits a rapid response in the females, but with males it is slow and uncertain, depending upon the amount of testicular degeneration which has taken place.

The richest and most convenient form of supply of Vitamin E is in wheat germ oil, but this is rather expensive if fed to all and sundry. Stud dogs seem to call for a course of treatment now and again (the vitamin can be stored in the body), and any bitch who has shown herself doubtful, either by 'missing' or a false conception, should be treated before coming in season again. Another source of the vitamin, though not to be compared with WGO, is fresh lettuce, which can be cut up and mixed with the food over longer periods.

VITAMIN B.12 is a most useful drug. Apart from its anti-anaemic value it can be used as an adjunct to treatment in most illnesses, though much has yet to be learned about it and how it works. It can do no harm.

CHAPTER XI

THE DIGESTIVE SYSTEM

O F course we all know how and on what to feed our dogs; we are continually being told; we can read about it in countless books and articles in the canine Press. If this is not enough, we can seek advice from breeders, though not all of them will agree, and if we were to listen to all of them we should find ourselves in a mental fog. We know that the food goes in at the mouth and the waste products, which the body is unable to use, are voided at the other end. We know that the stomach, being filled, gives a feeling of repleteness; we experience this ourselves after a good dinner. We know, in a vague sort of way, that the food does them good, that it is digested (though we may not clearly discriminate between digestion and assimilation), and that by some mysterious provision of nature the whole thing is turned to good account in the body; the animal is enabled to live, to breathe, to move about, to grow and reproduce its species, rear its young and live to a good old age. But how many of us really understand what goes on 'inside the works'?

A comprehension of the bodily processes by which the food is converted into bone, flesh, muscle, all the complex organs of the body, and energy, enables us to take a much more intelligent interest in our feeding and gives us an understanding of the individual idiosyncrasies of our dogs. It is because I have never seen the subject given more than cursory treatment in any of the books on dogs that I am devoting some space to it in the belief that readers will find it both interesting and instructive.

The Alimentary Canal (See Fig. 12)

This is the tract which starts at the mouth, continues in the oesophagus or gullet, through the stomach, the small and large intestines, finally terminating in the rectum and anus. Let it be noted that all food and food nutrients while in the alimentary tract are regarded as being, for all practical purposes, *outside the body*; they can be of no benefit whatever to the animal until they have

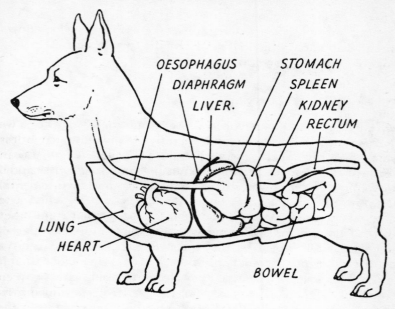

Fig. 12
The principal internal organs

been *absorbed* – mostly through the wall of the small intestine – and then *assimilated* into the blood and lymph by which they are carried to every organ and tissue.

SALIVARY DIGESTION

In the mouth are three pairs of glands which excrete saliva and which are excited by the presence of food in the mouth. They are also often stimulated to excretion by the sight or smell of food; this is what we mean when we say that some appetizing dish 'makes one's mouth water'. It is, of course, a nervous reflex. Saliva contains ferments which take part in the first process of digestion, but in the case of the dog and other carnivores, whose natural habit is to tear off and bolt lumps of flesh, there can hardly be said to be any appreciable salivary digestion in the mouth. Dry biscuit, which takes a little time to chew, will certainly undergo a very limited digestion in the mouth, and both biscuit and lumps of meat will carry some saliva down with them into the stomach where a certain amount of salivary digestion may take place. The walls of the gullet have a peristaltic action, forcing the food down into the stomach, which it reaches by the cardiac entrance. (It is possible to eat upside down.)

DIGESTION IN THE STOMACH

On entering the stomach the food comes in contact with the *gastric juice* which is poured out from digestive glands situated in the stomach walls. There is considerable muscular activity in the walls of the stomach, giving a churning movement to the food mass, breaking it down into smaller particles and mixing it with the powerful gastric juice. The first stage of protein digestion is now taking place. At the same time the food is being gradually worked along by muscular movement to the pylorus, that part of the stomach occupied by the food before it passes through the pyloric valve into the small intestine.

The *Pyloric Valve* deserves a paragraph to itself. This valve, or sphincter, regulates the passage of the partly digested food from the stomach into the small intestine, and it is interesting to see the way it works. The opening and closing of the sphincter is governed by two factors. First, the size of the food particles; second, their chemical condition. The sphincter will not allow particles to pass if they are too large, but will close against them, sending them back with the churning movement to undergo further subdivision. The gastric juice consists largely of hydrochloric acid, so that in mixing with the food the latter develops an ever-increasing degree of acidity. Until this acidity has developed to the requisite extent the pyloric valve will not allow it to pass; more gastric digestion is necessary.

The food, now in a softened and semi-fluid state, is called *chyme*. Carbohydrate foods develop acidity much more rapidly than proteins, and in consequence are retained for a shorter time in the stomach. For this reason a dog will be hungry again sooner after a cereal meal than after one of, say, raw meat. We all know that a breakfast of cereals gives a feeling of repletion which soon wears off. A well-balanced feed of proteins, fats and carbohydrates is much more satisfying than a cereal meal.

None of the digested products is absorbed from the stomach, nor is water. Curiously enough, the stomach of the dog, as with other flesh eaters, is not so essential as one would suppose. It acts as a food reservoir, macerates the food mass, and regulates the temperature of the food by bringing it to the normal body heat. Yet the whole of the stomach can be surgically removed without impairing the animal's health or digestive processes: an interesting experiment but not one likely to commend itself to my readers, who would no doubt prefer their dogs to keep their stomachs!

INTESTINAL DIGESTION

The chyme on entering the first part of the small intestine (the duodenum) now meets with some anti-peristaltic action tending to force it back towards the pylorus. (Peristalsis: the worm-like, muscular movement which takes place in the intestine and other tubular organs.) Thus the churning and mixing of the food constituents continues, and at the same time their acidity becomes neutralized by alkaline fluids, the bile and the pancreatic juice. Practically all absorption takes place from the small intestine; such is the efficiency of this organ that a large portion can be removed without any serious impairment of its functions.

The *Liver*, the largest gland in the body, excretes *bile* which passes into a reservoir, the *Gall Bladder*, from which it is poured through the bile duct to the duodenum as required. *Bile*, an alkaline fluid, when associated with pancreatic juice plays a large part in the digestion of fats. It also carries with it waste products of the liver, and promotes intestinal peristalsis, a lack of it causing constipation. An obstruction of the bile duct forces the bile to pass into the blood, producing jaundice. It is the bile which gives the characteristic colour to the faeces.

The *Pancreas*, or Sweetbread, pours its digestive juice into the duodenum which it enters close to the bile duct. The *pancreatic juice* continues the digestion of proteins started in the stomach, splits up the carbohydrates into sugars and the fats into simpler substances.

Any food not fully digested by the foregoing is dealt with by the *succus entericus*, or intestinal juice, produced by the intestinal glands, a very complex substance which completes the protein digestion and the splitting up of the carbohydrates into soluble sugars.

THE LARGE INTESTINE

This consists of the *Colon, Caecum* (absent or rudimentary in the dog) and the *Rectum*. It plays a minor part in digestion compared with the small intestine, though it is of greater importance in herbivorous animals in whom the intake of plant food introduces bacteria which have digestive functions in the intestines, splitting up the cellulose and also acting upon the fats. Dogs which have been regularly fed a proportion of vegetable food may carry what is called an 'intestinal flora', and so have some bacterial activity in the intestine. We must ever bear in mind, however, that the dog is carnivorous; to turn his digestive tract into that of a vegetarian would probably take a few million years.

ABSORPTION AND ASSIMILATION

THE LYMPHATIC SYSTEM

There are two fluids which circulate in the body – blood and lymph. We all know that if we scrape a piece of skin off the back of our hand, a colourless, watery fluid exudes over the surface of the abrasion, forming a protective coating over the wound. This is *Lymph*. It contains salts similar to the blood plasma, and corpuscles resembling the white corpuscles of the blood. The material by which the tissues are directly nourished, it also collects from them waste materials and carries them back into the blood stream. Certain tissues, such as cartilage and the cornea of the eye, rely entirely on lymph for their sustenance. The lymph is carried round the body by the *lymphatics*, or absorbent vessels, passing through lymph glands, and provision is made, by way of valves, for a one-way traffic only. Muscular contractions during exercise keep forcing the lymph through the valves, leaving a space behind for the exudation of more lymph.

Lymph glands also act as a defence against invading bacteria and prevent impurities entering the blood. The existence of the lymphatic system is one argument for giving dogs at least one daily gallop.

THE VILLI OF THE INTESTINE

The greater part of the wall of the small intestine is covered with tiny, knob-like projections, known as villi, which are in constant contact with the food passing through it. Each villus has a blood supply and a *lacteal*, the latter leading into the lymphatic system. The lacteals absorb fat from the intestine, and after a meal contain large amounts of fat globules in the form of a milky emulsion.

Water passes quickly through the stomach to the intestines and is rapidly absorbed. With the exception of fats, all other food substances are absorbed through the medium of water.

Protein is broken down during digestion into its component amino-acids, which are absorbed into the blood stream, passing to the liver and thence to the general circulation.

At this point it is convenient to mention the so-called *'Hay Diet'*, that of taking only proteins at one meal and carbohydrates at another, which was given tremendous publicity a few years ago and was swallowed 'hook, line and sinker' by a large and credulous public. The brief facts, as attested by leading nutritionists of the day, are that the proteins cannot be properly made use of unless accompanied by carbohydrates. A protein-only meal results in loss of amino-acids by conversion into urea which is excreted in the urine; it amounts to protein starvation. My readers can take it that the 'Hay Diet' has been blown sky-high and is definitely undesirable.

Carbohydrates after absorption are carried mainly to the liver where they are stored as glycogen, or animal starch, then released into the circulation, as required, in the form of glucose.

Fats are absorbed by the lacteals, entering the lymphatic system and ultimately the blood stream.

Minerals are absorbed through the walls of the digestive tract and undergo no chemical changes in the body.

All the products of absorption are carried round the body by the blood and lymph, from whence the appropriate nutrients are picked up by the body cells, the surplus being stored, either as fat deposited under the skin or around the muscles, or as glycogen in the liver.

The Organs of Excretion

These may be classified as the large intestine, kidneys, lungs and liver.

The *Large Intestine* excretes undigested or indigestible food residues, passing them out per rectum. It also excretes some nitrogenous products, minerals and water.

The *Kidneys* excrete surplus nitrogen through the urine. Toxic substances, if present in the body, are also excreted in the urine.

The *Lungs*, through which the body receives its oxygen, are also excretory in the sense that they pass out carbon dioxide and water vapour, the latter ridding the body of surplus heat.

The *Liver* excretes various substances through the bile.

Ch. Gay Dancer of Beecroft

Ch. Hildenmanor Crown Prince

Am Ch. Pennington Gloriand

Aust Ch. Dygae Super Spark

Sally Anne Thompson

Ch. Lees Rhiwelli Blue Ray and puppies

Ch. Withybrook Caesar

Marjorie Baker

Ch. Lees Melody and Int. Ch. Lees Symphony

Diane Pearce

Ch. Cordach Golden Plover

CHAPTER XII

FOODS AND FEEDING

M cCOLLUM and Becker, of Johns Hopkins University, Baltimore, USA, writing in *Food, Nutrition and Health*, say:

Animals on certain faulty diets become nervous and apprehensive, whereas normal ones are free from these defects. In our rat colony of 2,000 to 3,000 animals which have been kept for nutrition investigations for a period of twenty-one years we have seen evidences of physical inferiority only in those groups in which the diet either of the parents or the young was unsatisfactory. Partial deprivation for any essential factor may not cause the well-defined deficiency disease, but will surely undermine health. The absence of these dietary diseases is no guarantee of the excellence of the food supply. In the aggregate the most important thing is to avoid the borderline states of malnutrition which result from taking a diet which is not well constituted.

The dog being by nature carnivorous, it seems only common sense to treat him as such. His digestive system is not designed to deal with quantities of carbonaceous and vegetable foods, and though we go outside nature so far as to feed some amount of biscuit and other cereal in supplying the carbohydrate part of the ration, there is no doubt in the minds of enlightened dog owners that meat must form the basis – and preferably raw meat. Certainly many dogs are fed a proportion of vegetables, and appear none the worse for it, but it must be borne in mind that in the non-carnivorous animals vegetable foods are subjected to considerable bacterial activity in the intestine. It is believed that the dog can, to a limited extent, be 'educated' to the digestion of green foods by the gradual development of an intestinal flora, but he will never be a vegetarian, and there is nothing which vegetables supply which cannot be better supplied in other ways. The fact that dogs are frequently seen eating grass proves nothing to the contrary, but only that they are seeking a natural emetic or expellent of stomach worms.

Mr A. J. Sewell, MRCVS, one of the leading canine pathologists, is quoted as saying: 'I do not like vegetables for dogs, and I think the less given the better. Dogs living in the country can eat grass if they want anything green; and even London dogs have a chance of going into the parks.'

The stomach and digestive system of the dog are very much smaller, in proportion to the size of the animal, than those of the herbivores and less qualified to deal with large quantities of bulky foods. The herbivore in a state of nature can be eating many hours a day; not so the carnivore, who kills and eats his prey and may not get another meal for a long time. It is therefore essential that he should have a more concentrated food which will not overload the stomach and yet will stay with him for some time. Raw meat fulfils these conditions.

The feeding of soft, sloppy foods is condemned by the best authorities as unnatural and undesirable. A dog needs some hard tack which he has to chew – dry biscuit or raw bones – to bring his masticatory muscles into play and to keep his teeth free from tartar. While he cannot deal with quantities of bulky foods, a large percentage of which is water, he must still have enough bulk of concentrated food comfortably to fill the stomach. Also – and the importance of this cannot be over-emphasized – there must be variety, for the following reasons:

(1) Variety is more likely to provide all the essential constituents;
(2) It increases palatability, which becomes lost in monotonous diets;
(3) Palatability and variety stimulate appetite.

If a healthy dog will not eat good, varied and palatable food, he should not be tempted with all sorts of flavourings, condiments and appetizers. Let him go without for twenty-four hours; he will eat when he is hungry enough. And never on any account leave him with an untouched or unfinished dish; that is the best way to sicken him of the sight of it. I do not want to be too hard and fast on this matter; dogs, like humans, can have their idiosyncrasies; they should be individually studied and one should try to feed them what they will not only eat but enjoy. 'A little of what you fancy does you good.' This is equally true of dogs and humans. Some dogs eat best in company; others alone.

It is probably correct to say that more dogs, particularly house pets, suffer from an excess of food than from a lack of it. Moreover, the house pet gets far too many meals between meals, and is stuffed up with sugar-cake and all sorts of tit-bits calculated to give him fatty degeneration and a shorter life than he might enjoy if rationally. fed. A lady brought a Pembroke bitch to me after I had judged a championship show, complaining that she was a very bad doer and asking what I would advise. Some questioning elicited the astonishing news that she fed her six times a day! What she called 'little and often'. If there ever was a dog sick of the sight of food it was that one. The expert feeder of fattening poultry, a business at which some of the old hands are extremely clever, likes to remove the mash just when the bird fancies one more mouthful. A dog should eat his food, polish the dish, and just be wanting a little more. Of course this does not go for the glutton, who will eat his own and several other dinners if given the chance. The comparison with the fattening bird, which it is desired to get as fat as possible as soon as possible, is really applicable only to the shy feeder.

Whether adult Corgis should be fed once or twice a day is a matter on which opinions differ, but if fed twice it is best to give a light feed in the morning and the main meal at night. In the summer I do not think it matters much either way, but in cold weather, when more food is needed to keep up the body temperature, an extra feed is to be recommended. House dogs may well have their main feed at mid-day.

Dogs should not be fed immediately preceding or after heavy exercise, nor when they come in overheated or the reverse, or very tired. Half an hour's rest first is advised. Drastic changes in feeding should not be introduced suddenly. Any new food, to which the dog is not accustomed, is best brought in gradually.

MEAT

In this we include lean beef, horse, paunch or tripe, udder, rabbit, mutton, liver, heart, bullock or sheep's heads; plenty of variety here. The breeder in more than a very small way will patronize the knacker's yard. All sorts of animals find their way into these establishments and very good dog meat can usually be obtained from them. It is always advisable to fetch your meat yourself, then you can see what today's 'fare' is like and you may have some choice in the matter. The knacker makes a distinction (though not a difference in price!) between 'dead' and 'live' meat. The former comes from a beast which may have died out in the field, and possibly lain there many hours before it could be collected; the latter has been killed on the premises and properly bled. Sometimes an animal has been heavily physicked before death, and there is some danger in feeding this meat to dogs. But if you are on good terms with your supplier he will tell you this and advise you to cook it thoroughly and throw away the liquid.

It is not infrequently recommended that all knacker's meat be well boiled in any case, advice with which I strongly disagree; the superiority of raw over cooked meat is too great, and I have had very little trouble, nothing serious, over many years. In hot weather it will have to be cooked sooner or later, unless you have a large refrigerator or a freezer; but I always feed raw as long as I can. Dogs don't mind it a bit 'high' and it does not seem to do them any harm.

I have never been partial to *Horse* for dogs, though I have often had to feed it when beef was not available. It is a richer and more concentrated food than beef, liable to upset the digestion, and should be fed a smaller ration: say ¾ lb horse for 1 lb beef. If boiled, the rich, greasy gravy should be thrown away. I prefer *Beef*.

Paunch is a most useful food, not so rich in protein as muscle meat but very digestible, containing a good proportion of fat and relished by most dogs. Its high digestibility renders it a satisfactory food for puppies. As received from the knacker, it needs to be thoroughly washed, then lightly cooked. A raw paunch hung in the meat safe will keep well; portions can be cut off and cooked as required for use. *Tripe*, as sold in butchers' shops, is paunch cooked and refined. *Neck of Mutton*, fed with boiled rice, is very good for putting on flesh.

Sheep or *Bullock's Heart* (cooked) makes a pleasant change, but *Liver* should be fed only in small amounts; it is said to irritate the intestine and be too laxative if used to excess. I have often fed *Udder*; I cannot say what its analysis is, but the dogs appreciate it and it provides variety. *Rabbit* should be cooked and carefully separated from the bones; it is very useful for tasting up a meal for a shy feeder, while its digestibility makes it an excellent food for young puppies and invalids.

Dehydrated meat cannot be compared with the genuine raw article. In war or other times of shortage one may be glad of a supply on hand to tide over emergencies. *Tinned foods* of any sort should be used only when nothing better is available.

The knacker's yard and the abattoir have a big role in providing meat for the bigger kennels, but today some very good dog feed can be found at many of our excellent pet stores. Most of the canned dog food today is very good and useful to have in the larder, but I would always prefer to give my dogs fresh food if it is easily available.

Milk

Analyses of milk as given in various publications differ a good deal; the following is taken from *Animal Nutrition*, by Professor L. A. Maynard, Director of the School of Nutrition, Cornell University:

	Water	Protein	Fat	Lactose	Ash	Calcium	Phosphorus	Calories
Cow	87·2	3·5	3·7	4·9	0·72	0·12	0·095	74
Goat	86·5	3·6	4·0	5·1	0·81	0·13	0·104	79
Bitch	75·4	11·2	9·6	3·1	0·73	—	—	163

It will be seen that bitch's milk is over three times as rich in protein, and nearly three times as rich in fat, as cow's milk, so that the latter can never be a substitute for it unless reinforced with cream or casein, or eggs. A raw egg, beaten up in a cupful of milk, gives a very close approximation to bitch's milk.

Eggs are very similar to milk in many ways, though containing less calcium and sugar, and are rich in iron.

Fish

Fish cannot take the place of meat but it is a convenient change and provides mineral salts and iodine. Cod and haddock are rated as lean fish, providing protein but little fat. Herring and mackerel (fat fish) provide fat in addition. A pressure cooker is useful, bones and heads being reduced to a pulp. Rabbits can be dealt with in the same way.

CEREALS

Wholemeal biscuit or meal, stale or rusked brown bread, rice, oatmeal and flaked maize are all good cereal foods to feed in conjunction with meat. As already mentioned, sloppy feeding should be avoided; biscuits are better fed dry than soaked, advice which is endorsed by leading canine nutritionists in America as well as this country.

Biscuit meal, flaked maize and oatmeal should be soaked with boiling water or gravy to the limit of what they will take up but no more. Boiled rice is easily digested. But the wholemeal cereals are the sheet anchor. Care must be taken in storing them, and not too much should be bought at one time. The best storage bin is the ordinary household dustbin, rounded inside at the bottom, which is easy to clean. The long, four-compartment bin, with square corners, is a trap for weevils, mould and dirt, and can never be properly cleaned.

POTATOES

As a food potatoes provide starch and ascorbic acid, but little else, and are best left out of our calculations both for kennel and house dogs.

FEEDING THE ADULT CORGI

The objective to be kept in mind is a healthy fit dog, neither too fat nor too lean, adjusting the amount of food to the exercise, the weather, and if required for the show ring or hard work. I never weigh food; if I saw a kennelman doing this I would consider he was either wasting his time or did not know his job. The skilled feeder uses his eyes, not the scales, and studies the condition of his charges. But for the initial guidance of the novice an adult Pembroke will eat about half a pound of meat a day, with an equal quantity (not weight) of cereal, this ration being increased somewhat for the Cardigan.

In winter he should get a teaspoonful each of cod liver oil and calcium, and three or four yeast tablets daily in alternate months. Meat should be fed in fair-sized lumps, and the condition of the dog watched, the amount of food being regulated accordingly. House pets getting a minimum of exercise should have their carbohydrate cut down, leaving a larger percentage of lean meat. I do not consider it necessary to feed CLO to adults in summer when sunshine irradiates the ergosterol in the skin to produce Vitamin D.

FEEDING THE BROOD BITCH

No extra food is needed during the first few weeks of pregnancy, but after that she should have her ration gradually increased, CLO, calcium, iron and Vitamin B being added. When she begins to appear unmistakably in whelp the daily food should be divided into two or three meals in order not to overload the stomach. Milk is a good food in pregnancy, but many bitches seem to go off milk at this time. However, let her have what she likes in reason, and keep her happy. She is likely to refuse food when close to whelping, after which event she may have light meals for a few days. Newly born pups do not take a great deal out of her for the first week or so, and it is a mistake to press her with food. Later her ration must be gradually increased so that she gets pretty well all she will eat. A high protein ration is called for, with plenty of CLO and calcium, Vitamin B, and a small quantity of orange juice daily.

FEEDING THE STUD DOG

Stud dogs should be fed exactly as the other adults, except for an extra ration of raw meat. They need to be kept in good active condition with plenty of exercise. (See Chapter on Vitamins in connection with Vitamin E for stud dogs and brood bitches.)

ANTI-OBESITY FEEDING

This is not always easy; some dogs, and especially bitches, have a tendency to put on superfluous flesh with very little food. Lean meat should be the basis and all fattening foods avoided. A somewhat drastic treatment for the over-fat dog is 3 oz raw meat per day with just a very small scattering of Allbran and no more. This will take a week or so to show results, but I assure you it will. One needs a hard heart to get surplus weight off a dog. But bear in mind it is very much for their benefit, they will become brighter more alert and far more active.

Conditioning for Show

The Welsh Corgi is shown in what may be called good natural condition, but for the show ring he is required to carry rather more flesh than would be the case in one kept solely for work. If correctly fed there is no necessity to make any change in the feeding. It is more important to have him in good coat and well muscled-up; a dog which handles 'soft' is not looked upon with favour by judges. Good feeding and good exercise (not *too* much of the latter) are therefore the key to condition for the show ring.

Attention to daily grooming, which has been stressed elsewhere, is vitally important; one sees in the ring many dogs which would have looked better for more grooming.

A good *conditioner for dogs* is the following:

> 10 oz cod liver oil;
> 2 oz Parrish's Food.

A half-teaspoonful daily, gradually increased to a dessertspoonful.

Fresh Herrings, when they can be got, are splendid for putting a bloom on a dog. Put them in a saucepan of cold water, bring to the boil, then mash them up and feed either alone or with biscuit meal soaked in the herring water.

Feeding Corgi Puppies

This begins before they are born, for they are being fed through the dam, who cannot pass on to them anything she is not given or cannot draw from her own reserves. We must not allow her to deplete her reserves, to which end her feeding should be as varied and complete as possible.

The weaning stage is dealt with in the Chapter on rearing. From then the pups must be kept growing on, not losing their puppy flesh, getting plenty of raw meat cut up in lumps of increasingly large size as they grow and are able to deal with them. The growing puppy needs a higher proportion of protein than the adult, while its demands for calcium and phosphorus are also greater. The sooner they get on to dry, solid food, the better; too much milk and 'pappy' food will not grow a firm, solid dog.

Young puppies should be encouraged at an early age to play

with and chew a hard biscuit or an unsplinterable raw bone. Bone flour, a pinch on the food daily, with CLO, will supply calcium and phosphorus, and a yeast tablet will take care of the Vitamin B complex. The orange juice can be discontinued at three or four months, at which age the feeds can be reduced to three a day. At six months two feeds daily will be sufficient; at twelve months or so the feeding may be the same as for adults.

CHAPTER XIII

TRAINING THE CORGI

THE early lessons in training have been described in the Chapter on rearing Corgi puppies. Before going on from there let me make a few general observations and mention some considerations to be kept in mind when educating a dog; to forget them would make the task more difficult for the trainer and less pleasant for the dog. First, let it be categorically stated that an animal does not think, in the sense that it is capable of reasoning from cause to effect. A great many sentimental people will disagree with this; they are full of pity for the lion whom they picture lying behind his bars dreaming nostalgically of the jungle, and they will quote remarkable feats by dogs which – superficially, at least – could be ascribed only to a thinking brain. But the biologists do not confirm this. On the contrary, they will tell you that the lion is doing nothing of the sort; comfortably housed, well and regularly fed, he is quite happy, and I am bound to say he looks it. Unlike the village yokel, who 'sometimes sits and thinks, and sometimes just sits', he is not troubled by the 'thinking' part of it – which perhaps is fortunate for him.

Of course a lion, or any other animal, including dogs and humans, can be ill-treated by confinement in dark, dirty or cramped quarters, but this does not vitiate the argument. The examples of reasoning credited to dogs can, if fully investigated, be shown to be due to memory and association of ideas. Most animals have good memories – 'an elephant never forgets' – and just as a horse will 'shy' at a spot on the road where he has been frightened at some time, so will a dog associate one thing with another. To take a simple case, he will be quite uninterested when his master walks out of the house wearing his bowler hat and umbrella, but will jump with delight when he is clad in garb which is *associated* with a walk. Similarly, a puppy in course of being house-trained learns to associate the act of decorating the carpet with a scolding, and will run to the door, which he associates with being let out to do his business. It is all as simple as that. It is on these two factors, memory and association of ideas, that all animals are trained.

There is also instinct, something handed down from primeval ancestors through countless generations; the instinct to hunt and kill for food, the jungle law of tooth and claw, the herding instinct in the Welsh Corgi and other breeds, and, strongest of all, the care of a mother for her offspring. Some of the instincts in our Corgis — and in our children, if it comes to that — we wish to encourage, others to suppress; otherwise both dog and child will grow up into little hooligans.

The cardinal virtues in a successful animal trainer are Firmness, Kindness, unlimited Patience, and, above all, Understanding. I think I would place the last first, because without it there can be no Trust, no ability to get inside the mind of the pupil, to establish the link of Confidence between pupil and teacher which transcends all other considerations. If any reader believes that an animal can be trained by harsh, cruel methods, omitting the Trust, then I recommend a book called *The English Circus*, by Ruth Manning Sanders. But in stressing the kindness, understanding and all that, we must not forget Firmness. Young dogs, like small boys, feel rebellious sometimes; they like to fool their teacher, and will get away with it if they can. I believe some ultra-modern educationists advocate letting the child do pretty well what it likes; what they call self-expression, or something. I tremble to think what would happen if we were to apply this system to our dogs who, after all, are only children themselves. By all means temper justice with mercy; but justice there must be, and the dog in training must never be allowed to 'get away with it'. Let that be made clear to him.

You want to teach your puppy to do what he is told, and to leave undone those things he should not do. But first he must be shown what to do, and then given a word (or, rather, a sound, for he does not understand words as we do) which he will learn to associate with the doing. We have seen how you have taught your puppy to sit down on command; you have shown him what to do by pressing him down into a sitting position, and you have given him a word, or sound, by saying 'Sit'. With a little practice he will learn what the sound 'Sit' means and will obey the command. He will also learn, because you will teach him, that he must not move till he gets another command, which may be the word 'Up' or any other word you care to use. You must never alter either the words or the tone and inflexion of the voice in any command. That would only confuse him, and it is terribly easy to confuse him. Nor must you ever forget to finish off the exercise properly, not calling him, patting him on the head or saying 'Good dog' without first giving him the 'Up'. In all his exercises there must be no ragged ends. Everything must be crisp and clear, and nothing must be introduced that is likely to cause any doubts or uncertainties in his mind.

When training your puppy it is very advisable to do so in some place where he will have no distractions. To attempt it where some unthinking member of the family may at any moment pop his or her head round the corner to ask how you are getting on is hopeless, and unfair to the pupil. He should be free from all such temptations until he has really mastered an exercise; then will be time enough to ask him to work in less cloistered surroundings.

Clearly the first thing a puppy should learn is his name, by which I mean one name, not two or three. If you decide that it shall be Bobby, then do not on occasions abbreviate it to Bob, nor allow anyone else to call him Bob. I have known pet dogs addressed by four names by their owners and other members of the household. One dog, one name; and stick to it. He will learn his name at a very early age if you call him by it when you feed him or make a fuss of him, and will come to you when you call him. Make sure that the sound of his name will always evoke a pleasurable feeling in his mind, so that he will never associate it with something unpleasant, such as a scolding, but will come to you when he hears it.

For scoldings or corrections make use of some other word ('Ah! bad dog!', or what you will) which tells him he has done wrong. You can also make use of the word 'No', which he will come to associate with something wrong that he is doing or about to do. 'No' is a very useful word and one you will have to use quite often in the early stages, though naturally you will try not to overwork it. Young dogs, like their human counterparts, are full of mischief, and a very good thing too. They will be all the better for it when they grow up. 'Riotous puppies make the best hounds' is a truism which any huntsman will endorse. So, while coming down promptly on anything which may become a bad habit, do not adopt the attitude of 'Nurse, go and see what Master Richard is doing and tell him not to.' Keep your pupil happy by working and playing with him, enjoying his high spirits, and do not expect a three-months-old puppy to learn more than a few very elementary lessons. If you can teach him his name, house cleanliness, and not to chew up anything which happens to be left about, that is about all you can expect, though you can start lead-training at about four months. In regard to chewing things, it is better to keep him out of temptation by providing him with a large raw bone, or a hard biscuit, to amuse himself with. An old knotted sock or stocking is a good plaything for what I call a 'tiddle-pup'; he can be encouraged to play with it and leave other things alone.

The training of a dog demands an ability really to get inside the pupil's mind and that indefinable quality which establishes a sympathetic link between master and dog. If the link is there, then the whole business will be easier, happier and more fruitful. And what satisfaction we feel when our pupil has passed out with honours, an obedient and well-behaved dog who refrains from barking at nothing, putting up muddy paws on visitors, chasing bicycles, biting the postman and other crimes too numerous to mention, making him a nuisance to all and sundry. Moreover, he himself will enjoy life more fully for his obedience training. A disciplined dog is a happy dog.

CORRECTION, PUNISHMENT AND REWARD

Now we will get on to a more advanced stage, which can start at about five to six months; one cannot be dogmatic about this as much depends upon the puppy's temperament. Professional trainers usually like to take them in hand at six months or later, but the amateur may be recommended to start earlier, before the puppy has got into bad habits which will be difficult to cure. It is generally easier to teach a good habit than to cure a bad one.

We will assume that you have taught him to lead properly without pulling, and to sit for a few minutes on command. Rewards and Corrections are the basis of training, so that the pupil gets to associate well-doing with the former, wrong-doing with the latter. Tit-bits can be used as rewards but should not become a regular practice, or the dog will get to a stage when he will not work without them. Your unmistakable expression of approval should generally be sufficient reward and will be quite satisfying to the dog if you have already earned his affection.

I make a distinction between Correction and Punishment. When a dog in the course or learning an exercise does it wrongly it is just as likely to be your fault as his, in that you may not have made it absolutely clear to him what you want him to do. Or, though he did it all right yesterday, he may have fogotten it today; or perhaps he is not feeling on top of his form today, and is not working so well in consequence. Dogs can have their 'off' days just as we can; you must be understanding and make allowances for this. I associate Punishment only with wilful wrong-doing, when it should be hard and prompt, leaving no doubt whatever in the recipient's mind as to what it is for, and making an impression on him which he is not likely to forget. As a general axiom, a puppy should never be punished, only corrected, or he may get cowed – and that is fatal to all your plans. The best way to scold a puppy is described in the Chapter on rearing.

One of the most important considerations in training is to make the lessons short and never let the pupil get bored. If you keep him at it till he gets bored and slack you are likely to finish the lesson with some bad work. It is better to end while he is doing well, so that you can praise him. Then he will associate the lesson with a feeling of pleasure. Regular training is essential; just a little every day, or at most twice a day, with no intervals of several days in which he can forget what he has learnt.

The reader must decide whether he wishes to train his dog to be a pleasant, obedient companion, or with a view to competing in Obedience Trials, for the standard required in public competition is very much more exacting in many ways that that necessary for the pet dog.

Coming When Called

Many a dog will cheerfully obey this injunction when he has nothing better to do, but will ignore it when it suits him to do so. We see this every day of the week, the irate owner shouting unparliamentary remarks after him; then, when he eventually does catch him, giving him a walloping. 'That'll teach him to come when I call him!' Of course it teaches him nothing of the sort, for he now associates returning to his owner with a hiding and will not come at all next time. A young puppy can be partially trained by associating food or a tit-bit with coming when called by name, but the tit-bit should be replaced by praise. You want more than cupboard love. The next treatment, when the puppy is used to collar and lead, is the check cord, a light line five to ten yards long attached to the collar. Hold the end in your hand and let him run about; then, before he takes out all the line, call him. If he comes, well and good; praise him; but if not, continue calling, at the same time hauling him in by the line. As soon as he reaches you praise and make a fuss of him.

Next day take him out on the cord where temptations abound. He may see the neighbour's dog and will dash towards it; immediately call him sharply, at the same time jerking him back on the cord. (How vigorous you make the jerk depends on the age and temperament of the puppy, and I cannot advise you. It must be sharp enough to stop him in his tracks but not to cow him.) Now haul him in, calling him, and make a fuss of him. Note that we are still working on memory and association of ideas; he will associate disobedience with a hard jerk, and the return to you, however unwillingly, with praise.

You can practise this quite often, but do not let him realize that he is on the lead; many dogs behave well when they know they are under control. In theory, the correctly trained dog will always run back to his owner when called, but it does not always work out that way in practice. If he is engaged in the exciting occupation of hunting a hedgerow or chasing a rabbit, he may be deaf to all abuse or entreaties. The common reaction of the owner is to catch him, if he can, and thrash him. Associating rejoining his owner with a thrashing, he will be a great deal more difficult to catch on the next occasion. An impasse is arrived at, the owner wanting to punish the dog for an offence, the dog associating, not the offence but the act of coming back, with the punishment. Stop shouting at him, and don't run after him; you will stand a much better chance by just walking casually, when you may be able to grab him when he is not expecting it.

The most likely cure for this sort of thing is to take him out on a long drag cord, the cord trailing behind him. Do not let him get further away from you than the length of the cord, or rather less. When he 'runs in' put your foot on the cord (you will have to be very quick in this), thus pulling him up with a jerk. If you can grab the end of the cord, instead of putting a foot on it, let him go to the full extent and give him a really sharp pull – hard enough to pull him right over backwards. Such treatment may be too severe for a puppy, but not for an adult. Be careful to let him associate the jerk with the word 'No', or whatever word you use; then call him to you. Face your dog and walk backwards as he comes, so that he comes right up to you. Never walk towards him.

WALKING TO HEEL

This corresponds to 'Heel free' in the Obedience Tests. It should follow, not precede, the 'Come when called', as also should the next exercise, the 'Sit', because the dog is now free and subject to no control except the sound of your voice. In making the change from 'lead' to 'free' it is as well to do a little insurance by making use of the check cord, holding most of it in your hand and paying it out so that the dog does not realize that he is on it. But give him only a little rope at first, so that you can jerk him in, with the sharp command 'Heel', the moment he errs. Again, take him amongst temptations in all sorts of places before chancing him entirely free.

In any exercise, if you try a dog too highly and he badly blots his copybook it will put his education back a long way, which means you will have to go with him and do a lot of your work over again. It is inevitable sometimes, but avoid it if you can.

SIT AND STAY PUT

Similar considerations apply here. It is easy to teach a dog to sit or lie down, not so easy to persuade him to stay there ten or fifteen minutes while you are out of sight. First of all he will not understand why he is being left there at all; then all kinds of distractions are liable to unsettle him, apart from simple boredom. It is entirely a question of patience and lengthening the time very gradually, but well worth while when the pupil has learnt the lesson.

Leave the collar and lead on him at first. Having got him sitting, now back very slowly away from him, repeating the word 'Sit'. Every time he gets up, which he will frequently do, lead him back to the spot – always the same spot – and sit him, saying 'Sit' in a firm voice, and, if you like, giving him a light tap on the nose at the same time. As he improves you can walk about, within sight, always keeping an eye on him, even when your back is turned, so that you can correct him at once when he moves. Now walk round him. The first time you go round him he will probably move – but keep persevering.

You will now ask him to stay put while you are out of sight, sound or scent. It is imperative, when teaching this, to take up some vantage point not far away where you can watch him, for you must be in a position to correct him without a moment's delay. This is an important principle in dog training. Do not always wait till you have to correct him; it is all the better if you can go back to him and praise him for doing well. The time you expect him to sit without moving can be gradually extended, and you can also teach him the 'Down', a more comfortable posture if he is to stay there long. Make sure he understands and can distinguish between the commands 'Sit' and 'Down'. Do not be unfair to him by trying him too highly; this is an exercise in which I have often seen professionally trained Obedience dogs go wrong. *Make lessons short!*

BEHAVING IN COMPANY

We all know the dog which jumps up at visitors (and not only visitors) with muddy paws, sits up and begs for food at every meal, is always asking to be picked up and cuddled by somebody or other, barks inordinately without any good reason, chases the postman, and prefers getting under everybody's feet to lying quietly in his own corner. Some of these undesirable habits are most difficult to cope with, for the simple reason that one gets no co-operation from visitors and others, who call him a 'dear little dog' and caress him, offer him tit-bits without any with-your-leave or by-your-leave, and generally encourage him to behave like a little gangster.

To mess about with someone else's dog, particularly to offer it food, should be listed as a punishable crime! What is the use of you teaching him good manners when these inconsiderate people stultify all your work in this way? It is frequently someone whom you do not know very well, and have to be polite to, so that the very natural and rude reaction which surges up in your breast has to be stifled. Of course you will not let your dog behave in this unruly manner, but will put him in his basket and tell him to stay there. You will have to be more insistent with the visitors than with the dog. Rather than expose him to this undesirable treatment it is better to put him another room till they have gone.

Senseless Barking

No dog can be blamed for barking when he hears some unusual sound. In a house dog it is a very good trait, and that is why burglars don't like a house with a dog. But senseless barking, whether in house or kennels, is a habit which should be nipped in the bud. It is easily cured. In kennels, where one dog may set the others off, producing a good old chorus, I go down and crack a whip, or give the outside of the kennel a few resounding whacks with a stick, at the same time shouting 'Quiet!' in a loud voice. The great thing is to frighten the whole lot of them (the innocent have to suffer with the guilty), so that they will associate the word 'Quiet' with a command to stop making a row. After this has been done a couple of times it will only be necessary, when they make a noise, to put one's head out of the window and shout 'Quiet!', when there will be instant silence.

Biting the Postman

A dog will sometimes acquire this and other bad habits through no fault of his own. It may be that at some time in his formative age he has had a clout from a man in a peaked cap or carrying a bag over his shoulder. This has frightened him, with the result that he takes an instant dislike to anyone appearing to answer the description photographed in his brain, and expresses his fear, as dogs often do, by attacking the object of his fear. It is very seldom of any use to punish in these cases; in fact it generally does more harm than good. The only way is to remove the fear, and unless you have a very obliging and dog-loving postman, prepared to spend a few minutes each morning in convincing 'Towser' that his fears are groundless, then I am afraid there is little you can do beyond keeping him shut up till after the mail has been delivered.

I might mention here, as an aside, that a dog will never bite you if you stand still, a fact I have had (unwillingly) opportunities of proving to my own satisfaction scores of times. But you must stand really still and not move a muscle, however threatening the situation appears. When he has had a good smell all round you, and seems more or less satisfied, you can start, very slowly indeed, to back away. This is the ticklish part of the business and you cannot move too slowly.

Dogs and Livestock

A great deal has been heard recently on the subject of damage done by dogs to sheep, poultry and other livestock, the blame for which should be attached not to the dogs but to their owners, who could have prevented practically all of this if their dogs were properly brought up and controlled. Puppies fortunate enough to be reared in the country can generally be given ample opportunities at a tender age of meeting various kinds of farm stock; the sooner and the more they do so, the better. A farmer who would object, naturally enough, to an adult dog being tried amongst his sheep or poultry would view with less disapproval a request to introduce to them a twelve-weeks-old puppy who could not do any damage and would more likely put his tail between his legs and run away. A good frightening at an early age was the method adopted by a Master of Hounds of my acquaintance, who used to tie his foxhound puppies in a narrow corridor and drive a flock of sheep over them. The experience ensured that they would leave sheep strictly alone in future, and no doubt saved them a few good hidings.

The town dog, taken into the country for a holiday, can be a potential menace, especially when there are two together. By all means let your dog run about and enjoy himself, but do keep your eyes open and put him on the lead when likely to be near sheep or cattle. All your careful training may not avail if the temptation to run them becomes too strong for him. Rabbits are vermin, and the killing of one or two does nobody much harm; but one thing leads to another, and a dog which goes off rabbiting may very easily be led into less innocuous pastimes.

Some General Observations

The foregoing notes are not intended as a complete treatise on training your Corgi. That would take a book, and there are several excellent publications, written by expert trainers, which readers sufficiently interested can buy for themselves. I hope, however, these notes will have given the ordinary Corgi owner an idea of the right way to go about it and to bring up his puppy as a decently behaved and true companion from whom he will get the maximum of pleasure over many years.

Remember that the first essential is mutual trust; then your dog will delight to please you. If you have children, do teach them how to treat a puppy, to be quiet with him and not over-tire him in prolonged games. Let all your orders be firm and clear, so that he understands what is expected of him. Do not nag.

Make haste slowly in your training lessons; a little every day, and let him master one exercise before starting the next. If he is having an 'off' day, or you feel a bit livery yourself, do not persevere; give him an easy task in which he can do well and earn your praise, then pack up for the day.

If you ever have to punish him let retribution follow immediately upon the crime. It is no use telling him he is being punished for something he did ten minutes ago; he will not understand and he cannot think back. He can only associate the punishment with what he is doing at the time he receives it, which may be something perfectly right. No one is fit to train a dog who cannot get into the dog's mind and see things from his viewpoint.

CHAPTER XIV

GENERAL MANAGEMENT

I AM afraid this is a 'bits and pieces' chapter, into which I have collected all sorts of odds and ends which come into my mind. Some might perhaps have been appropriately dealt with elsewhere, and yet they mostly do seem suitable for inclusion under the above heading. In running a kennel of show dogs there are a hundred and one things to think of; we are apt to lose sight of them sometimes, occasionally to turn a blind eye to some job which we know very well needs doing; some we may just forget. 'Always put off till tomorrow what you don't want to do today' is a bad motto and a practice certainly not to be encouraged. We all suffer, to a greater or lesser extent, from the usual human frailties and it is not for any of us to cast a stone. It is as well, however, to bear in mind that livestock of any sort or kind are not inanimate objects which can be left to take care of themselves when not wanted. Nor are they able or willing to do for themselves the things which we have to do for them. If ever we forget or neglect them, then they are liable to suffer in body or in mind, for the dog has a mind even if he cannot think or reason for himself as we do. He can be happy or bored, just as he can be comfortable or the reverse. And one thing of which we can be absolutely certain is that a happy dog will do better in every way then a bored one. It is therefore important, if only from the material aspect, to see that our dogs are contented in mind as well as in body.

ROUTINE

Of course I am in favour of routine; aren't we all? Regular hours of feeding, kennel cleaning, exercising, and all the rest of it; we are bound to have some thought-out plan of action or we should always be in a muddle and half the work would never get done. It is worth while for any kennelman, employed or self-employed, to study how to save time so as to get through the chores efficiently and quickly. The time thus saved can be spent in other ways very profitably on the dogs themselves. I have sometimes wondered how many miles, without going off the place, I must have walked in a week, and how many I could have saved if I had had the sense to work out a better plan or cultivate a better memory. It is such silly things as going back for the shovel, or a bag of sawdust, which one should have remembered, that add to one's troubles.

Dogs no doubt appreciate a routine – up to a point. That is, they like their dinner at the appointed time, and are liable to let you know if it is late. Similarly, if they are accustomed to being taken out for exercise at a certain hour they will get restless as the hour approaches. Again, if it is a kennel routine to let them out in their runs last thing at night to relieve themselves they will be expecting this, and will delay in settling down until it is done. But, apart from such very necessary and advisable routines, the less dogs are subject to fixed plans the better. Many kennels dogs are forced to lead far too monotonous lives. They live in the same kennel, go out in the same run or paddock, see the same dogs and people, are taken on the same old walk day after day, week in, week out. It is only when they are put in the car and taken to a show that they get any real change – and even then they spend most of the time on their benches.

This indictment is not intended for all kennels, by any means, but I am sure it applies to a good many. Such a state of affairs is not necessary; there are several ways in which their lives can be brightened up, even in fairly large establishments. For instance, many kennel owners I know make a point of having a few of the kennel dogs in the house for an hour or so; not every day, as there are too many of them for this. But they take turns and all have their little session, which they enjoy, and they feel they are being noticed. They need not be in the house all the time; they can run about in the garden and generally amuse themselves round the place. It is good for the owner, too, who will get to know their individual characters much better and will draw out of them latent qualities which he did not know they possessed. Human companionship is a splendid thing for dogs.

Most dogs like an outing in the car. This is another way to give them a change; it does not matter much where they go, if only on a shopping expedition; the thing is to give them variety – the spice of life. I am sure they enjoy seeing fresh places, a run in a bit of country they have never seen before. As they sit looking out of the window they are full of interest in the 'passing show'.

Exercising

The factors governing the amount and kind of exercise are: the condition of the dogs at the time; the condition aimed at; the terrain available; the common sense and energy (or indolence) of the owner. In no matter is there such variation from one kennel to another as in this. It goes from the one extreme of turning dogs out into a small paddock to exercise themselves (which they never do) to the other of walking them for miles every day as though their lives depended on it. I read an article somewhere in one of the dog papers appealing for a balanced view on the question of exercise, and I have no doubt that the majority of Corgi owners do treat it with common sense.

The first point I want to stress is the need to make exercise interesting for the dogs. Not everyone has facilities for running them loose across country, but those who have are lucky and no doubt take advantage of their position. They also, no doubt, are careful to ensure that all dogs, though loose, are under control; the importance of this where farm stock are about needs no emphasizing. These are the lucky dogs. But even where only roads can be used it is often possible to introduce some variety, by going another way, or a different way round, or perhaps getting them into a park occasionally. 'Country' dogs should go on the roads as often as thought necessary for the sake of their feet. Roadwork will not turn bad feet into good ones, but it can make a lot of difference. Rough, gritty roads will tighten up feet much better than smooth macadam; the latter will not do much more than harden the pads.

When at exercise every dog should be observed for bowel action and the evacuations noticed for any abnormality. Slow exercise encourages bowel motion, fast work has the opposite effect. It is satisfactory when they get this job done in the first part of the walk; therefore take them steady at first. With a number running loose they are liable to get out of hand, and often one has a particularly adventurous spirit and will be only too glad to lead the others astray. A collar and lead should be carried for this sort and put on before any damage is done. On returning from exercise dogs should be put away in their kennels for an hour or so, first being washed and dried if necessary.

BATHING AND DRYING

The necessities for bathing a dog – which, by the way, need not be done very often – are: a sink or tin bath to stand the dog in; two buckets of warm water; a small jug; a chamois leather, and a couple of warm towels. Fill the jug with the washing material, which can be one of the excellent shampoos available or even Stergene; this ready mixed in warm water. First thoroughly wet the dog all over with plain water, making sure it goes right down to the skin. Then slowly pour the wash over him, starting at the head end and working it well in with the hands. On no account let water or soap get into ears or eyes. Do not forget to work the wash under the belly, elbows and stifle, and especially the legs and feet.

Now rinse with plain water, repeating till all soap is out. While the dog is still in the sink squeeze out as much water as possible with the hands, then put him on the floor and use the chamois leather; if this is frequently wrung out the dog will then be half dry. Finish with the warm towels and keep him in a warm place till completely dry. This latter is important. On a hot sunny day the dog can go on to a piece of clean grass to dry off; otherwise a warm room is best.

There are several ways of cleaning and drying dogs which come in wet and dirty after exercise. Here again the chamois leather and a bucket of warm water are hard to beat, finishing with towels. A rough and ready way of drying, though quite satisfactory, is the sawdust box. This can be any box large enough for the Corgi to stand in, about two feet deep and two thirds full of dry pine sawdust. (Dust from imported timber is the best; English is seldom dry enough.) The dog is popped into this and the sawdust quickly rubbed all over him, avoiding eyes and ears, of course. He is then allowed to jump out and shake himself.

The sawdust box is *not* recommended before a show.

CARE OF FEET

His feet are what the dog has to go upon! This is a self-evident fact which one would think is sometimes forgotten by many owners whose dogs' feet bear every signs of neglect. As the horseman says, 'No foot, no 'oss', so one might equally say 'No foot, no dog'. Long nails which tend to spread the foot out every time it touches the ground; dewclaws left on and never trimmed; soft, squashy pads.

Whether oval, as in the Pembroke, or round, as in the Cardigan, the foot should be tight, the toes slightly arched, the pads thick and firm, the nails always kept short.

In some breeds the front dewclaws are left on; in Corgis it is usual to take them all off. The dewclaw is of no use and is liable to get torn; but if left on it must be kept as short as possible without injuring the quick. The time to begin *cutting nails* is when the puppy is a few days old. This can be done with small sharp scissors. The quicks then are very short and, if the nails are consistently kept back, will not grow much. If this early cutting is missed the quicks will grow to such a length that it becomes quite impossible to take the nails back properly; and this, from the exhibition angle, is unfortunate.

When you buy your puppy it will already have become accustomed to having its nails attended to regularly, and this practice must be continued. Some owners like to use strong nail clippers. Inexpertly used, this can be painful to the dog and cause a nail to bleed. I personally prefer to use a strong file holding the foot firmly and filing each nail downwards. This enables the nail to be kept blunt, short and smooth and obviates any pain or bleeding. If this is made a regular routine job, at least once a week, your dog's feet will be kept neat and tidy. If by some mischance a toenail has been allowed to grow too long, it should be filed back to the required shape and length gradually, a little every other day for the next week or so.

In all nail-cutting, care must be taken not to hurt the dog or he will probably not stand for it next time. Some dogs seem to keep their nails down pretty well without much attention; others, kept under the same conditions, grow them to an inordinate length.

Firm, thick pads are acquired by suitable exercise on hard ground. This desirable point can also be helped by the provision of a clinker path along the wire netting where dogs like to run up and down.

Cracked pads can be treated by well rubbing in zinc and castor oil cream.

Tar on the feet is easily removed with lard or margarine.

COAT SHEDDING

A dog usually casts its coat twice a year. This is a natural process, which, however, can often be a nuisance in show dogs, which have a habit of starting to shed just after they have been entered for one or more important shows. Some moult and get it over fairly quickly; others take much longer. The weather may have a hand in it, a very hot spell encouraging rapid fall of hair. Casting the coat is not a habit which should be prevented, even if it were possible to do so. It can, however, be hurried along by rigorous daily grooming, and will be further assisted by bathing as soon as it starts. This will bring out a lot of loose hair. The new coat cannot grow until the old is out. Frequent use of a fairly stiff brush, and hand rubbing, are advisable.

SOFT EARS

All prick-eared breeds are liable to suffer from this fault and the Welsh Corgi is no exception. Both Cardigan and Pembroke puppies vary in the age at which ears become erect, some getting their ears up while still in the nest, others going to six months or more. A few exceptions have one or both permanently down. It is to guard against this latter misfortune that ears must have attention in cases where there is any doubt.

A puppy's ears will generally sag during teething, but if they have been up, or nearly so, before this process begins they will almost always come all right again. We prefer to be on the safe side, not letting them go beyond 3½ to 4 months with the ears down. The treatment is to stick them up by one method or another. We use Boots' one-inch surgical tape, from which we cut off a length of about 7 or 8 inches. The ear is drawn up into the erect position and folded to form a hollow tube; the tape is then wound round from the base upwards. It is important to start as low down as possible, and also to ensure that air can reach down into the ear; there should be room to insert a little finger or lead pencil. No more tape should be used than is necessary, otherwise there will be too much weight which will tend to drag the ear down. The tape can be left for about a week, when it can be removed with a piece of cotton wool soaked in methylated spirit.

If sagging takes place before the week is up, remove and try again. Repeat the process as often as necessary, and persevere. If a Corgi's ears are not permanently erect by twelve months he may be looked upon as a hopeless case.

It is always worth while taking some trouble over doubtful ears.

A dog with an ear down is ruined for the show ring, and in any case is unsightly with a thoroughly untypical appearance.

Points about Kennels

When siting wooden kennels with wood floors it is important to keep them well off the ground. Many make the mistake of raising them only a few inches, when they can become a harbour for rats. It is better to place them on brick piers with a clearance of about ten inches, so that a cat or a dog can get underneath if necessary. The whole should be surrounded with heavy gauge small mesh wire netting, let well into the ground, a removable panel being provided so that the cat can be popped in occasionally. The windward side or sides can be protected with tin or zinc sheets to prevent cold draughts under the floor. Alternatively, the kennel can be set on a concrete or cement base.

All kennels should be treated yearly using a good wood preservative, which will last longer without attention. It pays to line all outside walls. Cold does not matter so long as the dogs have snug sleeping boxes; but draughts are taboo.

It is as well to assume from the start that every dog will bite every bit of woodwork it can get its teeth into. But all this can be prevented by the use of zinc sheeting, which is easily cut as required with a pair of tin shears and can be fastened with flat-headed nails.

Doors should have inside as well as outside fasteners.

A few strong benches or tables somewhere handy to the kennels are very useful for showing off a dog to visitors (or, indeed, for training puppies for the show ring); they may be three feet by two feet, at a convenient height from the ground.

Travelling Boxes

Customers are not always very prompt in returning these, so it is as well to have one too many than too few. You will require both adult and puppy size. A visit to the trade stands at Cruft's or any of the more important shows will reveal any amount of choice in well-built, lightweight boxes of all sizes. Those with a ventilated ridge roof have the advantage that they cannot be packed round and on top with other luggage in a guard's van; a dog can be nearly suffocated in this way. Have your name, kennel prefix, station and

telephone number painted on them, and see that they have bolt
fastenings as well as a hasp and staple which can be padlocked.
Some excellent hampers are also obtainable. Whatever the re-
ceptacle used, it should be roomy enough to enable the dog to
stand up and turn round with something to spare, have good
ventilation without draughts, and be provided with a carrying
handle at each end.

DEALERS AND DOG SHOPS

Whether these are reputable or disreputable, it is certain that a
dog or puppy purchased from either will cost more than the same
dog bought from the breeder. And why not? Both have to make
their profit and pay their overhead expenses which, in the case of
the shop, may include a rent of some hundreds of pounds a year. It
is unreasonable to buy a puppy for £200 in the West End of
London and afterwards complain that it could have been obtained
from the breeder for £100.

Apart altogether from cost, there are many advantages in going
to the fountain-head for a dog and buying from a Corgi breeder
who has a reputation to lose. There you will see a much wider
choice from which to make your selection; the breeder will be
interested in the puppy after it has passed into your possession;
will give you sound advice on correct feeding and management,
and so on. If you are in any doubt as to where to go, write to the
secretary of one of the breed societies listed in this book; there you
will get all the help you need. But do not expect a young puppy to
be sent on approval; breeders have had too many come back with
chills or ailments caused by lack of proper care while away.
Wherever you live, a reliable Corgi breeder will be found within
reach.

NURSING THE SICK CORGI

A few notes on nursing may usefully come into this Chapter, and I
first make the point that nursing is not infrequently of more
importance than drugs. Some, especially women, have a flair for
this sort of thing and need no advice here. They use common
sense, seem to know exactly how the patient is feeling, and
anticipate its every want, even though they may have had very
little previous experience with dogs. After all, a sick puppy is

much like a sick child. It is not to such, but to others, that I address the following observations.

Warmth, comfort, fresh air, extreme cleanliness in all things, suitable feeding; these are the primary considerations in nursing a sick animal. And, one might add, rest. The eyes, nose and external genital organs should be sponged twice daily with water containing a little mild antiseptic, all bedding changed as necessary and well boiled before being used again, dishes kept scrupulously clean, the attendant's hands frequently washed with antiseptic soap. The patient will be freshened up by sponging the face and head every day with a little cold water. In illness and all infectious complaints, complete isolation is essential. Having done all one can, unnecessary interference with the patient is to be deprecated.

The bowels must be kept in working order and the dog encouraged to use a tray filled with earth or ashes.

Feeding should be very light. Glucose or honey and water at first, then, when the condition improves, such invalid diet as milk, Benger's, Brand's Essence, egg flips and a little fish. Clean water (boiled) and glucose to drink.

TEMPERATURE, PULSE AND RESPIRATION

The average *Temperature* of a dog is 101·5°F; anything over 102° is cause for some investigation; 103° is serious. Young puppies in good health frequently carry a temperature of 102°. A short-bulb thermometer is advised for insertion in the rectum.

The *Pulse* has a wide range of variation and may be anything from 70 to 100 beats a minute. The best place to take the pulse is at the femoral artery on the inside of the thigh. It is seldom that a breeder has occasion to take a pulse. A fast pulse is less serious than a very slow one.

Respirations in the Corgi will usually vary between 18 and 35 per minute.

The amateur will not learn much from taking pulse and respirations unless sufficiently interested to practise sometimes and thus be able to recognize any abnormality.

CHAPTER XV

THE NOVICE'S GUIDE TO EXHIBITING

THE exhibiting of dogs in the United Kingdom is governed by the Kennel Club, 1–4, Clarges St, London, W1, through its elected committee, which constitutes the ruling body, just as flat-racing comes under the aegis of the Stewards of the Jockey Club and steeplechasing under the National Hunt Committee. Each of these constitutes what is the best form of government – a benevolent autocracy. Unlike popularly elected parliaments, they are not subject to the whims and caprices of vast masses of voters, most of whom have not the vaguest idea of what they are voting for, and are not swayed by irresponsible clamour. On the contrary, selected as they are for the discharge of their onerous task by a strictly limited number of persons well qualified to do so, they comprise people of experience and integrity, *sans peur et sans reproche*, having no axes to grind nor salaries to consider, concerned only to further the best interests of the game.

As the doggy fraternity comprises all sorts and conditions of men and women it is only to be expected that we always have with us a disgruntled element, whose numbers are by no means to be compared with the noise they make, and whose fulminations in the canine Press and elsewhere should be accepted by the newcomer with considerable reserve. We also have, of course, the well-meaning 'reformers' with new and wonderful ideas for improving everything, ninety-nine per cent of which are entirely unpractical or impracticable. No doubt they get some fun out of it and they do nobody any harm.

The registration of dogs, their transfer to new owners, the licensing of shows, Obedience and Working Trials, awarding of Challenge Certificates, punishment of offenders, the rules and regulations touching every facet of the game, all are centred in the governing body. They also publish the *Kennel Gazette*, the monthly official journal of the Club, and every year the *KC Stud Book*. The novice reader will realize that he will come in contact with the Kennel Club at every turn, and will, I hope, also appreciate that he will derive great help from it. Without it, indeed, there would be chaos.

REGISTRATION, TRANSFER AND PREFIX

The first thing to do is on buying a pedigree dog is to register it at the Kennel Club, if it has not been registered by the breeder or seller. It cannot be shown until this has been done. The appropriate form can be obtained from the KC. You may also, if you wish, register your own kennel Prefix, which will be exclusive to dogs owned by you.

I have purposely omitted the various charges laid down by the Kennel Club as their fees vary so often. I suggest therefore that for all charges you may want to know e.g. export pedigree costs, registering your prefix, transferring a puppy, you apply to the Kennel Club at the time you intend using their services for a full and up-to-date list. Their address is 1–4 Clarges Street, Piccadilly, London W1Y 8AB.

CLASSES OF SHOWS

(a) *Championship Shows* are open shows at which KC Challenge Certificates are offered. These are the only shows at which it is possible for a dog or bitch to acquire the coveted title of 'champion' by winning three CCs at three different shows under three different judges.

(b) *Open Shows* at which there is no restriction as to exhibitors making entries in such classes as are provided.

(c) Shows limited to members of clubs or societies, or to exhibitors in specified areas or otherwise, known as *Limited Shows*. What are called *Sanction Shows* come in this category.

(d) *Exemption Shows*. The KC may grant to agricultural and horticultural shows, fêtes and the like, permission to hold a show of not more than four classes for dogs which need not be registered. Anyone not on the KC list of disqualified persons may turn up, there are no entry forms, and entry fees are paid on entering the ring.

Obedience – Shows and Classes

Most breed championship shows provide classes for obedience in addition to classes for beauty. These are graded according to previous wins and at the highest point, i.e. Test C, obedience championship certificates are awarded. As with the normal breed class competition, three first placings gained without losing more than ten from the maximum number of points, all gained under three different judges, qualifies the dog as an Obedience Champion. The only exception to this is at the annual Crufts Show where the winner, who must have previously won at least one challenge certificate, automatically acquires the much valued title. There are literally hundreds of obedience societies in Britain holding regular weekly classes to teach dogs this highly specialized work, concentrating mainly on the set exercises laid down by the Kennel Club.

Matches

There are sometimes held Matches, a match being between two dogs the property of members of the association, club or society authorized to hold the matches. These do not aspire to the title of shows but are popular in some parts of the country and can provide a pleasant evening's entertainment while being inexpensive for all concerned.

A few are held without the authority of the Kennel Club, all dogs and persons involved then being liable to suspension by that body. These should be avoided.

The Junior Warrant

This award was introduced a few years ago to meet a demand for some sort of recognition of the young dog which has put up a meritorious number of wins before reaching the age of eighteen months. It depends upon the number of points scored at championship shows where CCs are on offer for the breed, and open shows. A win at the former counts three points, at the latter, one point, twenty-five points in all being necessary to qualify, whereupon the exhibitor applies to the Kennel Club for the Junior Warrant. Be it noted that wins in classes for more than one breed or variety do not count towards qualification.

A typical litter of Pembroke puppies, aged seven weeks

Int. Ch. Barngremlin of Braxentra

Thomas Fall

Ch. Apollinaris Angel Clare

Ch. Lisaye Rebecca of Greenfarm

Diane Pearce

Ch. Ringinglow Morys' Treasure

Thomas Fall

Ch. Evancoyd Personality Girl

Hugh Henderson

Ch. Hannaford Roy

Diane Pearce

Ch. Olantigh Black Diamond

While the Junior Warrant is always well worth having it is not all that it is cracked up to be. A smart, flashy puppy may do a lot of winning for a time, then go off a good deal, so that by the time he is twelve or eighteen months old one wonders how he ever got his JW.

Stud Book and Kennel Gazette

The *KC Stud Book* contains a record of the dog or bitch placed first, second or third in the Open Classes at all championship shows held during the year, or is awarded a Challenge Certificate or Reserve Challenge Certificate. The Kennel Club will automatically notify you of the number and it will be published in the *Kennel Gazette*.

BITCHES ON BREEDING TERMS

Not infrequently it is found convenient for the owner of a bitch to loan her to another breeder, the conditions being mutually agreed between the parties. I am often asked what are the usual breeding terms, a question incapable of exact answer inasmuch as the terms may be any that are decided upon by the parties concerned. A bitch may be lent for a stated time, or for one or more litters. It must be specified which party to the transaction is officially to be considered the breeder, in whose name the puppies are to be registered, how and by whom they are to be disposed of, together with any other conditions that may be agreed.

If the loan is for not less than six months the transaction may be registered at the Kennel Club, who will charge a fee of £5. Any disputes arising must then be referred to the Club, whose decision is final and binding on the parties. It is very easy for some (possibly quite friendly) dispute to arise, and this form of registration is greatly to be recommended.

PREPARING A DOG FOR SHOW

The first consideration in entering a dog for a show is to make sure that he is in what is called 'show condition'. One sees many dogs in the ring who fall short of this description, but that is no reason why yours should follow suit. Your dog should be well covered with flesh, but not fat; he should be muscular and not flabby; his pads firm and thick – all qualities acquired by sound feeding and proper exercise. There is no secret about it. He should be in good coat; if he is not, let him stay at home. One often hears an exhibitor say: 'I am showing so-and-so; he is out of coat, but probably most of the others will be, too.' This is generally in late spring or early summer when there are usually a lot of dogs out of coat. I can assure you it is a mistake to show a dog unless he is looking his best.

His nails should have been kept short and his teeth cleaned. If he has had distemper, resulting in marked teeth, do not hesitate on that account to show him. While some judges will penalize distempered teeth I think the majority recognize that this is a misfortune rather than a fault, which will tip the scales only if he comes up against a dog equal in other respects but whose teeth are perfect. If, however, the teeth are very badly pitted, loose or otherwise unsound, then I am afraid he is not very likely to get away with it.

GROOMING

One of the most important, and most neglected, operations in a kennel; and by grooming I mean 'elbow grease', not a perfunctory going over with a brush.

During the first winter of the 1914 War I had a troop of Yeomanry on the East Coast. It was bitterly cold and our horses stood in open sheds; except for a roof over their heads they were pretty well exposed to all the elements. I knew nothing about soldiering, but all about strapping horses. I had every man straightaway make himself a hay wisp, and took care to show him how to use it. Every morning, when we came in from work, I had them strapping till they must have got sick and tired of it. But they were Nottinghamshire miners, some of the best chaps in the world, and they nearly pushed those horses over with the vigour they put into it. We had our reward when the GOC, a beautiful horseman himself and a VC to boot, came round on an inspection. He followed up his congratulatory remarks with an order to the commanders of the other two squadrons to come and see our horses and to get theirs in similar condition. I never told them how it was done!

This little anecdote is put in only to illustrate the value of elbow grease, which is just as effective for dogs as for equines. First go through the coat with a comb; follow with ten minutes of hard brushing, finishing with a few minutes' vigorous hand rubbing the way of the hair. Don't do this for a week and then forget about it; keep it up.

SHOW TRAINING

It is an extraordinary thing that one should see so many half-trained and badly behaved dogs in the ring. The only connection they appear to have with their handlers is a long lead, at the end of which they seem to do much as they like, particularly when the handler is engaged in gossip with a fellow exhibitor. These dogs are a nuisance to others and to the judge, and are lessening their own chances of winning. Make up your mind that your dog shall be a model of deportment in the ring; and, making allowances for inexperienced, light-hearted puppies, he can be so if you will take the trouble to teach him manners at home. It is not sufficient for him to run by your side on a loose lead, though this is of great importance in the show ring. He must also learn to stand still when required, nicely (but not too much) stretched out, and to take an intelligent interest in something, be it only a piece of liver concealed in your hand.

Practise your dog daily, both on the ground and on a table, for many judges examine the dogs on a table. Discover some means of exciting his intense interest. A glutton will generally show for a piece of liver, rabbit or other tit-bit, though this is not always the case. I have shown dogs who would have jumped through fire at home for a bit of liver, yet would completely ignore it when in the ring. This is often the case with shy ones. There is only one thing that a dog loves more than food, and that is sport. If he is accustomed to hunting and killing rabbits or rats, make a point of saying some word of encouragement to him while he is engaged in this thrilling occupation, so that he will associate the word, and the tone of voice in which it is spoken, with the sport. Then, when you spring this on him in the ring, he will instantly become alert and on his toes. But resort to this only at the moment when the judge is looking at him; if it is overdone, he will realize that he is being fooled and will lose interest. Then you can do nothing and may have the mortification of seeing him just lose to another which he might have beaten if only he had cocked his ears up at the psychological moment.

As well as learning to stand, run on a loose lead, and show

himself off, your dog must submit cheerfully to having his mouth opened and his teeth inspected by the judge. To ensure this it is advisable to get any friend who comes along to make such an examination, thus getting him used to it. While one dog will raise no objection at all another may be all the better for some practice. It is a KC recommendation, though not a rule, that judges should allow exhibitors to show their dog's mouth themselves, but not all of them do so.

BATHING

It generally pays to bath a Corgi a couple of days before a show; not nearer to the show than that as the natural oils will not have had time to get back into the coat, which will have a fluffy look. Needless to say, he must be kept out of the dirt meanwhile. What exhibitor has not had a beautifully clean dog thwart his good intentions by rolling in some awful filth just before a show? Accidents will happen in the best regulated kennels and one cannot always avoid them. (*See* Bathing and Drying in the Chapter on General Management.)

TEETH CLEANING

Like grooming, this is another job which is frequently spasmodic or neglected altogether, and I am afraid it is a human frailty sometimes to 'forget' the ones who make the most fuss about it. It is worth while to spend odd minutes occasionally messing about with your dogs' mouths, then they will learn that they are not going to be hurt. A dog which trusts its owner or attendant will seldom raise any objection. Teeth can be kept clean with a rag dipped in peroxide of hydrogen, or a tooth brush may be used. But if there is a fast deposit of tartar it is necessary to 'scale' them, for which purpose a scaler can be purchased cheaply from any firm supplying dog requisites. It is better to get an experienced friend to give you a demonstration before attempting it yourself, as injury can be done to the gums. Finish up by washing out the mouth with a mild antiseptic such as TCP in warm water.

MAKING AN ENTRY

Now you will have to decide at which show to take the plunge with your exhibit. If he is a real good one, up to championship form, it is a waste to put him in some small local affair, where he may win some prizes which will disqualify him from competing in some of the lower classes at a championship event where a win is very much more worth while. You will probably have your doubts about this and feel inclined to go for the 'small game', but you may know an experienced exhibitor or judge who will have a look at your dog and advise you. Welsh Corgi exhibitors are a friendly crowd and you will get an honest opinion, though, as I have pointed out before, not all judges think alike.

Consult the advertisement columns in the doggy Press, select your show and write to the secretary for a schedule. Now study very carefully the Definitions of Classes. If you enter and win a prize in a class for which your dog is not qualified – a mistake which, through carelessness, is sometimes made by experienced exhibitors – not only will the prize be taken away from you but the Kennel Club will impose a fine which you will have to pay. So be careful; the definitions are not always the same at different shows. Complete your entry form and send it off in good time. In due course you will receive your admission ticket bearing your dog's bench number, but always keep some proof of posting in case entries go astray.

OFF TO THE SHOW

Be in good time! There is nothing more harassing than arriving late, dashing in, trying to find your bench, your class perhaps already in the ring, milling through a crowd of people with your unfortunate dog who doesn't know whether he is coming or going and is given the worst possible chance of doing himself justice. So start off early, having got everything ready overnight.

You may require a strong collar and bench chain, show lead, a small blanket for the bench, a coat for him if the weather is very cold, a bottle of milk and glucose to give him a drink on arrival, some food, and a dish. You would also be well advised to take some food and drink for yourself. Lunches and refreshments at many shows are expensive or bad, or both, and nearly always overcrowded. It is very much pleasanter, especially at a summer show, to take a picnic lunch.

On entering the show, find your bench and install your exhibit, tying him up by a short chain so that he cannot possibly jump off and hang himself; one sees scores of dogs tied up on dangerously long chains. Give him a drink and leave him to settle down. In the case of a puppy at its first show, stay with him for a while to make sure he is happy and not worrying at his strange and noisy surroundings. When all is well you can leave him, buy a catalogue, find your ring, which may be some distance away, and try to discover what time you are likely to be judged. Take your dog off the bench occasionally for exercise, but not for more than fifteen minutes at a time; this is a KC rule. Give him a quick run a few minutes before he goes into the ring to loosen him up.

In the Ring

You will have taken a great deal of trouble over this dog; perhaps reared him from a small puppy, and spent heaps of time in feeding, exercising, grooming and training him. You have now arrived at a moment when all of this can be thrown away by bad and inefficient handling; failure to show him off to the best advantage; failure to conceal as far as possible any points in which he is not as good as he might be. It is all very well to say that it is the dog and not the handler that is judged. Quite true; but the judge can appraise only what he sees, and if by bad or careless handling you present the dog in such a way that his good qualities are not fully apparent, then you are clearly placing a handicap on him. Similarly, it is perfectly legitimate to try to keep his defects on the blind side of the judge if you can, though the best judges may not be deceived. For instance, if one foreleg is not quite aₛ good as the other, you will take care to stand him, whenever possible, so as to present the best leg to the judge. But do not make a 'business' of all this or the judge's suspicions may be aroused and he will have another look. This may be your undoing. Go about the job in a quiet and unobtrusive way, always keeping one eye on your dog and the other on the judge, ready at a second's notice to obey the latter's instructions.

Do not throw a ball or bits of liver about the ring, to the annoyance of other exhibitors, nor use squeaky toys to make your dog show. These habits are a pest and should be stopped.

At outdoor shows the rings are sometimes on a slope. Whenever possible stand your dog so that he is facing uphill, and avoid placing him so that his front feet are on lower ground than his hind, which would throw his hindquarters up and spoil his outline. If he fails in action, try to find out at what pace he moves best, so that you can run him down for the judge to the best advantage.

Let him rest when he is not required to show himself off. This can be done whenever the judge is some distance away; but keep a close watch on the judge so as not to be caught napping. Never let him see your dog standing slackly or awkwardly, but always at his best. Concentrate on the business in hand and resist temptations to gossip with fellow exhibitors. Keep your dog close up to you, so that you have him under perfect control, not roving about at the full extent of the lead. If you have any difficulty in getting him to stand to the best advantage it is quite legitimate to kneel by him, holding the lead a few inches from the collar so that he cannot move about. From this position, too, you can give hind feet a little push back if he is inclined to stand with his hocks underneath him. But do not copy the handlers in some of the terrier breeds who string their dogs up so that their feet hardly touch the ground, and pose them like so many dummies. The Welsh Corgi, Pembroke or Cardigan, whether standing or moving, should always have an alert and natural look.

If you should win a prize, put the card in your pocket; it is not permitted to display prize cards in the ring.

Exhibiting brings many disappointments, and a few triumphs. Never be disconsolate when you lose, nor unduly elated when you win. Treat these two impostors both the same, then you will earn the respect of your fellows. If you think your dog deserved a higher place than the judge has awarded him, keep your opinion to yourself; nobody else wants to hear it, and may not share it, anyway. When this happens to me, as it frequently does, I console myself by thinking of the occasions when I have done better than I consider I deserved. 'It all comes out in the wash', so why worry?

AFTER THE SHOW

Whether you give your exhibit a feed after he comes out of the ring, or wait till he gets home, is a matter calling for common sense, depending a good deal upon how far you are from home. In the ordinary way I prefer to let him have something light, then a good supper when he gets back to kennels. To sustain him at the show there is nothing better than milk with glucose or honey. Mix the honey with (boiled) warm water, then add the milk.

On your return home you should take such precautions as you can to prevent the carrying of infection into the kennels. Some of the winter indoor shows are hotbeds of infectious disease and one cannot be too careful. Ideally the dog should be isolated for ten days, and you should most certainly change your outer clothes and shoes before going amongst the other dogs, especially puppies. All collars, leads, blankets, dog coats, etc., should be hung out on the line for a few days. Vera Lister-Kaye once asked the veterinary surgeon what was the best disinfectant; his answer was 'the weather'. Exposure to frost, rain, sun, changes of temperature; if this is done I do not believe there is any necessity to soak them all in disinfectant.

Watch your dog carefully during his isolation period, and take his temperature at once if you notice anything unusual.

With the really superb inoculations available to each and every one of us these days the ten days isolation is not so vital as it used to be. And it is not always easy for the small kennel to have such isolation facilities. However, I do strongly urge the necessity of anyone returning from a dog show not to go near a nursing bitch or young puppies without first having changed clothing, shoes and thoroughly washed one's hands. And it should go without saying that the dog or dogs who have been to the show should not be allowed to come into contact with un-inoculated stock, i.e. puppies under twelve weeks of age.

CHAPTER XVI

JUDGING AND STEWARDING

(This Chapter is based on contributions by the author
to the *Handbook of the Welsh Corgi League*.)

JUDGING

I SUPPOSE it is the ambition of most of us, when we start to breed dogs, to be honoured some day with an invitation to judge. We may not realize it at first, but there are very few of so retiring a disposition that all requests to occupy the centre of the ring are firmly and consistently refused. Judging is an interesting, if thankless, task, not to be taken lightly, and calling for more qualities than merely a knowledge of the breed. Integrity is such a *sine qua non* that it is hardly worth mentioning and, in any case, the majority of judges I believe are honest. Much more dangerous than the deliberately dishonest judge, because very much more numerous, is the judge who lacks complete confidence in his own opinion, who is afraid of offending somebody, who hesitates to put a big winner down, or an unknown up, for fear his placings will incur hostile criticism, who gets 'cold feet' as soon as he enters the ring, who goes home and lies awake half the night pondering over all the mistakes he thinks he may have made. Just as the golfer needs the 'match temperament', so the judge of dogs requires the temperament enabling him to give no thought to the business before he goes into the ring and to have no qualms when he comes out of it. He has given his opinion, which is all that he is supposed to do, and that is all there is to it. What anybody else thinks or says, either to his face or behind his back, is of no interest to him. His conscience is clear.

What I write here is intended to apply only to so-called specialist judges, who know (or profess to know) only one or two breeds, and not to the all-rounders. The latter are a class by themselves, one for which I personally have a great respect. Certainly there are good, bad and indifferent all-rounders, and not all of them possess a full knowledge of the finer points of every breed in which they award Challenge Certificates – a fact which gives rise to some well-justified grumbling sometimes. Nevertheless, the all-rounders can be of great benefit to a breed, bringing a fresh mind and a balanced view, which is not always the case with specialist judges, some of whom are inclined to over-emphasize their own particular fads and fancies. The dog must be judged as a whole and not necessarily turned out of the ring for failure in some point which happens to be the judge's pet aversion.

It is said that a judge is born and not made, a sweeping statement which carries more than a grain of truth. I would prefer to say that a good judge of livestock had at least some latent ability before he started, without which he could never be a good judge. I have known men, some of them long since departed, who could judge anything on four legs; they possessed a flair. If one of them, who had never judged dogs in his lifetime, were to be wafted back and put into the Corgi ring he would know nothing at all of the breed points, but I guarantee he would know unsoundness when he saw it – which is more than can be said for many of today's aspirants. He would also be quick to recognize 'quality' and 'style', and I would not expect his placings to be so very far wrong.

Quality and style! How many exhibits in the ring today can really be said to boast these two indefinable attributes? And yet, without them, though they measure up to every specification of the standard, they are still sadly lacking. I would give any dog a big credit for quality and style.

What are the qualifications required in a judge, and how is he to get started? (The word 'he' in this book can almost invariably be read 'he or she'.) Endless controversy goes on in the doggy Press on this subject; all kinds of suggestions are made but agreement seems as far off as ever. Some advocate classes for judges, pupil judges in the ring, and so on. I have never been in favour of wet-nursing for the novice, for the simple reason that I do not consider it is of any use to him. If he has the ability it will come out; if he has not, then the wet-nursing is a waste of time. Let him come into the ring and consistently show good, sound stuff, leaving the bad ones at home. If he is capable of appraising the merits of his own dogs, then he can judge others, will in due course be invited to judge and will be supported by his fellow exhibitors. This, when all is said and done, is the acid test.

There is certainly something to be said for the idea of pupil judges, a practice frequently carried out with the larger breeds of livestock, I believe successfully. The pupil goes into the ring with the judge; he has no official standing and does nothing except keep his eyes open and his brain working. He watches the judge go about his work, tries to anticipate his decisions, all the time getting his eye in and listening to any words of wisdom the judge may have time to drop for his benefit. I am not sure whether the judge reports on the pupil; but after the latter has been through so many shows under different judges he will stand a good chance of being recommended for a judicial engagement. This system might well be given a try-out in the field of dogs.

I read an article recently in a breed magazine in which the writer discussed the question of comparing a dog with a horse, and the value of such a comparison in assessing soundness and movement, coming down heavily with the view that nothing whatever could be gained. Having had a good deal of experience, from my earliest days, of both animals I have no hesitation in expressing an entirely contrary opinion. A very great deal can be learnt from the show hunter or hack, and if more novice judges would study them whenever they have the chance they would learn more about sound action than I could tell them in a dozen pages of this book. (But they should keep away from the extravagant action of the Hackney.)

In addressing the following remarks to the novice or prospective judge let me make it clear that they are only my own views and my own methods. Others may have better ones, or more suited to their own individuality, and they need not take the slightest notice of my exhortations unless they want to. It is, however, desirable to work on some set plan when in the ring and stick to it consistently, otherwise one may get into a muddle, especially if the classes are big, or the stewards not very efficient, as sometimes happens. It is, perhaps, an exposition of the obvious to say that before one enters the ring in a judicial capacity one should have as complete a knowledge as possible of the subject and of the breed. Therefore do not be in too much of a hurry to make a start. Sorting out a moderate lot, which is probably what you will get at your first small show, is a great deal more difficult than judging good ones. It is necessary to acquire an 'eye' for a dog and not be taken in by mere flashiness. Try to judge the dog as a well-balanced whole and do not over-indulge pet fancies or aversions of your own. There is a tendency in all breeds, if a particular point such as short legs is stressed, to think that still shorter legs must be better still. Thus we should eventually breed a Corgi so low to the ground as to be incapable of work. Remember what the breed was intended to be used for and ask yourself the question: Is this one fitted for the job?

Resolutely put aside such thoughts as: I wonder if I am doing right? and remember always that the best dog in the class is a matter of opinion and not of fact. The exhibitors have come for *your* opinion and you have nobody to satisfy but yourself. Don't be afraid to put a big winner down if you honestly consider it is only second best, and avoid the besetting sin of trying to play for safety by favouring a big kennel over an unknown one. Therein lies disaster. Corgi exhibitors by and large are a sporting crowd; they will forgive your mistakes if they are honest mistakes, will bear you no ill-will, and will show cheerfully under you again. But they will expect you to learn by and profit from your mistakes.

Have a look round the class and get a general idea of the level of merit, then have your first dog out in the middle. Don't touch him; let him stand. One inclined to be shy will often show himself off better before he has had a stranger lay a hand on him. You cannot see a dog under your feet, so stand well away from him. Now you can begin to run the rule over him. Examine his mouth, take his head in your hands and note size, shape and colour of eyes, fineness of muzzle, set-on of ears, etc. Pick up a foreleg for bone, feet and pads; go over the body for well-set shoulder blades, spring of rib, firmness of flesh and condition; run your hand against the lay of the hair for length and texture of coat, and look for muscle on the second thighs. Finish up with movement, making sure you can really see his action both coming and going; some exhibitors are very clever at concealing bad movement, but they will not get past a judge who knows his job. You may have suspicions when a handler 'brisks' his dog down the ring, so insist on a steady trot with a loose lead. The important thing is to go over the points of each dog in the same order, otherwise it is possible to miss something. I have seen a judge go through a large class and some of the exhibits never had their mouths looked at.

When you have selected, say, seven or eight from which you are sure your first four must come you can forget the others, or, if you want more room, have your steward turn them out. There is not much fun in being turned out of the ring; therefore it is a duty which should be performed with a smile by the steward and a pleasant word of thanks; some seem to forget this.

In judging subsequent classes take the best of the new exhibits and work him up into his rightful place among the old ones, following with the next, and so on.

Never forget that in showing under you the exhibitors are doing you an honour, whether you are a young judge or one of long standing. Extend to them every consideration you can and help them to get the best out of their dogs. Be very quiet and very patient with a young puppy, probably making its first appearance, perhaps its first time away from home. If it will not show, don't bother it; put it back in the line till you have gone over the others, then bring it out again, when you may find it has gained confidence and will give quite a good show. While being scrupulously considerate, at the same time be firm. When you are in the ring you are boss and the exhibitors are expected to do what you tell them, either directly or through your steward. Do not allow dogs to be 'placed' by their handlers as though they were made of plasticine, nor to be held up by both ends as is permitted – I can never think why – with some breeds. You want to see the dog stand himself, not have it done for him. Penalize shyness more heavily in a dog than in a bitch; one can forgive a little diffidence in the fair sex, but a dog, particularly if he has any pretensions to the stud, should walk into the ring as though he owned the place. I never like to see them looking apologetic.

In reporting a show it is necessary to apportion fairly the praise and the blame. A purely whitewash report is of little value, while one that mentions all the faults without at the same time giving credit for the good points is an unnecessary cruelty. Bear in mind that your report does not state which dog was the best, but only which *in your opinion* was best. They may meet another judge next week, whose opinion is entitled to at least as much respect as yours and who may differ from you. So do not stress faults as such unless you are fairly sure that any reasonably good judge would agree with you; and if you allow yourself any bias let it be on the side of being 'to their virtues ever kind and to their faults a little blind'. Some judges in their reports make a point of thanking the exhibitors for the sporting manner in which they received the awards; this always strikes me as the reverse of a compliment, giving the impression that there could be some doubt. Among Corgi fanciers? Surely not!

Finally, let me commend to young judges my three golden rules which, if carried into the ring, will stand them in good stead: Know what you want; go for it; hang the consequences.

STEWARDING

The duties of stewards are not fully appreciated by the novice exhibitor, to whom these notes on this very essential task are addressed. They may also serve as a reminder to the 'old hands' who, equally with the less experienced, are sometimes inclined to take the stewards for granted, to give them little credit for the somewhat thankless task they perform and to blame them when, usually through the owner's carelessness, an exhibit misses its class – which of course it would undoubtedly have won. Let me say straightaway that dog show stewards are doing a public service, without any reward beyond a free lunch, and not always that, for which both judge and exhibitor should be duly grateful. They are there to help us, and we should reciprocate by making their task as easy for them as possible.

Two stewards are usually allotted to each ring. Their first obligation is to arrive at the show in good time, certainly not less than fifteen minutes before judging is timed to begin, and to report at the secretary's office. They will be given a catalogue apiece, the ring number cards and prize cards. In the case of a championship show they will also take charge of the Challenger Certificates, Reserve Best of Sex and Best of Breed cards. These should be taken care of and not left lying about during the luncheon interval. The ring numbers and prize cards for each class will usually have been separated by rubber bands. Show secretaries who fail to do this will come in for some not unmerited protest from the stewards whose work is unnecessarily added to, particularly if it is a big entry.

Having repaired to the ring and made the acquaintance of the judge, the stewards' duties will now begin in earnest. They must see that the various 'props' are there; a table, one or two chairs, award board, chalk and duster.

When the judge is ready to start, get the first class in the ring. Stewards are not responsible for bringing dogs into the ring. Having taken steps to inform exhibitors that judging is to commence it is thereafter the exhibitors' responsibility to get their dogs into the ring. A good steward however will make an effort to ensure exhibitors do not miss their classes. It is always advisable to give the steward a written note if you are exhibiting in another ring. It also helps if you inform them if any of your dogs are absent.

Having got all the exhibits in the ring and handed out the ring numbers, advise the judge of any absentees so that he can mark them in his book. The stewards should now take a back seat, but be at hand in case the judge requires them.

Do not forget that it is a Kennel Club rule that the four placed dogs must be lined up in the middle of the ring to receive their award cards; this is for the benefit of the spectators. The judge will hand his stewards two award slips, one of which is to be pasted on the award card at the back of the board, the other left on the table for collection by a show official. Now chalk the class number and winners on the board.

Subsequent classes are dealt with in much the same manner, except that all exhibits which have appeared in an earlier class will be lined up on one side of the ring and the new dogs on the other side. Sometimes an exhibitor will wander into the wrong side, so this has to be watched. While the judge is engaged with the new entry the old ones must be placed in their right order; that is to say, those which have been in the awards should be placed accordingly. There is no difficulty about this, but complications may arise in later classes when two or more dogs, all prize winners, have not met each other. Be sure and get this right and advise the judge exactly what the position is. The best of judges can, on occasions, accidentally reverse a decision. See that he does not do so.

At championship shows it used to be the practice for unbeaten exhibits to 'challenge' for the certificate, but this has been stopped. It is within the competence of the judge to send for any dogs which he may wish to consider for the award of the CC or Reserve Best of Sex cards, but there is no automatic right to take a dog in unless sent for.

Here are a few thoughts which stewards should have in mind:

You are there to help both judge and exhibitors. Do not let exhibitors crowd into the centre of the ring; push them back when they start doing so.

Similarly, when running round see that they make full use of the ring; the judge will see them better and rings at many shows are small enough without making them smaller. Keep the award board up to date.

Be always on the alert to carry out or anticipate the judge's wishes.

In your dealings with exhibitors be firm but polite.

I have said nothing about division of duties between the stewards. It is a curious thing, and very satisfactory, that though I have stewarded many times there has never been any discussion as to who shall do what. There has always seemed to be some tacit understanding and everything has just fallen into place. I suppose the answer is that stewards go into the ring to do what they can to help everybody, including each other. It may be thought that stewarding is a dull job, to be avoided if possible, but I have never found it so. The steward has a first-class view of the proceedings, not always obtainable in a crowded ringside, and can do a bit of private judging on his own account and see how it pans out. For the young aspirant to the judges' list I can thoroughly recommend stewarding, as much of it as he can get. There he will be immeasurably closer to the heart of things than any ringsider, will be free of distractions, and will all the time be learning something about the breed. Not only that; when he does eventually enter the ring in a judicial capacity he will feel much more confident than he would otherwise.

CHAPTER XVII

EVERYDAY CARE AND COMMON AILMENTS

I N the last edition of *The Welsh Corgi* there was a chapter
specially written by a veterinary surgeon. This time it was felt
that with the ever-changing face of medicine, new drugs, new
ideas, it would possibly be of more practical use to our readers to
have a chapter on everyday care and common ailments. I in no
way recommend d-i-y medicine, but there are several common-
sense treatments and suggestions that can be used. With any truly
sick dog, nothing can take the place of professional advice. I have
throughout my many years as a dog breeder always relied tre-
mendously on a thermometer. If a dog has a temperature – in a
puppy anything approaching 103·5°F, in an adult anything
approaching 103°F – then the advice of a vet should be sought.
Always remember, do not take temperatures immediately after an
animal has had a bowel action, wait for half an hour or so.

A puppy from good stock and a reliable breeder is usually a well
reared puppy which has been given a good start in life, and should
therefore basically be healthy and strong. Welsh Corgis are as a
rule tough, hard wearing little dogs with few congenital problems,
who will always be one step ahead of their owner, if he or she
doesn't learn at the start to say 'NO' and mean it. There is very
little difference in the upbringing of a small child and a puppy. A
well disciplined child is a joy to you and to him or herself. So too, is
a puppy!

Dog Bites

If your Corgi becomes involved in a fight, or is attacked by another
dog, examine him very carefully for bites. Corgis possibly are
luckier than the shorthaired breeds, as they carry such a thick
undercoat, but this must not deter you from looking thoroughly
for puncture wounds, which are likely to occur on the body, neck
or throat. The punctures seldom bleed very much and may be
difficult to find, but they are usually deep and cause bruising and

swelling, and rapidly become septic. It is essential to keep these puncture wounds open and thoroughly bathed with a good anti-septic such as TCP. These wounds must heal from the base otherwise your dog will end up with a bad abscess. It is a good idea anyway to take the injured animal to the vet for an antibiotic jab and he can then check him for any further damage.

STINGS

Dogs snapping at insects frequently get stung near the lip or in the mouth. Bees leave their stings behind, wasps do not. If the sting is left behind it should be extracted with tweezers. Again I fall back on my unfailing remedy, TCP. I have found that, applied neat to the sting site, this works every time, bringing down the swelling incredibly quickly. Antihistamine cream can also be used.

METRITIS (inflammation of the uterus)

A complication after a whelping, often caused by the introduction of unwashed hands or the retention of an afterbirth. After a whelping a bitch usually has a bloody discharge, which should be a healthy red in colour. If after approximately three days this discharge looses its healthy colour and has an unpleasant smell, and you find her temperature has risen, then veterinary help is necessary.

PYOMETRA

This is acute inflammation and infection of the uterus that normally occurs about two months after a bitch has had a season. It is possibly more frequent in older bitches, 7 years or so, but not necessarily so. The bitch goes off her food, drinks a lot and you might see a pink discharge from the vulva. Veterinary advice must be sought, and will possibly result in your bitch being spayed. This is a total hysterectomy, when the uterus and the ovaries are surgically removed.

CONSTIPATION

A teaspoonful of liquid paraffin on either a main meal or in a drink of warm milk will usually work wonders.

FITS

Fits in puppies are often brought about by the presence of worms; sometimes also at the cutting of the permanent teeth. There is no excuse for the former; the use of reliable worm medicine at not later than six weeks of age is a must. Fits are a symptom and not a disease. It is the latter which should be sought and treated. A puppy in a fit should be wrapped in a blanket and taken to a vet at once.

DIARRHOEA

In adults place on a light diet, white of egg and arrowroot with barley water to drink. Obstinate cases in adults may be treated with bowel active antibiotics, available through your vet. In puppies, worms should be suspected and treated, if this has not already been done fairly recently, but it may be merely indigestion. I have found summer puppies are more likely to get diarrhoea. I normally scatter a good sized teaspoonful of Kaolin powder over a main meal and that usually does the trick. Kaolin may be bought from any small local pharmacist who does his own dispensing. Diarrhoea is not a matter to be treated lightly. Unless cleared up within a few days, veterinary advice should be sought.

ECLAMPSIA

This is associated with the nursing bitch, in layman's jargon, milk fever. It comes on very suddenly and the bitch can collapse very rapidly. She becomes extremely restless with staring eyes, pants a great deal and has a temperature. A prompt injection of calcium must be given by a vet. If neglected the symptoms become worse, convulsions occur and death results.

FADING PUPPIES

Much as been written on this subject and still very little is known as to the cause. Probably virus or bacterial infections are the commonest causes. All the puppies may be born dead, some or all may die in five days, or in up to six or seven weeks. It is essential to obtain a pathologist's diagnosis to help find the cause of death. The 'seagull cry' is a typical fading symptom.

I would advise anyone who has lost all or part of a litter in this manner and who intends mating the bitch another time, to ask the vet to take a vaginal swab a few days before the bitch is likely to be mated. Sometimes tests show evidence of infection which can be treated prior to a mating and the next time the bitch can have a normal, perfectly healthy litter.

EARS

These present very few problems in Corgis, but that doesn't mean that an occasional check shouldn't be carried out. Dogs who run over grassland may have picked up a grass seed which can work it's way into the ear channel. Also around harvest time, mites can be a nuisance. Ask your vet for some eardrops for these.

FLEAS, LICE AND TICKS

These three are a menace to all dogs, and even more so in the summer months. Prevention and treatment of the ordinary dog *flea* is by dusting with a reliable flea powder, well rubbed into the coat, the whole of the dog being treated. It is essential to treat all benches and bedding, also the corners and cracks between the floorboards which harbour the eggs and larvae. An aerosol spray, Nuvan Top, is also obtainable.

Lice are recognized as small bluey-grey parasites adhering to the skin. Here again the whole dog must be treated with a reliable insecticide shampoo, the process being repeated at an interval of five to six days to destroy the nits which have hatched out in the meantime. I must stress that any treatment of this kind must be kept away from the eyes of the animal.

Ticks are easily recognized. They attach themselves firmly, burying their heads beneath the skin, and their bodies become bloated and purplish grey in colour as they fill with blood. Attempts to pull the tick off its host usually result in leaving the head still buried in the skin. To remove without damage to the skin of your dog, soak a piece of cotton wool in ether, surgical spirit or paraffin, and hold it over the area for a few minutes. The tick dies and will release its hold. It can then be picked off and burnt. Wipe the area of punctured skin with a little diluted antiseptic, such as TCP. To be on the safe side apply some antibiotic cream or powder.

But here I must stress *never* treat a bitch for parasites if she is suckling a litter. Make sure the bitch is free of parasites *before* she is due to whelp.

Eye Injuries

The eye is an extremely delicate organ and a vet should always be consulted.

Fractures

In the event of severe injury or accident, or any suspected fracture, wrap the dog in a blanket, support the injured part and get to a vet as quickly as possible.

Obstruction by a Foreign Body

If you *know* your dog has eaten something poisonous (e.g. slug pellets etc.), try to make him vomit it back up as quickly as possible. The best emetic is washing soda. A few lumps forced down his throat should make him vomit immediately. If you *know* he has eaten something made of metal, plastic, lead or any other sharp edged material, it is safer to help him to try to pass it through the bowel in the normal way. Give him something stodgy immediately, such as sponge cake, bread lumps soaked in gravy, or anything you have that he may enjoy eating, but it must be stodgy. This helps to protect his intestines against any sharp edges which could cause damage. Any foreign body swallowed unknown to the owner can lodge inside the dog and cause an obstruction. Signs are discomfort and pain, the dog may vomit or try to vomit. He may strain as if constipated and not want his food. Veterinary examination should be sought as soon as possible.

I always try to impress on people buying puppies from me, not to let them have small balls to play with, but something much larger than their open mouth can accommodate. I have known dogs choke to death on tennis balls and the like thrown for the dogs to catch by their owners.

Poisoning

Today there are chemicals and drugs in all forms, shapes, sizes, and liquids. Some of these can be deadly to a dog if consumed. If you have any reason to suspect your dog has done such a thing, for instance while out walking, notify your vet immediately. If it is something you *know* they have taken in your own home or garden then take the packet or container with you to the surgery. And please, I beg of all dog owners, do read full instructions on every bottle, packet or container *before* you use it, thus maybe avoiding what can be a very traumatic experience for all concerned.

BLEEDING

Blood loss must be checked at once by applying pressure to the wound. Hold your thumb over the place to staunch the flow and encourage clotting, while a pad is prepared and then applied to the wound. Bandage firmly. Do *not* apply a tourniquet. Keep the wound under direct pressure while getting the dog to the vet as quickly as possible.

INOCULATION

In a previous chapter mention has been made of the importance of having your dog inoculated. For the benefit of readers who are pet owners I will go into further detail on Distemper, Hardpad, Hepatitis, Leptospirosis (both forms), Parvovirus and Kennel Cough.

Distemper It is seldom that a fully inoculated dog gets distemper but the virus is still active. Usual symptoms, any or all of which may be present, are a runny nose and discharge from the eyes, a dry cough with some retching and diarrhoea. The temperature rises to 104°–105°F. The dog is obviously feeling very poorly indeed. He must be isolated, kept warm and have veterinary treatment as quickly as possible. Urgency is the name of the game. Distemper often leaves after-effects such as chorea, paralysis, hardened pads, brown marks on the teeth and invariably impaired general health.

Hardpad used to be considered a separate disease but is in fact either a symptom or the result of distemper.

Hepatitis This attacks the liver and can cause sudden death. Symptoms are diarrhoea, vomiting and a high temperature. In advanced cases the eye may become blue and opaque. Prompt attention is vital for survival.

Leptospirosis One form is rare but deadly and is carried in rats' urine. The virus attacks the liver and kidneys, causing yellow jaundice and an insatiable thirst. The whites of the eyes have a yellowish tinge as do the gums. The dog develops a high temperature, vomits and passes blood. Immediate veterinary attention is essential.

The canicola form of the disease is less serious. A dog can become infected by sniffing the urine of other dogs with this condition. The virus affects the kidneys where it does permanent damage. Symptoms are lassitude and increased thirst. Veterinary treatment, careful nursing and restricted diet will help recovery, but it is still a serious disease.

PARVOVIRUS

Appeared in this country in 1978/79 and spread rapidly assuming epidemic proportions in some areas. Canine parvovirus is closely related to the virus which causes enteritis in cats. Symptoms are acute diarrhoea and sickness, and the dog is obviously very ill. Rapid dehydration can cause collapse and death, especially in puppies and old dogs. Urgent veterinary treatment is essential. A small or young puppy thus affected can die within a few hours as at this age the virus attacks the heart muscle. In 1981/82 a canine vaccine was developed and has become available for dogs of all ages. Bitches can pass on some immunity to their puppies, but this fades as the pups are weaned.

KENNEL COUGH

Can be transmitted from an infected dog anywhere in the vicinity. Training classes, boarding kennels, public parks, even the vet's waiting room are likely places for the spread of this virus. The dog may cough occasionally or suffer frequent bouts of coughing. Puppies and old dogs are particularly at risk. Junior Benylin expectorant, a cough mixture for children, is soothing. In 1981/82 a vaccine became available either as an injection or as nose drops and a single dose gives protection for up to six months.

If you have to put your dog in a boarding kennel during holidays then it is advisable to have him inoculated. I feel certain most good boarding kennels would not accept any dog today without an up-to-date certificate of *full* inoculation for all the foregoing diseases. This is why I always strongly advise anyone buying a puppy from me to have all inoculations that are available. Your local vet will advise you when and how often to take your dog in for its initial inoculations and thereafter booster jabs.

Dog owners today should realize how lucky they are to have the benefit of all these preventative medicines. In the old days many beloved and beautiful dogs as well as young puppies died through lack of know-how. As dog owners we can do lots to help ourselves and our dogs, but it should always be remembered that, when in doubt your vet is the person to contact. It costs money, of that there is no doubt, but it can save a lot of suffering for your animal and heartache for yourself.

THE CORGI AS A CATTLE DOG

By John Holmes
(Reproduced from the *Handbook of the Welsh Corgi League*)

Before starting on this article I should like to point out that what experience I have had of Corgis as workers, although gained the hard way by actually working the breed over a number of years, is entirely my own experience with my own dogs. I have never lived in a district where the breed is used extensively for work, although from what I have seen of Wales I should say that the working conditions there are very similar to those where I was in Scotland. Having had very much greater experience of Working Collies, I realize that the abilities and style of working varies very considerably in different individuals and strains, and it is quite probable that other strains of Corgis may work in a very different manner from that I shall endeavour to describe. These few qualifying remarks are made in the knowledge that this article may be read by some whose experience of Corgis as cattle dogs is much greater than mine; and I also wish to guard against the danger of some novice arguing with a Welsh farmer and saying: 'But it must be so; I read it in the *Corgi Handbook*!'

TRAINING

The majority of Corgi breeders, and breeders of all show dogs, are very hazy or entirely ignorant of what are the essentials of a herding breed and what makes it different from any other breed. I shall first of all try to explain this difference. If a Terrier puppy gets into a field with cattle or sheep it will probably chase them, in spite of all attempts by its master to prevent it doing so. If a Corgi puppy gets into the same field it will also chase the cattle or sheep, and probably a good deal faster as it will nip their heels. To the uninitiated there is no difference; but there is one very big and important difference. Whereas the Terrier chases here, there and everywhere, the Corgi will run round the outside, either keeping the cattle in a bunch in the middle of the field or chasing them into a corner and keeping them there. That is the herding instinct on which all future training is based, and without which no dog is of the very slightest value as a worker.

Shepherds in Scotland refer to a pup as 'starting to run' when it first shows the desire to herd or round up sheep, and there are very great variations in the age at which different puppies do so. Until it starts to 'run' a puppy should be taught to follow its master at heel, and to stay seated or down, and it is a great mistake to allow it to work until it is sufficiently matured as there is every possibility that it will either become stale or develop bad habits in its attempts to 'shorten the journey'.

If a puppy is keen to work, old enough and well grown, then it should be encouraged to make use of that instinct to herd; and, although Corgis usually start to run much younger than Collies I never allowed them to work until nine or ten months old at least. Some need no encouragement at all, and, in fact, are the very devil to get away from cattle, while others, especially if they have been kept strictly to heel, are afraid they may be doing wrong and need encouragement to get them to leave their handler. Many people think that a young dog learns from an old one, but I know of no surer way of ruining a young dog than allowing it to run with an old one. It will certainly learn all the old dog's bad habits, and develop several of its own in its attempts to get there first.

Having succeeded in getting the puppy to run round cattle on command, the next stage is to get it to bring them to the handler. Some will do this without any teaching but the majority will run round and round making a complete circle and keeping the animals on the same spot. This can be overcome by the handler getting as near to the cattle as possible and stopping the puppy when it comes round towards him, which will be very easy if it has already been taught to sit down on command but practically impossible if it has not. It should then be sent back and stopped when it comes round the other side, and in a very short time it will learn to run forward and backward behind the cattle in a half-circle instead of round and round. The handler should walk away and the puppy will bring the cattle along behind him. Of course it is much better to start with cattle which know where they are going and will go there in any case, even if the puppy makes a mistake.

That is the first and most important stage, and in my opinion no puppy should be allowed to do anything else until it does that properly. From that stage the distance it is sent for the cattle is gradually increased and it is taught to 'run to both hands': i.e. run round the right- or left-hand side of the animals, which will be more easily taught if it has already been taught to walk to heel on both sides. This is very important, as a dog which will run only to one hand is worse than useless at times. If a puppy is under perfect control, will run to either hand, and fetch cattle to its handler, it can be expected to do almost any job, some of course being much better at it than others, and only experience, combined with instinct, will teach it the rest.

Working

Having touched very briefly on how a Corgi is trained (a whole book could be written on the subject), we now come to how a Corgi works, and I shall try to answer the question so often asked as to how such a small dog can control a whole drove of wild cattle. Actually a Corgi will turn cattle which no Collie would face, and I have won many bets by turning cattle which were considered unmanageable by any dog. I think the real reason for this is the Corgi's great courage and tenacity, and its almost unbelievable agility. I read in a magazine devoted to dogs a query by a Corgi owner as to how she could stop her dog yapping, and the 'expert' replied advising her to get a Cocker, as Corgis, he or she said, always yap, having been bred to yap in their work. This expert's knowledge of a working dog must be extremely limited, to say the least of it, as it will be found in dogs as in humans that those which make most noise almost invariably do least work, and certainly never do it so well. Sheep will run from a barking dog, but cattle respect one only if they know that it is capable of making itself felt, and a dog whose bark is worse than his bite is never much use for cattle. Corgis do bark a great deal when working but are always ready to nip the heels or nose, and the incessant yapping type is usually more of a nuisance than anything else.

If a bullock is trying to get past a Corgi – or any dog, for that matter – he invariably charges with his head down, and it is then that the Corgi grips him by the nose. I should think that a Corgi must have a much stronger grip than a Collie, as I have never yet

seen a bullock wait for a second dose, and it is when it turns away
that the dog gets it by the heels, keeping it on the run. All this takes
a very long time to tell, but in actual fact, unless one is very
observant, and close up on the dog, it is impossible to see what
happens; the movements are so quick, and it can dart from one to
the other keeping a whole herd on the move. A Corgi never draws
back! I have seen them attacked by a herd of twenty to thirty cows
with suckled calves at foot, and, for the benefit of those who have
had no experience of same, I might mention that the bellowing of
these cows can be heard quite plainly a mile away or more, but
even then the little Corgi will stand its ground, gripping here,
there and everywhere until it gets the cattle turned and running in
the direction wanted.

I have heard different descriptions of the Corgi's method of
avoiding kicks, the most usual one being that every time it grips a
heel it claps down flat; but I wonder where the cattle would be if it
spent at least half its time lying down and getting up. It avoids
being kicked, with practically one hundred per cent success, by a
much simpler method than that, and is assisted in doing so by its
low stature. It grips very low, in the tender part just above the
hoof, and as it does so it keeps moving forward in the same
direction as the bullock, at the same time swerving slightly to one
side or the other, depending on which heel it has gripped. The
bullock usually lashes out at where the Corgi was a split second
beforehand. Even if the dog misjudges its movement, which is
very unusual, it still has its head nearly on the ground, and the
nearest I have ever seen a Corgi to being kicked was a muddy
mark across the back of the neck.

All cattle do not require the rough treatment I have just tried to
describe, but the Corgi has sufficient intelligence to enable it to be
trained to bring in the two or three milk cows quite gently, and I
have had several which were very good with sheep, especially for
road work, etc. No day is too long for them, and I have worked
them ten or twelve hours at a time, rushing and barking all the
time, but they are always ready for more.

Before leaving the working side I should like to mention another
job on the farm for which the Corgi is admirably suited, and that is
ratting. In my opinion there is no Terrier to equal it, as it is much
more easily trained, is as quick as lightning, has an excellent nose,
and that jaw which will terrify the wildest of cattle can kill a rat
instantly without even shaking it. There are many other classes of

work to which a Corgi can easily adapt itself with training, but I mention only the above as it is one of the jobs which it is expected to do naturally in the normal course of events on the farm.

APPENDIX B

THE BREED CLUBS

In the United Kingdom there are fifteen Welsh Corgi breed clubs, and one only caters exclusively for Pembroke Welsh Corgis – the Welsh Corgi League. Two cater for the Cardigan Welsh Corgi – the Cardigan Welsh Corgi Association and the Cardigan Welsh Corgi Club of Northern Ireland. The remaining twelve breed clubs cater for both types of Welsh Corgi: the Welsh Corgi Club; the Midland Welsh Corgi Club; the Welsh Corgi Club of Cambria; South Wales Corgi Club; Northern Counties Welsh Corgi Club; the Pennine Welsh Corgi Association; the Yorkshire Welsh Corgi Club; the Eastern Counties Welsh Corgi Club; the South East Corgi Association; the West of England Corgi Association; the Devon and Cornwall Corgi Club and the Welsh Corgi Club of Ulster. For up-to-the-minute information on the names and addresses of any of these secretaries, application should be made to the Kennel Club, 1–4 Clarges Street, Piccadilly, London, W1Y 8AB (Telephone: 01-493 6651), and written enquiries should be addressed to the secretary.

There are two clubs in Eire – the Welsh Corgi Club of Ireland and the Munster Welsh Corgi Club.

Around the world there are many Corgi clubs. Each state in Australia has a Welsh Corgi Club, catering for both types of Welsh Corgi. New Zealand has three Corgi clubs, one in South Island and two in North Island. America have Corgi clubs extending over the whole range of North America. There are at least two clubs in Canada, three in South Africa, and one in Rhodesia, Sweden, Holland, Switzerland, Norway, Finland and Denmark each have one.

Our own London-based Kennel Club has reciprocal arrangements with all Kennel Clubs around the world, and each breed club in turn is governed by the Kennel Club of their own country or state. Therefore the ideal arrangement for any one of our readers who may be requiring information on a Corgi club abroad would be well advised, in order to get up to the moment data, to write first to our Kennel Club, asking for the address of the Kennel

Club in whatever country you require the name and address of the secretary of a particular breed club. In this way you might just write an extra letter or two, and possibly wait a week or two, but the ultimate information will be correct. This is preferable to letters going astray, having written to a secretary who has long since relinquished the office and possibly even moved away entirely.

APPENDIX C

KENNEL CLUB REGISTRATIONS

Pembroke and Cardigan

1925	10	1929	80
1926	29	1930	56
1927	89	1931	80
1928	76	1932	115
	1933	202	

	Pembroke	Cardigan
1934	240	59
1935	360	110
1936	562	81
1937	919	96
1938	975	78
1939	695	58
1940	302	11
1941	293	14
1942	409	19
1943	837	45
1944	1,306	41
1945	1,956	61
1946	3,142	136
1947	3,660	153
1948	3,709	135
1949	4,331	169
1950	4,342	168
1951	4,595	229
1952	4,348	192
1953	5,021	311
1954	5,794	294
1955	6,873	360
1956	8,190	314
1957	7,953	334
1958	8,580	323

	Pembroke	Cardigan
1959	8,713	371
1960	8,933	321
1961	8,666	308
1962	7,923	314
1963	7,004	281
1964	6,310	240
1965	5,706	241
1966	4,625	197
1967	4,459	197
1968	4,593	210
1969	4,165	192
1970	3,897	228
1971	2,979	218
1972	3,180	252
1973	2,936	223
1974	2,621	245
1975	1,922	159

Note: In April 1976 the Kennel Club changed its registration system, thus preventing the continuation of the previous method of listing annual registration totals.

D.A.

BRITISH PEMBROKE CHAMPIONS, 1960 to 1989

Name	Sex	Sire	Dam	Owner	Breeder	Born
1960 Ch. Cogges Teal	D	Ch. Maracas Masterpiece	Cogges Rozavel Supersarong	Mr E. Mathias	Mrs D. H. Lee	18.12.57
Ch. Cornflower of Cowfold	B	Ch. Maracas Masterpiece	Ch. Cowslip of Cowfold	Miss M. Murray Wright	Miss M. Murray Wright	24.1.57
Ch. Domabelle of Wey	B	Sportsman of Wey	Gaytime of Annley	Mrs K. Butler	Mrs K. Butler	29.12.58
Ch. Layston Saracen	D	Crusader of Cowfold	Layston Turandot	Miss J. S. Kite	Miss E. Cradick	17.7.54
Ch. Lees Fairygold	B	Lees Jackpot	Lees Firefly	Miss P. L. Curties	Miss P. L. Curties	11.12.58
Ch. Medlloyd Makeway	D	Askari of Elsdyle	Medlloyd Mascara	Lady Lloyd	Lady Lloyd	11.6.58
Ch. Point Duty	B	Ch. Zephyr of Brome	Gossamer	Miss A. V. Lambert	Miss A. V. Lambert	24.5.56
Ch. Stormerbanks Indigo	D	Stormerbanks Icebreaker	Ch. Stormerbanks Superfine	Miss P. Hewan	Miss P. Hewan	6.4.57
Ch. Stormerbanks Invader	D	Ch. Stormerbanks Indigo	Stormerbanks Flashback	Miss P. Hewan	Miss P. Hewan	26.3.59
Ch. Teekay Danceaway	B	Ch. Zephyr of Brome	Teekay Dinah	Miss A. G. Biddlecombe	Miss A. G. Biddlecombe	21.5.56

Name	Sex	Sire	Dam	Breeder	Owner	Date
1961 Ch. Cherquita of Wey	B	Int. Ch. Gayelord of Wey	Chinese Cracker	Mrs K. Butler	Mr F. C. Tomlinson	30.12.57
Ch. Banhaw Dawn	B	Int. Ch. Gayelord of Wey	Aurora of Banhaw	Mrs Watts Russell	Mrs Watts Russell	25.5.57
Ch. Saffid Sorceress	B	Ch. Maracas Masterpiece	Saffid Dream Girl of Broadwood	Mrs B. Faithfull	Mrs B. Faithfull	23.4.57
Ch. Caswell My Fair Lady	B	Ch. Layston Saracen	Eggerness Fascination	Mrs G. Rainbow	Mrs G. Rainbow	14.8.58
Ch. Stancis Cockrow Darksome David	D	Leonine Maestro of Gwynt	Larkwhistle Lucilla	Mr S. Wharton	Mrs M. Hudson	5.2.59
Ch. Kentwood Cogges Woodpecker	D	Ch. Maracas Masterpiece	Cogges Rozavel Super Sarong	Mrs Godden	Mrs D. H. Lee	7.7.58
1962 Ch. Bowman Puesedown Passport	D	S.A. Ch. Falaise Huntsman of Almadee	Harhams Sandy Mary	Mrs J. Vaughan	Mrs Aspinwall	27.7.58
Int. Ch. Crowleythorn Ladomoorlands	D	Ch. Crowleythorn Snowman	Crowleythorn Celebration	Mr and Mrs J. Kearney	Mr Duckworth	2.6.60
Ch. Cogges Pirate	D	Aus. Ch. Cogges Periwig	Cogges Wimbrel	Mrs D. H. Lee	Mr J. M. Evans	18.12.59
Ch. Winrod Rob Roy	D	Ch. Kentwood Cogges Woodpecker	Winrod Vanessa	Mrs E. J. Busby	Mrs E. J. Busby	1.4.60
Ch. Bradwellane Kingfisher	D	Newbas Penguin	Bradwellane Carousel	Mrs J. Lee	Mrs J. Lee	5.4.59

Name	Sex	Sire	Dam	Owner	Breeder	Born
Ch. Barney of Braxentra	D	Ch. Kentwood Fairytale	Zuzie of Braxentra	Mrs V. Palmer Cummings	Mrs V. Palmer Cummings	11.1.58
Ch. Beretta of Braxentra	B	Ch. Barney of Braxentra	Zenith of Braxentra	Mrs V. Palmer Cummings	Mrs V. Palmer Cummings	10.2.59
Ch. Stokeplain Fandancer	B	Stokeplain Stargazer	Stokeplain Sweet Dream	Mrs D. Irlam	Mrs D. Irlam	30.9.61
Ch. Seamist of Wey	B	Int. Ch. Sealord of Wey	Ch. Cherquita of Wey	Mrs K. Butler	Mrs K. Butler	18.12.59
Ch. Corgwyn Merrylegs	B	Corgwyn Llanberis Farmers Boy	Corgwyn Lucky Lady	Mrs E. Collins	Mrs E. Collins	9.1.60
Ch. Saffid Surprise Packet	B	Copper of Cowfold	Saffid New Surprise	Mrs B. Faithfull	Mrs B. Faithfull	2.11.58
Ch. Mabinogi Maori	B	Mabinogi Muffler	Mabinogi Moth	Mrs H. Griffith	Mrs H. Griffith	23.11.58
1963 Ch. Barngremlin of Braxentra	D	Ch. Barney of Braxentra	Zenith of Braxentra	Mrs Palmer Cummings	Mrs Palmer Cummings	8.4.61
Int. Ch. Peregrine of Elsdyle	D	Gay Deceiver of Elsdyle	Distaff of Elsdyle	Mrs Drummond	Mrs B. M. Morgan	16.5.59
Ch. Mynthurst Carousel of Cellerhof	B	Helarian Raven	Tigbourne Blackcurrant of Cellerhof	Mrs M. Roberts	Mrs Middleton	5.7.59
Ch. Winrod Rhapsody	B	Ch. Kentwood Cogges Woodpecker	Winrod Vanessa	Mrs E. M. Busby	Mrs E. M. Busby	1.4.60

Name	Sex	Sire	Dam	Breeder	Owner	Date
Ch. Dronlow's Dancing Lady	B	Ch. Stormerbanks Sabreflash	Griselda of Charavigne of Wey	Mrs and Miss Glover	Mrs and Miss Glover	20.10.61
Ch. Costons Cherokee of Wey	B	Sealion of Wey	Costons Halfyoke Gay Princess	Mrs K. Butler	Mrs J. Newbold	18.4.61
Ch. Leonine Tansy	B	Leonine Maestro of Gwynt	Halmor Sequin	Mrs J. Froggatt	Mrs E. M. Gregory	15.2.59
Ch. Stormerbanks Vanessa	B	Ch. Stormerbanks Invader	Stormerbanks Stardream	Miss P. Hewan	Miss P. Hewan	31.5.60
Ch. Evancoyd Cover Girl	B	Evancoyd Brockencote Benedictine	Evancoyd Romance	Mrs B. Thompson	Mrs B. Thompson	16.8.59
1964 Ch. Crowleythorn Miss Mink	B	Int. Ch. Crowleythorn Ladomoorlands	Crowleythorn Sundew	Mrs D. Winter	Mr and Mrs Duckworth	1.6.61
Ch. Peersbrook Pynto	D	Peersbrook Gynt	Pennylass of Rode	Miss S. Peel	Miss S. Peel	17.11.59
Ch. Lees Sunsalve	D	Lees Jackpot	Lees Firefly	Miss P. L. Curties	Miss P. L. Curties	24.8.60
Ch. Falaise Maccaboy	D	Stormerbanks Boniface	Falaise Merleybourne Miracle	Mrs P. Brown	Mrs P. Brown	12.4.62
Ch. Sealion of Wey	D	Int. Ch. Sealord of Wey	Ch. Cherquita of Wey	Mrs K. Butler	Mrs K. Butler	18.12.59
Ch. Benomley Dafydd	D	Benomley Demetrius	Auriole of Benomley	Mrs M. Hills	Mrs A. Melling	1.9.61

Name	Sex	Sire	Dam	Owner	Breeder	Born
Ch. Stormerbanks Foxyface	D	Stormerbanks Boniface	Stormerbanks Valencia	Miss P. Hewan	Mrs Brooks and Miss Powell	6.3.63
Ch. Rockrose of Wey	B	Red Rock of Wey	Michele of Wey	Mrs K. Butler	Mrs E. Evans	20.11.62
Ch. Benomley Fenella	B	Ch. Benomley Dafydd	Stormerbanks Supervite	Mrs M. Hills	Mrs M. Hills	17.8.62
Ch. Winrod Pollyanna	B	Helarian Raven	Ch. Winrod Rhapsody	Mrs E. J. Busby	Mrs E. J. Busby	4.7.62
1965 Ch. Caswell Duskie Knight	D	Caswell Marcus	Mynthurst Duskie Princess	Mrs G. Rainbow	Mrs G. Rainbow	15.3.63
Ch. Tigertim of Wey	D	Ch. Sealion of Wey	Lena of Buckingham	Mrs K. Butler	Mrs Gray	21.4.63
Ch. Stormerbanks Vagabond	D	Ch. Stormerbanks Invader	Stormerbanks Chaffinch	Miss P. Hewan	Miss P. Hewan	29.4.60
Ch. Banhaw Renard	D	Banhaw Bendigo of Corgay	Banhaw Helarian Rosemary	Mrs E. Hardy	Miss S. Watts-Russell	18.3.63
Ch. Mynthurst Duskie Broadwing	B	Int. Ch. Barngremlin of Braxentra	Mynthurst Costons Can Can	Mrs M. Roberts	Mrs Palmer Cummings	21.8.63
Ch. Whielden Copper Penny	B	Ch. Kentwood Cogges Woodpecker	Whielden Susannah	Miss J. Wadge	Miss J. Wadge	21.1.61

Ch. Lees Chintz	B	Ch. Lees Sunsalv	Lees Glamour	Miss P. L. Curties	Miss P. L. Curties	25.6.63
Ch. Helarian Jessamy	B	Helarian Raven	Helarian Juniper	Miss E. Forsyth Forrest	Miss E. Forsyth Forrest	21.3.63
Ch. Benomley Frolic of Wey	B	Ch. Benomley Dafydd	Lees Viola	Mrs K. Butler	Mr P. F. Hopwood	3.7.63
1966 Ch. Lees Wennam Eagle	D	Ch. Winrod Peregrine	Wennam Snowbunting	Miss P. L. Curties	Mrs M. New	14.6.63
Ch. Golden Prince of Llwynog	D	Ch. Flanagan of Wey	Honeysuckle of Wey	Mr D. C. Smith	Mr D. C. Smith	25.4.64
Ch. Corwgyn Shillelah	D	Pennywise of Wey	Corgwyn Lucky Lady	Mrs E. Collins	Mrs E. Collins	8.9.62
Ch. Winrod Peregrine	D	Helarian Raven	Ch. Winrod Rhapsody	Mrs E. J. Busby	Mrs E. J. Busby	4.7.62
Ch. Banhaw Chaffinch	B	Banhaw Bendigo of Corgay	Banhaw Braxentra Beverlee	Mrs S. Watts-Russell	Mrs S. Watts-Russell	27.2.64
Ch. Belroyd Enchantress	B	Pennywise of Wey	Belroyd Confetti	Mr J. B. Taylor	Mr I. Jones	29.6.62
Ch. Kydor Maldwyn Melisande	B	Int. Ch. Crowleythorn Landomoorlands	Maldwyn Melissa	Mrs D. M. Winter	Mrs E. Montgomerie	9.8.63
Ch. Lees Pennyfarthing of Treland	B	Lees Scherzo	Snowpenny of Treland	Miss P. L. Curties	Mrs R. M. Tresidder	21.6.63
Ch. Kathwyners Mona-Lisa of Wey	B	Gerona's Woodvale Miitagong	Crowleythorn Celebrations	Mrs K. Butler	Mrs E. Duckworth	9.10.65

Name	Sex	Sire	Dam	Owner	Breeder	Born
Ch. Stokeplain Loveday	B	Ch. Kentwood Cogges Woodpecker	Ch. Stokeplain Fandancer	Mrs W. Irlam	Mrs W. Irlam	4.1.63
Ch. Helarian Trouble	B	Int. & Nordic Ch. Helarian Jacob	Helarian Pandora	Miss E. Forsyth-Forrest	Miss E. Forsyth-Forrest	19.3.63
1967 Ch. Hildenmanor Crown Prince	D	Hildenmanor Bonilad	Hildenmanor Gold Crown	Mrs D. Albin	Mrs D. Albin	6.2.65
Ch. Clive of Pendcrest	D	Mabinogi Masquerade	Celia of Pendcrest	Misses Laverick, Leslie and Waterfield	Misses Laverick, Leslie and Waterfield	18.6.64
Ch. Rockgail of Wey	D	Red Rock of Wey	Michele of Wey	Mrs K. Butler	Mr E. Evans	22.6.64
Ch. Gerona's Craythornes Golden Eagle	D	Ch. Lees Wennam Eagle	Craythornes Fleur de Lys	Mr and Mrs J. Kearney	Mrs H. Sheldon	27.4.66
Ch. Lees Opalsong of Treland	B	Ch. Hildenmanor Crown Prince	Penny Songster of Treland	Miss P. L. Curties	Mrs R. M. Tresidder	21.2.66
Ch. Gay Dancer of Beecroft	B	Ch. Stormerbanks Invader	Coranton Sherry	Mr and Mrs T. D. Brown	Mr and Mrs T. D. Brown	22.10.62
Ch. Craythornes Spellbound Melody	B	Ch. Lees Sunsalve	Spellbound Star of Delight	Mrs H. Sheldon	Mr N. G. P. Kelsey	18.4.64
Ch. Bella of Bulcorig of Wey	B	Lees Jackpot	Annabel of Bulcorig	Mrs K. Butler	Miss C. C. Lewis	18.11.63
Ch. Belroyd Kismet of Sturmorg	B	Carnival of Cowfold	Belroyd Highlight	Mr W. J. Sturgess	Mr I. Jones	4.7.65

Name	Sex	Sire	Dam	Breeder	Owner	Date
Ch. Bedor Daffodil	B	Ch. Benomley Dafydd	Bedor Starlet	Mrs S. Calland	Mrs S. Calland	8.10.65
1968 Ch. Jomaro Midnight Special	D	Int. Ch. Corgwyn Shillelah	Jomaro Winrod Juno	Miss J. Ross	Miss J. Ross	2.8.65
Ch. Claudia of Pendcrest	B	Mabinogi Masquerade	Celia of Pendcrest	Mr and Mrs W. Overend	Misses Laverick, Leslie and Waterfield	18.6.64
Ch. Dusky Muffin of Kathla	B	Blands Telstar	Kathla Roxi of Edlands	Mr and Mrs E. Lacy	Mr and Mrs E. Lacy	22.1.64
Ch. Cherryhome Clipper	D	Blands Telstar	Cherryhome Candy	Mrs I. Rodgers	Mrs I. Rodgers	8.12.65
Ch. Peggysmill Whistler	D	Black Satan of Braxentra	Peggysmill Stormerbanks Vogue	Mrs M. Banks	Mrs M. Banks	28.11.66
Ch. Kaytop Marshall	D	Kaytop Martin	Kaytop Ruby	Mrs L. K. Moore	Mrs L. K. Moore	8.5.67
Ch. Stokeplain Sealord	D	Stokeplain Lovelace	Stokeplain Sea-Nymph of Seacourt	Mrs W. Irlam	Mrs W. Irlam	29.12.64
Ch. Lees Cracknel	D	Ch. Lees Wennam Eagle	Lees Biscuit	Miss P. L. Curties	Miss P. L. Curties	7.4.65
Ch. Evancoyd Personality Girl	B	Ch. Caswell Duskie Knight	Evancoyd True Love	Mrs B. J. Thompson	Mrs B. J. Thompson	18.2.67
Ch. Evancoyd Secret Love	B	Ch. Caswell Duskie Knight	Evancoyd True Love	Mrs B. J. Thompson	Mrs B. J. Thompson	18.2.67
Eng. & Am. Ch. Winrod Rosanna	B	Ch. Winrod Rob Roy	Ch. Winrod Pollyanna	Mrs A. Black	Mrs E. J. Busby	29.5.65

Name	Sex	Sire	Dam	Owner	Breeder	Born
Ch. Penholm Sunglow of Wey	B	Ch. Lees Sunsalve	Lees Minuet	Mrs K. Butler	Mr R. Daniels	6.4.65
Ch. Belroyd Jenny Wren	B	Ch. Kentwood Cogges Woodpecker	Belroyd Delilah	Mr I. Jones	Mr I. Jones	9.1.65
1969 Ch. Blands Ambassador	D	Pinochio of Kathla	Blands Belinda	Mrs M. Gamble	Mrs M. Gamble	11.7.67
Ch. Camway Court Jester	D	Ch. Caswell Duskie Knight	Camway Gay Finality	Mrs H. Basford	Mrs H. Basford	1.8.64
Ch. Penholm Sunglade	D	Ch. Lees Sunsalve	Lees Minuet	Mrs R. Daniels	Mrs R. Daniels	6.4.65
Ch. Masongill Courier	D	Ch. Bowman Puesedown Passport	Braxentra Baggage of Masongill	Mr & Mrs G. W. Peacock	Mr & Mrs G. W. Peacock	7.12.64
Ch. Newville Pandora	B	Ch. Caswell Duskie Knight	Newville Daphne	Mrs J. Pillinger	Mrs J. Pillinger	18.8.67
Ch. Denrhyl Dresden	B	Int. Ch. Barngremlin of Braxentra	Denrhyl Dauphine	Mr E. T. Williams	Mr E. T. Williams	6.10.66
Ch. Byworth Foxash Juliana	B	Ch. Caswell Duskie Knight	Foxash Winrod Juliet	Mrs M. Roberts	Mrs V. May	11.11.66
Ch. Tehidybarton Falaise Blackbird	B	Ch. Falaise Maccaboy	Falaise Silver Sandels of Robrene	Mrs D. L. Roskruge	Mrs P. M. Brown	29.11.66
Ch. Falaise Suellen	B	Catamaran of Cowfold	Falaise Camelot	Mrs P. M. Brown	Mrs P. M. Brown	9.5.65
Ch. Donna Rosa of Rowell of Wey	B	Ch. Caswell Duskie Knight	Rowell Puesedown Prima Donna	Mrs G. McKay	Miss P. A. Date	5.5.67

Name	Sex	Sire	Dam	Breeder	Owner	Date
1970						
Ch. Kydor Cresta	B	Lenmau President	Kydor Benomley Chaffinch	Mrs D. M. Winter	Mrs D. M. Winter	24.1.68
Ch. Braxentra Barney Two	D	Aust. Ch. Braxentra Time Tag	Braxentra Black Brocade	Mrs V. K. Palmer Cummings	Mrs V. K. Palmer Cummings	26.11.66
Ch. Leonine Kathis	B	Ch. Leonine Adonis	Leonine Katrine	Mrs J. Froggatt	Mrs J. Froggatt	23.6.68
Ch. Fitzdown Sunflower	B	Hildenmanor Lees Gold Flake	Fitzdown Cygnet	Miss J. Fitz-Williams	Miss J. Fitz-Williams	13.3.69
Ch. Lees Chico	D	Ch. Caswell Duskie Knight	Ch. Less Chintz	Miss P. L. Curties	Miss P. L. Curties	14.1.69
Ch. Saffid Widgeon	D	Ch. Winrod Peregrine	Ch. Saffid Surprise Packet	Mrs B. M. Faithfull	Mrs B. M. Faithfull	18.11.64
Ch. Peggysmill Stormerbanks Gorse	B	Am. Ch. Stormerbanks Winrod Fergus	Stormerbanks Machine	Mrs M. Banks	Miss P. Hewan	24.11.68
1971						
Ch. Wyeford Roberto of Wey	D	Lees Antonio	Wyeford Maggie May	Mrs K. Butler	Mr & Mrs J. Ford	21.1.70
Ch. Brocade of Rowell	D	Ch. Hildenmanor Crown Prince	Black Sateen of Braxentra	Miss P. Date	Miss P. Date	4.8.68
Ch. Lees Orpheus	D	Ch. Lees Sunsalve	Ch. Lees Opalsong of Treland	Miss P. Curties	Miss P. Curties	15.8.68
Ch. Evancoyd Audacious	D	Am. Ch. Evancoyd Something Special	Evancoyd Golden Charm	Mrs B. J. Thompson	Mrs B. J. Thompson	20.3.70
Ch. Wyeford Black Tweed	D	Ch. Brocade of Rowell	Wyeford October Flame	Mr & Mrs Schmarr (Australia)	Mr & Mrs J. Ford	10.10.69

Name	Sex	Sire	Dam	Owner	Breeder	Born
Ir. & Eng. Ch. Cooneen Charm	B	Butterybar of Braxentra	Cooneen Earlybird	Mrs V. Deer & Mrs D. Mason	Mr C. Williamson & Mrs J. E. Richmond	1.2.69
Ch. Stormerbanks Mame	B	Ch. Kaytop Marshall	Stormerbanks Kernel	Miss P. Hewan	Miss P. Hewan	30.12.69
Ch. Evancoyd April Love	B	Ch. Caswell Duskie Knight	Evancoyd True Love	Mrs B. J. Thompson	Mrs B. J. Thompson	25.6.69
Ch. Georgette of Wey	B	Ch. Caswell Duskie Knight	Georgianna of Wey	Mrs K. Butler	Mrs K. Butler	24.11.69
1972 Ch. Banhaw Golden Prince of Llwynog	D	Can. Ch. Banhaw Lucas	Banhaw Tortoiseshell	Mr D. C. Smith	Mrs S. Watts-Russell	15.6.68
Ch. Jomaro Midnight Sun	D	Ch. Jomaro Midnight Special	Jomaro Blands Candida	Miss J. M. Ross	Miss J. M. Ross	16.5.70
Ch. Orangeade of Olantigh	D	Ch. Kaytop Marshall	Magnolia of Olantigh	Mrs W. V. Lepper	Mrs W. V. Lepper	10.10.68
Ch. Kydor Cara-mia of Maldwyn	B	Evancoyd Contender	Kydor Franjos Lace	Mrs D. Winter	Mrs E. S. Montgomerie	11.11.70
Ch. Mynthurst Peach Blush	B	Ch. Lees Chico	Mynthurst Shemoy Albertine	Mrs M. E. Roberts	Mrs M. E. Roberts	24.6.70
Ch. Pengavin Passing Delight	B	Ch. Kaytop Marshall	Pengavin Passing Joy	Mrs P. E. Franks	Mrs P. E. Franks	30.1.69
Ch. Stormerbanks Martha	B	Ch. Kaytop Marshall	Stormerbanks Kernel	Miss P. Hewan	Miss P. Hewan	7.10.68

Name	Sex	Sire	Dam	Breeder	Owner	Date
1973 Ch. Kydor Cossack	D	Evacoyd Contender	Kydor Franjos Lace	Mrs D. Winter	Mrs D. Winter	11.11.70
Ch. Kathlas Dusky Curacao	D	Ch. Jomaro Midnight Sun	Dusky Rosaday of Kathla	Mr & Mrs K. Lacey	Mr & Mrs K. Lacey	4.11.71
Ch. Penmoel My Fair Lady	B	Ch. Caswell Duskie Knight	Ashbarton Fantasia	Miss E. J. Evans	Miss E. J. Evans	15.6.68
Ch. Stormerbanks Vain Glory	D	Ch. Stormerbanks Invader	Ch. Stormerbanks Martha	Miss P. Hewan	Miss P. Hewan	10.12.70
Ch. Duskiana of Wey	B	Ch. Caswell Duskie Knight	Georgianna of Wey	Mrs K. Butler	Mrs K. Butler	24.12.69
Ch. Braxentra Pardal Maid	B	Ch. Hildenmanor Crown Prince	Braxentra Red Rosa	Mrs V. Palmer-Cummings	Mrs V. Palmer-Cummings	16.6.69
Ch. Kathlas Dusky Sparkler of Blands	D	Ch. Jomaro Midnight Sun	Dusky Rosaday of Katrla	Mr & Mrs K. Lacey	Mrs P. K. Gamble	4.11.71
Ch. Blands Impressario	D	Ch. Blands Ambassador	Blands Mythend Andromeda	Mrs P. Gamble	Mrs P. Gamble	28.5.69
1974 Ch. Gilburn Supermac	D	Ch. Kydor Cossack	Gilburn Fantasy	Miss P. Date	Mrs A. Gibson	29.11.71
Ch. Fitzdown Badger	D	Hildenmanor Red Duster	Fitzdown Cygnet	Miss J. Fitzwilliams	Miss J. Fitzwilliams	21.6.72
Ch. Pengavin Pure Rapture	B	Pengavin Proud Jubilation	Shallion Shamru	Mrs P. Franks	Mrs S. Burgess	21.3.72
Ch. Olantigh Christmas Carol	B	Blands Telstar	Olantigh Kay of Nilgreen	Mrs W. Lepper	Mrs W. Lepper	26.12.71

Name	Sex	Sire	Dam	Owner	Breeder	Born
Ch. Highlawn Black Diamond	B	Evancoyd Contender	Morning Cloud	Mr J. B. Howarth	Mr J. B. Howarth	25.10.69
Ch. Falaise Teazel	B	Ch. Hildenmanor Crown Prince	Ch. Falaise Suellen	Mrs P. Grogan	Mrs P. M. Brown	12.5.70
Ch. Apollinaris Andorra	B	Ch. Caswell Duskie Knight	Apollinaris Almari	Mrs V. Higgs	Mrs V. Higgs	24.9.70
Ch. Cordach Royal Crown	B	Ch. Hildenmanor Crown Prince	Faine of Bulcorig	Mr & Mrs A. Winsone	Mr & Mrs A. Winsone	17.5.72
1975 Ch. Lynfarne Pacesetter	D	Ch. Stormerbanks Vainglory	Stormerbanks Katie	Mrs L. M. Clarke	Mrs M. A. Carlyle	1.7.73
Ch. Penmoel Minstrel	D	Ashbarton Merry Monarch	Penmoel Sound of Music	Miss J. Evans	Miss J. Evans	1.7.72
Ch. Belroyd Date Line	D	Rowell Best Seller	Belroyd Willow Wren	Messrs Taylor & Jones	Messrs Taylor & Jones	4.1.73
Ch. Dream Girl of Evancoyd	B	Ch. Evancoyd Audacious	Kenzdine Girl	Mrs B. J. Thompson	Miss C. Dickenson	6.2.73
Ch. Kathlas Dusky Serenade	B	Jomaro Royal Flush	Dusky Rosaday of Kathla	Mrs D. Thrower	Mr & Mrs E. Lacey	26.9.72
Ch. Pengavin Passing Consent	B	Evancoyd Contender	Ch. Pengavin Passing Delight	Mrs P. E. Franks	Mrs P. E. Franks	7.6.73
Ch. Blands Silvana	B	Ch. Kydor Cossack	Blands Marmoset	Mrs M. E. Gamble	Mrs M. E. Gamble	19.6.72
Ch. Lees Octavia	B	Hildenmanor Lees Gold Flake	Ch. Less Opalsong of Treland	Miss P. L. Curties	Miss P. L. Curties	5.12.70

Name	Sex	Sire	Dam	Breeder	Owner	Date
Ch. Bardenford's Wood Fay of Jofren	B	Jofren Phoenix	Bardenford's Phaze Gipsy	Mr P. J. Hopwood	Mrs D. Bingham	9.8.72
Ch. Cordach Golden Plover	B	Ch. Hildenmanor Crown Prince	Faine of Bulcorig	Mr & Mrs R. Parker	Mr & Mrs A. Winsome	29.11.72
1976 Ch. Blands of Solomon of Bardrigg	D	Ch. Kathlas Duskie Sparkler of Blands	Blands Belinda	Mr & Mrs W. D. Noall	Mrs P. Gamble	28.10.74
Ch. Fitzdown Cygnus of Rowell	D	Ch. Gilburn Supermac	Fitzdown Cygnet	Miss P. Date	Miss J. Fitzwilliams	22.12.73
Ch. Olantigh Christmas Gift	D	Blands Telstar	Olantigh Kay of Nilgreen	Miss P. Date	Mrs W. Lepper	25.12.71
Ch. Alnsea Christmas Topper of Holmside	D	Ch. Stormerbanks Vainglory	Alnsea Honeysuckle Rose	Mrs J. A. Jones	Mrs Earle	23.12.72
Ch. Winkle of Wey	D	Bryherdene Black Prince of Wey	Yewbury Periwinkle	Mrs K. Butler	Mrs D. M. Herbert	20.9.74
Ch. Stormerbanks Patience	B	Ch. Lynfarne Pacesetter	Ch. Stormerbanks Martha	Miss P. Hewan	Miss P. Hewan	4.1.75
Ch. Wey Blackmint	B	Wey Magic	Caram of Wey	Mrs K. Butler	Mrs K. Butler	6.9.75
Ch. Blands Lisabelle	B	Ch. Kydor Cossack	Blands Marmoset	Mrs M. E. Gamble	Mrs M. E. Gamble	19.6.72
Ch. Gwithian of Tehidybarton	B	Ch. Wyeford Roberto of Wey	Tehidybarton Snow Jennie	Mrs P. Osborn	Miss P. Eberle	17.5.73
Ch. Telsima Pink Lady	B	Pengavin Proud Ambassador	Pengavin Pink Marygold	Mr & Mrs J. E. Knight	Mr & Mrs J. E. Knight	18.2.74
1977 Ch. Belroyd Firecrest	D	Stormerbanks Achilles	Hildenmanor Amber of Belroyd	Messrs Jones & Taylor	Messrs Jones & Taylor	21.8.75

Name	Sex	Sire	Dam	Owner	Breeder	Born
Ch. Jomaro Midnight Again	D	Ch. Jomaro Midnight Sun	Jomaro Inca	Mrs K. Chapman	Miss J. M. Ross	10.2.73
Ch. Penmoel Such Fun of Rivona	D	Ch. Penmoel Minstrel	Penmoel Time for Fun	Mrs M. L. Johnston	Miss J. Evans	15.3.76
Ch. Telsima Sweet Content	B	Evancoyd Contender	Telsima Prunella	Mr & Mrs J. E. Knight	Mr & Mrs J. E. Knight	23.9.74
Ch. St Breaca Sea Melody	B	Pengavin Petrovitch	Tehidybarton Shell	Mrs P. Osborn	Mrs P. Osborn	14.11.74
1978 Ch. Kathlas Melissa of Goronwy	B	Ch. Lynfarne Pacesetter	Kathlas Dusky Lulu	Mr & Mrs Lacey	Mr E. A. Woodrow and Mrs K. Lacey	12.1.76
Ch. Vanrell Dusky Gaylord	D	Ch. Kathlas Dusky Sparkler of Blands	Blands Kismet	Mr B. Wilson	Mr B. Wilson	14.9.74
Ch. Tymaur Empress	B	Ch. Fitzdown Badger	Honour & Glory of Tymawr	Mrs N. Kevill	Mrs N. Kevill	5.3.76
Ch. Knollmoor Secret Wish	B	Kathlas Sandeman	Dark Secret of Knollmoor	Mrs K. Godfrey	Mrs K. Godfrey	24.11.75
Ch. Rowell Mayfly	B	Ch. Olantigh Christmas Gift	Sturmorg October Morn of Rowell	Miss P. Date	Miss P. Date	16.5.76
Ch. Belroyd Firebird	B	Stormerbanks Achilles	Hildenmanor Amber of Belroyd	Messrs Jones & Taylor	Messrs Jones & Taylor	21.8.75
Ch. Foredowne Quixotic	D	Hildenmanor Red Duster	Foredowne Ophelia	Mrs V. J. Coker	Mrs V. J. Coker	10.1.73

Ch. Andersley Easy Rider	D	Ch. Kathlas Dusky Sparkler of Blands	Andersley Everlasting Love	Mrs E. Anderson	Mrs E. Anderson	3.10.75
Ch. Apollinaris Anastasia	B	Ch. Gilburn Supermac	Ch. Apollinaris Andorra	Mrs V. Higgs	Mrs V. Higgs	5.6.76
1979 Ch. Olantigh Black Diamond	D	Ch. Kathlas Dusky Sparkler of Blands	Ch. Olantigh Christmas Carol	Mrs W. Lepper	Mrs W. Lepper	25.1.78
Ch. Ashbarton Blackberry	D	Ashbarton Merry Monarch	Ashbarton Holly Berry	Mrs K. Haley	Mrs K. Haley	18.10.72
Ch. Lynfarne Poldark	D	Ch. Lynfarne Pacesetter	Lynfarne Querida	Mrs L. M. Clarke	Mrs L. M. Clarke	6.3.77
Ch. Apolinaris Angel Clare	B	Ch. Olantigh Christmas Gift	Apolinaris Amaryllis	Mrs V. Higgs	Mrs V. Higgs	20.12.77
Ch. Evancoyd Miss World	B	Ch. Olantigh Christmas Gift	Evancoyd Miss Daring	Mrs B. J. Thompson	Mrs B. J. Thompson	7.6.77
Ch. Camway Christmas Joy	B	Ch. Fitzdown Badger	Camway Bonnie Lass	Mrs A. Green	Mrs H. Bashford	14.12.73
Ch. Evancoyd Miss Daring	B	Ch. Fitzdown Badger	Ch. Dream Girl of Evancoyd	Mrs B. J. Thompson	Mrs B. J. Thompson	9.10.74
1980 Ch. Blands Likely Lad	D	Ch. Kathlas Dusky Sparkler of Blands	Ch. Blands Lisabelle	Mrs M. Gamble	Mrs M. Gamble	16.3.78
Ch. Limehurst Coeur de Lion	D	Anzil Proud Laird	Limehurst Charcoal	Mr & Mrs Daly	Mrs E. Pickford	3.8.74

Name	Sex	Sire	Dam	Owner	Breeder	Born
Ch. Pengavin Proud Jet	D	Ch. Benomley Concorde	Pengavin Lambrook Ladybird	Miss T. Maddox & Mrs P. Franks	Mrs P. Franks	29.6.74
Ch. Revelmere Cock-a-Hoop	D	Ch. Penmoel Such Fun of Rivona	Revelmere Charmian	Mrs D. Mason	Mrs D. Mason	1.1.78
Ch. Blands Sweet Someday	B	Ch. Blands Solomon of Bardrigg	Blands Marmoset	Mrs M. Gamble	Mrs M. Gamble	31.1.79
Ch. Carlton Cottage Frolic	B	Ch. Penmoel Such Fun of Rivona	Ch. Camway Xmas Joy	Mrs A. Green	Mrs A. Green	27.10.77
Ch. Kathlas Gigi	B	Ch. Lynfarne Pacesetter	Kathlas Dusky Lulu	Mr & Mrs Lacey	Mr & Mrs Lacey	20.2.77
Ch. Anzil Elegance of Blands	B	Blands Sonny Boy	Anzil New Penny	Mrs M. Gamble	Mesdames Walton & Hill	9.10.78
Ch. Fitzdown Starbelle	B	Ch. Fitzdown Badger	Dixie Belle of Fitzdown	Miss J. Fitzwilliam	Miss J. Fitzwilliam	8.8.77
Ch. Lees Liquorice	B	Am. Ch. Avonbridge Meteor of Blands	Lees Sugar Plum	Miss P. L. Curties	Miss P. L. Curties	3.6.76
Ch. Rowell Starling	B	Ch. Olantigh Christmas Gift	Sanjon Skylark	Miss P. A. Date	Miss P. A. Date	18.11.78
1981 Ch. Wey Spearmint	D	Ch. Blands Sonny Boy	Ch. Wey Blackmint	Mrs K. Butler	Mrs K. Butler	3.9.79
Ch. Avondale Dark Secret	D	Kay Cymbol of Lambrook	Avondale Hollyberry	Mrs J. Hale	Miss S. Randall	30.4.77

Name	Sex	Sire	Dam	Breeder	Owner	Date
Ch. Belroyd Hyperion	D	Ch. Jomaro Midnight Again	Ch. Belroyd Firebird	Mrs M. Roberts	A. Taylor & I. Jones	6.12.77
Ch. Blands Sonny Boy	D	Ch. Blands Solomon of Bardrigg	Blands Marmoset	Mrs P. Gamble	Mrs P. Gamble	26.6.76
Ch. Fanara Frazer	D	Ch. Evancoyd Mr Wonderful	Fanara Fern	Mrs B. J. Thompson	Mrs P. Grogan	17.12.79
Ch. Belroyd Jacana	B	Ch. Blands Sonny Boy	Belroyd Gaybird	Allan Taylor & Idris Jones	Allan Taylor & Idris Jones	9.5.79
Ch. Carlton Cottage Jolly	B	Ch. Penmoel Such Fun of Rivona	Ch. Carnway Christmas Joy	Mrs A. Green	Mrs A. Green	27.10.77
Ch. Forestop Welsh Pride	B	Ch. Vanrell Duskie Gaylord	Tontil Welsh Lady	G. & B. A. Littler	G. & B. A. Littler	9.11.78
Ch. Carabana Sandra Dee	B	Can. Ch. Foxash Dawn Piper of Rowell	Carabana Carolina	Mrs R. Huckle	Mrs R. Huckle	22.11.78
Ch. Evancoyd Irresistible	B	Ch. Blands Soloman of Bardrigg	Ch. Evancoyd Miss Daring	Mrs B. J. Thompson	Mrs B. J. Thompson	5.6.79
Ch. Rivona Minerva	B	Ch. Belroyd Hyperion	Rivona Matchmaker	Mrs M. L. Johnson	Mrs M. L. Johnson	11.8.79
Ch. Upperwick Joy and Glory	B	Ch. Stormerbanks Vain Glory	Upperwick Christmas Joy	Mr R. Webb	Mr R. Webb	5.11.77
1982 Ch. Apolinaris Annscome Lad	D	Ch. Evancoyd Mr Wonderful	Ch. Apolinaris Angel Clare	Mrs V. Higgs	Mrs V. Higgs	29.11.80
Ch. Fanara Farr of Maldwyn	D	Ch. Evancoyd Mr Wonderful	Fanara Fern	Mrs E. S. Montgomerie	Mrs P. Grogan	17.12.79

Name	Sex	Sire	Dam	Owner	Breeder	Born
Ch. Forestop Red Rorrie	D	Ch. Blands Sonny Boy	Tontil Welsh Lady	Mr G. & Mrs B. Littler	Mr G. & Mrs B. Littler	16.11.80
Ch. Stormerbanks Bearable	D	Stormerbanks Bertram Bear	Stormerbanks Christiania	Miss P. Hewan	Miss P. Hewan	16.6.79
Ch. Evancoyd Unforgettable	B	Ch. Blands Soloman of Bardrigg	Ch. Evancoyd Miss Daring	Mrs B. J. Thompson	Mrs B. J. Thompson	5.6.79
Ch. Belroyd Hecate	B	Ch. Jomaro Midnight Again	Ch. Belroyd Firebird	I. Jones & A. Taylor	I. Jones & A. Taylor	6.12.77
Ch. Evancoyd My Delight	B	Ch. Evancoyd Mr Wonderful	Evancoyd My Pleasure	Mrs B. J. Thompson	Mrs B. J. Thompson	16.12.79
Ch. Wey Such Joy	B	Ch. Penmoel Such Fun of Rivona	Arviivstan Shaney of Wey	Mrs N. Butler	Mrs N. Butler	7.12.78
1983 Ch. Kilvewood Over the Moon	D	Eng. & N.Z.Ch. Revelmere Cock-a-Hoop	Tolverne Princess Tanya	Mrs J. B. Lloyd	Mrs J. B. Lloyd	4.1.81
Ch. Brynelli Black Label	D	Can. Ch. Pengavin Plane Jet	Brynelli Sauterne	Mrs B. M. Ellis	Mrs B. M. Ellis	9.1.78
Ch. Brynelli Heineken of Cooneen	D	Shimisu Maundy Thursday of Penmead	Brynelli Sauterne	Mr & Mrs C. T. Williamson	Mrs B. Ellis	24.6.79
Ch. Blands Status Symbol	D	Ch. Olantigh Black Diamond	Ch. Blands Sweet Someday	Mrs P. Gamble	Mrs P. Gamble	4.7.82
Ch. Marstoanna Peter Pan	D	Ch. Jomaro Midnight Sun	Dusky Roseday of Kathlas	Mrs C. E. Hare	Mr A. Taylor	3.10.77

Ch. Rosewarne Old Ale	D	Ch. Belroyd Hyperion	Rosewarne Kirsch of Ridgewarne	Miss G. Moore	Miss G. M. Moore	30.1.80
Ch. Belroyd Lovebird	B	Ch. Penmoel Such Fun of Rivona	Ch. Belroyd Firebird	Allan Taylor & Idris Jones	Allan Taylor & Idris Jones	16.6.81
Ch. Blands Starflight	B	Ch. Blands Sonny Boy	Blands Shooting Star	Mrs P. Gamble	Mrs P. Gamble	4.4.82
Ch. Skokholm Choirgirl	B	Pemland Royal Command	Shimisu Maundy Bounty of Skokholm	Mrs P. Biles	Mrs P. Biles	6.3.80
Ch. Tymawr Moonfly	B	Tymawr Adam	Tymawr Charity	Mrs N. M. Kevill	Mrs N. M. Kevill	24.5.82
Ch. Tymawr Pink Heather	B	Wey Magic	Tymawr Wild Apple	Mrs N. M. Kevill	Mrs N. M. Kevill	6.6.79
1984 Ch. Fitzdown Dorian of Deavitte	D	Ch. Olantigh Christmas Gift	Ch. Fitzdown Starbelle	Mr S. J. Parsons	Miss J. Fitzwilliams	23.6.81
Ch. Spellbound Silver Dollar	D	Pengavin Petty Kash	Vanity of Spellbound	Messrs Kelsey and Dudeney	Messrs Kelsey and Dudeney	28.6.81
Ch. Pemland Magnus	D	Lees Mastermind	Pemland Royal Romance	Mr & Mrs Magness	Mr and Mrs Magness	22.12.82
Ch. Pemland Ambassador	D	Ch. Evancoyd Mr Wonderful	Hildenmanor Frederika	Mr and Mrs Magness	Mr & Mrs Magness	17.6.82
Ch. Pemland Royal Dream	B	Pemland Royal Command	Hildenmanor Frederika	Mr & Mrs Magness	Mr & Mrs Magness	27.12.80
Ch. Blands Imagination	B	Ch. Blands Status Symbol	Blands Glorianna	Mrs P. Gamble	Mrs P. Gamble	12.2.83

Name	Sex	Sire	Dam	Owner	Breeder	Born
Ch. Blands Expectations	B	Ch. Blands Status Symbol	Ch. Anzil Elegance Of Blands	Mrs P. Gamble	Mrs P. Gamble	12.3.83
Ch. Shesteph Amber of Pinewalk	B	Ch. Blands Likely Lad	Eton Way Tasmin	D. P. Cawthera	Mr S. Bazan	18.9.81
Ch. Masongill Ruby	B	Ch. Kathlas Duskie Sparkler of Blands	Masongill Sedormer Amethyst	Mrs D. Peacock	Mr & Mrs Peacock	14.5.76
Ch. Peggysmill Footpad	D	Blands Status Quo of Peggysmill	Peggysmill Pocket Picker	Mrs M. Banks	Mrs M. Banks	27.2.83
1985 Ch. Lees Mastermind	D	Ch. Penmoel Such Fun of Rivona	Lees Radiant	Mrs P. L. Curties	Mrs P. L. Curties	15.1.83
Ch. Cordach Lucinda	B	Stormerbanks Robson	Tweedbanks Lucy Locket of Cordach	Mr & Mrs Winsone	Mr & Mrs Winsone	30.3.82
Ch. Meres of Twilight	D	Kilvewood Turn to Gold	Caruan Sugar and Spice of Norecliffe	Mrs V. Watson	Mrs V. Watson	24.8.83
Ch. Bymil Black Nymph	B	Ch. Fitzdown Dorian of Deavitte	Bymil Sherry Spinner	Miss S. Taylor	Miss S. Taylor	29.12.83
Ch. Luther of Wey	D	Ch. Wey Spearmint	Dundryview Gemma	Mrs N. Butler	Miss Harvey	2.6.84

Name	Sex	Sire	Dam	Breeder	Owner	Date
Ch. Belroy Nut Cracker	D	Cordach Master Copy of Hildenmanor	Penland Court Dancer	Messrs Jones & Taylor	Messrs Jones & Taylor	28.11.83
Ch. Fitzdown Dorian of Deavitte	D	Ch. Olantigh Christmas Gift	Ch. Fitzdown Starbelle	Mr S. J. Parsons	Miss J. Fitzwilliams	23.6.81
Ch. Forestop Royal Salute	D	Pemland Royal Command	Ch. Forestop Welsh Pride	Mr G. & Mrs B. Litler	Mr & Mrs Litler	23.5.83
Ch. Lees Mastermind	D	Ch. Penmoel Such Fun of Rivona	Lees Radient	Miss P. L. Curties	Miss P. L. Curties	15.1.82
Ch. Meres of Twilight	D	Kilvewood Turn to Gold	Caruen Sugar and Spice of Norecliffe	Mrs V. Watson	Mrs V. Watson	28.4.85
Ch. Belroyd Nestling	B	Pemland Royal Command	Ch. Belroyd Jacana	Messrs Jones & Taylor	Messrs Jones & Taylor	28.11.83
Ch. Bymil Gold Sylph	B	Ch. Fitzdown Dorian of Deavitte	Bymil Sherry Spinner	Sarah Taylor	Sarah Taylor	29.12.83
Ch. Kaytop Dancing Daffodil	B	Tindervale Ramdrop of Burlocks	Kaytop Red Rose	L. K. Moore	L. C. Moore	10.12.80
Ch. Pemwell Pekoe	B	Ch. Blands Status Symbol	Kathlas Magic Moments of Pemwell	Mr C. Whitwell	Mr C. Whitwell	23.5.83
1986						
Ch. Perrymist Captain Scarlet	D	Blands Kiwi of Perrymist	Perrymist Scarlet Lady	Mr & Mrs Saxton	Mr & Mrs Saxton	2.5.84
Ch. Haresfoot Isaac	D	Ch. Evancoyd Mr Wonderful	Fitzdown Frolic	Mrs S. Harrison	Mrs S. Harrison	3.1.81
Ch. Ormareon Oddfellow of Ashburton	D	Ashburton Cardinal	Spellbound Marina of Ormareon	Mrs K. M. Haley	Mrs M. Carlyle	3.9.84

Name	Sex	Sire	Dam	Owner	Breeder	Born
Ch. Kiss Me Kate of Foxydale	B	Foxydale Snowmartin	Howman Honeysuckle	Mrs M. Neal	Mr E. I. Howells	20.2.82
Ch. Mynthurst Swinging Rhythm of Rynline	B	Ch. Penmoel Such Fun of Rivona	Mynthurst Speedy	J. & D. Powell	Mrs M. E. Roberts	29.5.83
Ch. Revelmere Rose Cocker	B	Ch. Pemland Magness	Vennwoods Tritoma of Revelmere	Mrs D. Mason	Mrs D. Mason	19.5.84
Ch. Evancoyd Unique	B	Ch. Haresfoot Isaac	Ch. Evancoyd Unforgettable	Mrs B. J. Thompson	Mrs B. J. Thompson	1.12.83
Ch. Forestop Lady Clare of Gemiro	B	Ch. Apollinaris Annsome Lad	Tontil Welsh Lady	Mrs M. Crane	Mr & Mrs Littler	8.4.82
1987 Ch. Blaizewood Crackerjack of Kilvewood	D	Ch. Belroyd Nut Cracker	Cinnonnie Star Choice	Mrs Barbara Lloyd	Mrs J. A. Logsdon	19.9.85
Ch. Apollinaris Agenot	D	Ch. Fitzdown Dorian of Deavitte	Ch. Apollinaris Angel Clare	Mrs V. Higgs	Mrs V. Higgs	19.12.84
Ch. Apollinaris Assen	D	Ch. Penmoel Such Fun of Rivona	Apollinaris Annabel	Mr Rod Thomas	Mrs V. Higgs	15.11.85
Ch. Bronteg Sians Mr Magic	D	Ch. Evancoyd Mr Wonderful	Lucky Charm of Wey at Bronteg	Mr Trevor Blake	Mr Trevor Blake	28.11.83
Ch. Belroyd Pipit	B	Ch. Belroyd Nut Cracker	Belroyd Kiwi	Messrs Jones & Taylor	Messrs Jones & Taylor	26.8.85
Ch. Marklynne Maid Marion	B	Ch. Peggsmill Footpad	Marklynne Issidora	Mr & Mrs A. Rhodie	Mr & Mrs A. Rhodie	24.9.84

Name	Sex	Sire	Dam	Breeder	Owner	Date
Ch. Belroyd Popinjay	B	Ch. Blands Status Symbol	Ch. Belroyd Jacana	Messrs Jones & Taylor	Messrs Jones & Taylor	15.8.85
Ch. Deavitte Treacle Parkin	B	Ch. Fitzdown Dorian of Deavitte	Deavitte Cinnamon Sedge	Mrs M. Parsons	Mrs M. Parsons	31.10.84
Ch. Evancoyd Style	B	Ch. Fitzdown Dorian of Deavitte	Evancoyd Intrigue	Mrs J. Thompson	Mrs J. Thompson	1.8.85
Ch. Kaytop M'Lady Miranda	B	Ch. Fitzdown Dorian of Deavitte	Kaytop Mazurka	L. Moore	L. Moore	27.6.85
1988 Ch. Blands Limited Edition of Belroyd	D	Ch. Belroyd Nut Cracker	Blands Lovelorn	Taylor, Jones & Gamble	Taylor, Jones & Gamble	16.5.84
Ch. Super Trouper of Drumbuie	D	Ch. Blands Status Symbol	Drumbuie Sweet Success	Mr J. & Miss P. Forgie	Mr J. Stewart	9.10.86
Ch. Belroyd Puffin	D	Ch. Blands Status Symbol	Ch. Belroyd Jacana	Messrs Jones & Taylor	Messrs Jones & Taylor	15.8.85
Ch. Irish Ch. Manto Red Earl	D	Ch. Penmoel Such Fun of Rivona	Irish Ch. Davilton Darling Lady	Mr T. Wilson	Mrs F. Toman	13.4.83
Ch. Rivona Twice the Fun	D	Ch. Belroyd Nut Cracker	Rivona Tricks	Mrs M Johnson	Mrs M Johnson	24.1.86
Ch. Belroyd Quite & Lark	B	Ch. Penmoel Such Fun of Rivona	Belroyd Olympic Star	Messrs Jones & Taylor	Messrs Jones & Taylor	29.3.86
Ch. Bulcorig Zenita	B	Bulcorig Queens Master	Bulcorig Xie Xie	Miss C. Lewis	Miss C. Lewis	11.11.85
Ch. Pendogett Prelude	B	Karenhurst Nut Crunch	Pendogett Pussy Willow	Mesdames Cholmondeley & Hickman	Mrs Cholmondeley	22.12.86

Name	Sex	Sire	Dam	Owner	Breeder	Born
1989 Ch. Kaytop Dice of Rossacre	B	Deavitte Golden Emblem of Rossacre	Kaytop Dancing Dawn	Mrs A. Boughton	Mrs Leila Moore	1.7.85
Ch. Ermyn Sugar Loaf of Lees	D	Kaytop Summer Sea at Ermyn	Kilvewood Twilight Moon	Miss P. L. Curties	Mary Davies	19.5.87
Ch. Blands Dedication	D	Ch. Belroyd Nut Cracker	Ch. Blands Imagination	Mrs P. Gamble	Mrs P. Gamble	24.10.86
Ch. Lion of Wey	D	Am. Ch. High Flyer Ryan	Bulcorig Zenana	Mrs K. Butler	Mr N. P. Cawston	29.4.87
Ch. Longrene Bon Bon of Pemland	B	Pemland Royal Command	Marisco Melody	Mr & Mrs Magness	Mrs W. Truman	30.6.86
Ch. Bymil Feather Duster	B	Kaytop Ming	Ch. Bymil Black Sylph	Miss S. Taylor	Mrs S. Taylor	14.2.87
Ch. Beaushae Christmas Joy of Mysweet	B	Avondale Aran of Kaytop	Beaushae Fantasy	Mr & Mrs Wood	Mrs Bovington	25.12.83
Ch. Belroyd Rosefinch	B	Pemland Ambassador	Belroyd Nestling	Messrs Jones & Taylor	Messrs Jones & Taylor	29.1.87
Ch. Rynline Elinor	B	Pemland Royal Command	Ch. Mynthurst Swinging Rhythm of Rynline	J. & D. Powell	J. & D. Powell	22.4.87
Ch. Kentwood Magic Moments	B	Ch. Kilvewood Over the Moon	Kentwood Mistress Mine	Mrs M. Godden	Mrs M. Godden	4.1.85
Ch. Lees Diadem	B	Ch. Lees Master Mind	Lees Delight	Miss P. L. Curties	Miss P. L. Curties	13.1.84

BRITISH CARDIGAN CHAMPIONS, 1960 to 1989

Name	Sex	Sire	Dam	Owner	Breeder	Born
1960 Ch. Kentwood Eirwen	B	Ch. Kentwood Hannaford Jose	Kentwood Violetta of Veryan	Mr and Mrs J. Cutler	Miss S. H. Godden	9.11.56
Ch. Parmel Pilot	D	Ch. Parmel Dambuster	Elkay Mandi	Mr J. E. J. Parkinson	Mr M. Sheehan	8.12.56
Ch. Kentwood Eirwen	B	Ch. Kentwood Hanaford Jose	Kentwood Violetta of Veryan	Mr and Mrs Cutler	Miss S. Godden	9.11.57
Ch. Rozavel Blue Rosette	B	Rozavel Blue at Last	Rozavel Blue Mist	Mrs T. Gray	Mrs T. Gray	28.2.58
1961 Ch. Parmel Stewardess	B	Ch. Parmel Pilot	Ch. Another Delight	Mrs A. Parkinson	Mrs A. Parkinson	2.7.60
Ch. Kentwood Hawen	B	Ch. Kentwood Dewin	Ch. Kentwood Curigwen	Miss S. Godden	Miss S. Godden	21.11.57
Ch. Kentwood Rhydlyd	D	Kentwood Mervyn	Ch. Kentwood Myfanwy	Miss S. Godden	Miss S. Godden	24.2.59
Ch. Konitz of Corfox	D	Kentwood Corwynt of Corfox	Fine Friend of Corfox	Mr A. Toomer	Mr A. Toomer	20.3.58
1962 Ch. Edenwell Black Ormig	D	Ch. Edenwell Gleghornie Barrister	Ch. Edenwell Elkay Mali	Miss Verity	Mr R. T. Eden	19.6.58

Name	Sex	Sire	Dam	Owner	Breeder	Born
Ch. Robgwen Fordwell Deborah	B	Ch. Parmel Pilot	Parmel Aureola	Mrs G. M. Roberts	Mr D. Bamford	8.5.61
Ch. Parmel Dandini	D	Ch. Parmel Pilot	Ch. Another Delight	Mrs A. Parkinson	Mrs A. Parkinson	2.7.60
Ch. Sandon Dilwell Quicksilver	B	Dilwell Monksford	Dilwell Gweno	Mrs W. J. Wood	Mr J. H. Jones	16.6.60
1963 Ch. Fordwell Belinda	B	Ch. Kentwood Cymro	Fordwell Parmel Aureloa	Mr D. Bamford	Mr D. Bamford	27.9.59
Ch. Ringinglow Gleghornie Brigadier	D	Ch. Gleghornie Elkay Miri	Gleghornie Ambition	Miss M. Thomas	Mrs E. M. Roberts	27.12.59
Ch. Joanne of Bealclose	B	Ch. Kentwood Jose	Knowland Tegwen	Miss D. Bagley	Miss D. Bagley	21.3.59
Ch. Kentwood Brenin	D	Kentwood Rozavel Blue Badge	Ch. Kentwood Hawen	Miss S. Godden	Miss S. Godden	3.2.61
Ch. Wildfowl of Willowbeach	D	Lisaye Ranger	Gleghornie Aquatint	Mrs C. Barker	Mrs C. Barker	28.4.58
1964 Ch. Pantyblaidd Pip	D	Pantyblaidd Ginger	Tresaith Mali	Mr O. Jones	Mr F. B. Jones	21.1.63
Ch. Hildenmanor Isolabella	B	Edleys Farmers Boy	Hildenmanor Tia Maria	Mrs D. Albin	Mrs D. Albin	11.9.58
Ch. Elkay Meridyn	D	Ch. Kentwood Rhydlyd	Elkay Mefus	Mr K. Lockyer	Mr K. Lockyer	27.5.62

	Sex	Sire	Dam	Breeder	Owner	Date
Ch. Parmel Gaiety Girl	B	Ch. Parmel Dandini	Parmel Frolic	Mrs A. Parkinson	Mrs A. Parkinson	7.1.63
1965 Ch. Haraudon Parmel Guardsman	D	Ch. Parmel Dandini	Parmel Frolic	Mrs Joughin	Mrs A. Parkinson	7.1.63
Ch. Kentwood Emrys	D	Ch. Kentwood Cymro	Ch. Kentwood Sian	Miss S. Godden	Miss S. Godden	1.1.62
Ch. Southpark Gerwyn	D	Teilo Bryn	Maethlon Miss Moppet	Mr and Mrs J. H. Jones	Mr and Mrs Gilmour	10.4.62
Ch. Calbridge Haughlands Magical Miss	B	Ch. Edenwell Black Ormig	Haughlands Pixie Girl	Mr Haigh	Mr Street	2.2.62
Ch. Dilwel Malen of Rode	B	Teilo Bryn	Dilwel Glesni	Mr Mortimer	Mr and Mrs J. H. Jones	25.6.62
Ch. Kentwood Sian	B	Kentwood Selwyn	Ch. Kentwood Myfanwy	Miss S. Godden	Miss S. Godden	14.11.60
1966 Ch. Bonvilston Syr Iago	D	Clemox Carioca	Bonvilston Meira	Mrs S. Evans	Mrs S. Evans	16.9.61
Ch. Parmel Digger	D	Ch. Kentwood Cymro	Parmel Delight	Mrs A. Parkinson	Mrs A. Parkinson	5.9.63
Ch. Dilwel Maggie	B	Teilo Bryn	Dilwel Glensi	Mr and Mrs J. H. Jones	Mr and Mrs J. H. Jones	25.6.62
Ch. Jezalin Josetta	B	Ch. Kentwood Cymro	Jezalin Fordwell Deena	Miss P. Walker	Miss P. Walker	10.11.62

Name	Sex	Sire	Dam	Owner	Breeder	Born
Ch. Rozavel Blue Tinsel	B	Rozavel Trecwn Stanhope	Ch. Rozavel Blue Rosette	Mrs T. Gray	Mrs T. Gray	16.12.63
1967 Ch. Pim of Critum	D	Langland Kontra of Bablake	Bloom of Bablake	Mrs Pratt	Mrs Pratt	6.10.65
Ch. Dilwel Gwynfil	B	Ch. Southpark Gerwyn	Dilwel Gweno	Mrs Hammond	Mr and Mrs J. H. Jones	25.3.65
Ch. Robgwen Black Beauty	B	Dilwel Gwilym	Ch. Robgwen Fordwell Deborah	Mrs G. Roberts	Mrs G. Roberts	2.6.65
1968 Ch. Echium of Hezelclose	D	Black Mawddach	Jasione of Bealclose	Miss Rob	Miss Rob	23.7.66
Ch. Dilwel Gweno-yr-Ail	B	Ch. Southpart Gerwyn	Dilwel Gweno	Mr & Mrs J. H. Jones	Mr & Mrs J. H. Jones	25.3.64
1969 Ch. Dilwel Maggie May	B	Ch. Southpark Gerwyn	Int. Ch. Dilwel Maggie	Messrs Stott & Winsome	Mr & Mrs J. H. Jones	1.3.66
Ch. Dilwel Auntie Maggie of Sillbrook	B	Ch. Southpark Gerwyn	Int. Ch. Dilwel Maggie	Mrs E. Baker	Mr & Mrs J. H. Jones	1.3.66
Int. Ch. Robgwen Welsh Fire	B	Dilwel Gwilym	Ch. Robgwen Fordwell Deborah	Mrs L. Vantrease	Mrs G. Roberts	2.6.65
Ch. Rozavel Blue Gynt	D	Ch. Kentwood Brenin	Rozavel Glynis	Mr and Mrs Carter	Mrs Wintour	7.1.67
1970 Ch. Parmel Duges	B	Ch. Parmel Digger	Parmel Cassandra	Mrs A. Parkinson	Mrs A. Parkinson	21.8.68

Name		Sire	Dam			
Ch. Robgwen Welsh Minstrel	D	Ch. Parmel Digger	Int. Ch. Robgwen Welsh Fire	Mrs G. Roberts	Mrs G. Roberts	24.6.68
Ch. Baileswood Gwlithyn	B	Black Mawddach	Dilwel Gwerfyl	Mrs S. Bailes	Mrs S. Bailes	25.7.67
Ch. Wendac Robgwen Midnight Special	D	Dilwel Gwilyn	Ch. Robgwen Black Beauty	Mrs D. Dodd	Mrs G. Roberts	28.2.69
1971 Ch. Lees Rhiwelli Blue Lamp	B	Rhiwelli Trilliw	Rhiwelli Blue Gem	Miss P. Curties	Mrs Young	18.1.68
Ch. Parmel Delfryn	D.	Ch. Parmel Digger	Joy Abounding Bridget	Mrs A. Parkinson	Mr Anderson	6.8.68
Ch. Dilwel Tony	D	Dilwel Regal	Dilwel Tegwen	Mr & Mrs Jones	Mr & Mrs Jones	5.8.68
1972 Ch. Baileswood Gwythyr	D	Ch. Echium of Hezelclose	Dilwel Gwerfyl	Mrs S. Bailes	Mrs S. Bailes	25.5.70
Ch. Bleacholme Celynen	B	Ch. Echium of Hezelclose	Baileswood Grainne of Bleacholme	Mr K. F. Lindley	Mr K. F. Lindley	27.4.69
Ch. Dilwel Tosca	B	Dilwel Regal	Dilwel Tegwen	Mr & Mrs Zimmerman	Mr & Mrs Jones	5.8.68
Ch. Deb's Delight of Grangefield	B	Ch. Wendac Robgwen Midnight Special	Tursdale Black Pearl	Mr & Mrs J. R. Page	Mr & Mrs J. R. Page	8.11.70
1973 Ch. Kentwood Helwen	B	Ch. Kentwood Emrys	Kentwood Dawn	Miss S. Godden	Mrs M. F. Davis	6.2.70
Ch. Rozavel Blue Lamp	B	Rozavel Blue Flashlight	Ch. Rozavel Blue Tinsel	Mrs T. Gray	Mrs T. Gray	19.7.70

Name	Sex	Sire	Dam	Owner	Breeder	Born
Ch. Apollinaris Cenydd	D	Ch. Robgwen Welsh Minstrel	Robgwen Solitaire	Mrs V. Higgs	Mrs V. Higgs	13.12.71
1974 Ch. Parmel Deenee	D	Ch. Parmel Delfryn	Ch. Parmel Duges	Mrs A. Parkinson	Mrs A. Parkinson	14.11.71
Ch. Winsdown Blue Disk of Robgwen	D	Winsdown Brymore Carbon Blue	Am. Ch. Winsdown Brymore Cat Ballou	Mrs G. Roberts	Mrs L. Vantrease	13.7.71
Ch. Joseter Mudwin	D	Ch. Pantyblaid Pip	Samantha of Joseter	Mr & Mrs P. Clifton	Mr & Mrs P. Clifton	31.5.71
Ch. Baileswood Blodeuwedd	B	Ch. Wendac Robgwen Midnight Special	Baileswood Tursdale Amethyst	Mrs S. Bailes	Mrs S. Bailes	11.9.72
Ch. Sirax Beeswax	B	Ch. Wendac Robgwen Midnight Special	Paschal Candle	Mrs J. Grace	Mrs J. Grace	1.2.72
1975 Ch. Baileswood Bryn Mawr	D	Ch. Wendac Robgwen Midnight Special	Baileswood Tursdale Amethyst	Mrs Serginson	Mrs S. Bailes	11.9.72
Ch. Apollinaris Ceinwen	B	Sirax Gregory	Apollinaris Carmen	Mr L. Day	Mrs V. Higgs	19.2.72
Ch. Pharoah of Joseter	D	Ch. Joseter Mudwin	Daleviz Inga	Mr & Mrs P. Clifton	Mr & Mrs Finney	24.6.73
Ch. Cainlock April Dawn	B	Dondor Cador of Wendac	Wendac Sirax Paschel	Mrs Lockton	Mrs Lockton	11.4.74
Ch. Geum of	D	Ch. Echium of	Dryas of	Miss J. Hunt	Miss K. Robb	17.3.68

1976 Ch. Wendac Astral	B	Ch. Wendac Robgwen Midnight Special	Wendac Sirax Paschal Joy	Mrs D. Dodd	Mrs D. Dodd	5.12.71
Ch. Doldrum Amanda	B	Black Mawddach	Baileswood Briallen	Mr & Mrs K. Littlefair	Mr & Mrs K. Littlefair	23.12.73
1977 Ch. Baileswood Dyddanwy	B	Ch. Baileswood Gwythyr	Ch. Baileswood Blodeuwedd	Mrs S. Bailes	Mrs S. Bailes	10.4.75
Ch. Beckrow Bandelero	D	Rozavel Merioneth	Rozavel Blue Lace of Beckrow	Miss S. M. Tonkyn	Miss S. M. Tonkyn	11.3.72
Ch. Willowbeach Bumble Bee	D	Ch. Joseter Mudwin	Contessa of Willowbeach	Mrs E. Baker	Mrs E. Barker	13.2.73
1978 Ch. Rowell Guilty Party	B	Ch. Joseter Mudwin	Rowell All Night Party	Miss P. Date	Miss P. Date	17.1.75
Ch. Baileswood Essylt	B	Ch. Baileswood Gwythyr	Ch. Baileswood Blodeuwedd	Mrs S. Bailes	Mrs S. Bailes	2.7.76
Ch. Bekonpenn Gwyneth	B	Ch. Joseter Mudwin	Apollinaris Columbine	Mr L. Needham	Mr L. Needham	12.6.74
Ch. Doldrum Brandy Snap	D	Ch. Baileswood Gwythwr	Baileswood Briallen	Mr & Mrs K. Littlefair	Mr & Mrs K. Littlefair	23.1.75
Ch. Sirax Pickwick	D	Ch. Apollinaris Cenydd	Ch. Sirax Beeswax	Mrs J. Grace	Mrs J. Grace	27.3.75

Name	Sex	Sire	Dam	Owner	Breeder	Born
Ch. Doldrum Barron Knight	D	Ch. Baileswood Gwythyr	Baileswood Briallen	Mr & Mrs K. Littlefair	Mr & Mrs K. Littlefair	23.1.75
Ch. Ringinglow Morys	D	Bridgemont Sentinal	Ringinglow Brynhall Tamarisk	Miss M. Thomas	Miss M. Thomas	5.5.74
Ch. Ringinglow Morys' Treasure	B	Ch. Ringinglow Morys	Ringinglow Tyddwen	Miss M. Thomas	Miss M. Thomas	21.3.76
Ch. Grangefield Rainchaser	D	Asoka Morgan	Veritas Mistral of Grangefield	Mr & Mrs B. A. Jones	Mr & Mrs J. Page	31.3.77
1979 Ch. Jubilee Joseph	D	Ch. Pharoah of Joseter	Beckonpenn Carmen	Mr & Mrs D. Baxter	Mr & Mrs P. Clifton	5.2.77
Ch. Apollinaris Catkin	B	Int. & Lux. Ch. Sirax Gregory	Apollinaris Caitlin	Mrs V. Higgs	Mrs V. Higgs	9.6.76
Ch. Robgwen Gregson	D	Int. & Lux. Ch. Sirax Gregory	Robgwen Pride of Place	Mrs G. Roberts	Mrs G. Roberts	23.2.76
1980 Ch. Grangefield Night Story	D	Asoka Morgan	Veritas Mistral of Grangefield	Mrs M. E. Aynscough & Miss S. Verity	Mr & Mrs J. Page	31.3.77
Ch. Kentwood Taglys	B	Ch. Joseter Mudwin	Kentwood Pansi	Miss S. H. Godden	Miss S. H. Godden	22.5.76
Ch. Downholme Silver Sand of Joseter	D	Ch. Joseter Mudwin	Downholme Golden Beauty	Mr P. Clifton	Mrs A. M. Hart	4.6.78

Name	Sex	Sire	Dam	Breeder	Owner	Date
Ch. Kentwood Anwyl	B	Bridgemont Suseman	Ch. Kentwood Heulwen	Miss S. H. Godden	Miss S. H. Godden	4.3.78
1981						
Ch. Kentwood Arnallt	D	Bridgemont Suseman	Ch. Kentwood Heulwen	Miss S. H. Godden	Miss S. H. Godden	4.3.78
Ch. Robgwen Welsh Flame	D	Ch. Parmel Digger	Robgwen Pride 'n Joy	Mrs G. M. Roberts	Mrs G. M. Roberts	31.3.76
Ch. Baileswood Geraint	D	Ch. Joseter Mudwin	Ch. Baileswood Blodeuwedd	Mrs S. A. Bailes	Mrs S. A. Bailes	8.6.78
Ch. Rowell Party Spirit	B	Ch. Joseter Mudwin	Rowell All Night Party	Mr P. Clifton	Miss P. Date	17.1.75
Ch. Wendac Javelin	D	Ch. Pharoah of Joseter	Wendac Specials Jubilation	Mrs D. M. Dodd	Mrs D. M. Dodd	19.8.79
Ch. Wendac Jaunty	D	Ch. Pharoah of Joseter	Wendac Specials Jubilation	Mrs D. M. Dodd later Miss S. M. Tonkyn	Mrs D. M. Dodd	19.8.79
Ch. Cavalay Silver Slippers	B	Ch. Beckrow Bandelero	Vennwoods Destiny	Miss S. M. Tonkyn	Mrs C. Lakin	30.11.77
1982						
Ch. Downholme Serena of Bridgemont	B	Bridgemont Suseman	Downholme Golden Beauty	Miss B. Witheridge	Mrs A. M. Hart	15.8.78
Ch. Magdor Black Velvet	B	Ch. Apollinaris Cenydd	Robgwen Love in a Mist	Mr & Mrs R. E. H. Dorsett	Mr & Mrs R. E. H. Dorsett	23.12.77
Ch. Wendac Sugar 'n' Spice	B	Ch. Baileswood Geraint	Wendac Charm	Mrs D. M. Dodd	Mrs D. M. Dodd	10.11.79

Name	Sex	Sire	Dam	Owner	Breeder	Born
Ch. Molead Must Bet At Allspark	D	Apollinaris Casanova	Halesmore Black Magic	Mrs F. Allsopp	Mr & Mrs A. A. Mole	9.9.80
Ch. Marycliffe Ceri	B	Baileswood Gethin	Marycliffe Annabelle	Mrs B. Serginson	Mrs B. Serginson	18.7.79
1983 Ch. Wendac Black Special of Jontays	D	Ch. Wendac Robgwen Midnight Special	Wendac Charm	Mr D. Johnson	Mrs D. M. Dodd	30.5.77
Ch. Robgwen Miss Muffet	B	Ch. Robgwen Gregson	Robgwen Pride 'n' Joy	Mr & Mrs R. E. H. Dorsett	Mrs G. M. Roberts	6.6.77
Ch. Lionoak Tiperty Witch	B	Robgwen Magic Moments of Lionoak	Lionoak Bronze Beauty	Mrs J. Cummings	Mrs J. Cummings	10.6.78
Ch. & Aus. Ch. Rhossili Itsa Special of Beckrow	B	Aus. Ch. Cambrian Just for Luck of Medea	Aus. Ch. Keerhos Beckrow Solo	Miss S. M. Tonkyn	Mrs J. Georgiou (Aus.)	27.6.80
Ch. Kentwood Elwyn	D	Ch. Kentwood Arnallt	Ch. Kentwood Taglys	Miss S. H. Godden	Miss S. H. Godden	6.11.80
1984 Ch. Doldrum Edwina	B	Ch. Pharoah of Joseter	Doldrum Barbarina	Mr & Mrs K. Littlefair	Mr & Mrs K. Littlefair	12.12.79
Ch. Jezalin Top Brass	D	Ch. Kentwood Elwyn	Jezalin Gypsy Moth	Miss P. Walker	Miss P. Walker	11.12.81
Ch. Halesmore Welsh Storm	D	Ch. Robgwen Welsh Flame	Halesmore Black Surprise	Miss N. Mortimore	Miss N. Mortimore	5.5.82

Name	Sex	Sire	Dam	Breeder	Owner	Date
Ch. Wendac Legionnaire	D	Ch. Wendac Robgwen Midnight Special	Wendac Joyful	Mrs D. M. Dodd	Mrs D. M. Dodd	1.2.82
Ch. Lees Blue Rose of Bymil	B	Joseter JP	Lees Blue Chevron	Miss S. E. Taylor	Miss P. Curties	19.6.80
Ch. Baileswood Lleucu	B	Ch. Wendac Javelin	Ch. Baileswood Essyllt	Mrs S. A. Bailes	Mrs S. A. Bailes	18.6.81
Ch. Kentwood Edwin	D	Ch. Kentwood Arnallt	Ch. Kentwood Taglys	Miss T. Maddox	Miss S. H. Godden	6.11.80
Ch. Antoc Cinnabar	B	Ch. Kentwood Elwyn	Lees Jet	Mrs A. Spedding	Mrs A. Spedding	23.10.82
Ch. Joseter Joson	D	Ch. Jubilee Joseph	Ringinglow Valentine	Mrs A. Baxter	Mr P. Clifton	17.1.82
Ch. Doldrum Hennessy	D	Ch. Wendrac Legionnaire	Doldrum Enchantress	Mr & Mrs K. Littlefair	Mr & Mrs K. Littlefair	19.5.83
1985 Ch. Gwenlais Croeso	D	Ch. Grangefield Rainchaser	Grangefield Milford of Gwenlais	Mr & Mrs Jones-Rees	Mr & Mrs Jones-Rees	27.8.83
Ch. Kentwood Bethan	B	Ch. Kentwood Arnallt	Kentwood Pansi	Miss S. H. Godden	Miss S. H. Godden	1.1.79
Ch. Bymil Silver Lining	B	Kerridas Ianto	Ch. Lees Blue Rose of Bymil	Miss S. E. Taylor	Miss S. E. Taylor	8.1.82
Ch. Beckrow Beverley of Willowglen	B	Beckrow Baronet	Beckrow Suzanne	Mr & Mrs C. Tonkyn	Miss S. Tonkyn	3.6.82

Name	Sex	Sire	Dam	Owner	Breeder	Born
1986						
Ch. Craigdam Thomas	D	Craigdam Ifor	Craigdam Whynne	Mr & Mrs Senior	Mr & Mrs Senior	12.7.83
Ch. Magdor Prince Hal	D	Robgwen Glint	Magdor Black Velvet	Mr R. Dorset	Mr R. Dorset	1.1.85
Ch. Beckrow Belle Suzanne	B	Ch. Pharaoh of Joseter	Beckfawn Minstrel	Miss S. Tonkyn	Miss S. Tonkyn	20.6.80
Ch. Baileswood Myfanwy Fechan	B	Ch. Jubilee Joseph	Baileswood Iariles	Mrs S. Bailes	Mrs S. Bailes	29.4.83
Ch. Dolly Dickon of Ringinglow	B	Ch. Molead Must be at Allspark	Bridgemont Sophie	Miss M. Thomas	Mrs Allsop	21.1.84
1987						
Ch. Beckrow Blue Cedar	D	Kerridas Ianto	Beckrow Blue Sapphire	Miss S. Tonkyn	Miss S. Tonkyn	28.5.85
Ch. Kerman the Sailorma::	D	Ch. Wendac Legionnaire	Kerman Rhynwyn's Rapture	Miss Fricker	Mrs K. J. Fricker	16.5.85
Ch. Enversue A Dream Come True	B	Ch. Jubilee Joseph	Bonnie Bell of Evensue	Mr & Mrs D. Luckman	Mr & Mrs Clarkson	5.8.84
Ch. Irish Ch. Grange Field Guinevere	B	Grangefield Elmet	Gwenlais Beauty of Grangefield	Miss M. Searson	Mrs D. Paige	15.3.85
Ch. Gwenlais Casiad	B	Ch. Grangefield Rainchaser	Grangefield Milford of Gwenlais	Mr & Mrs Jones Rees	Mr & Mrs Jones Rees	27.8.83
Ch. Marycliffe Dazeling Dina	B	Ch. Robgwen Welsh Flame	Ch. Marycliffe Ceri	Mrs B. Sergison	Mrs B. Sergison	31.5.83

1988						
Ch. Antoc Moonstone	B	Cardwyn Merrywen	Ch. Antoc Cinnabar	Mrs A. Speding	Mrs A. Speding	21.3.85
Ch. Ringinglow Troyanna	B	Wendac Legend	Ringinglow Magpie	Miss M. Thomas	Miss M. Thomas	2.12.85
1989						
Ch. Gorthleck Blue Danube	D	Lees Black Heckle of Gorthleck	Bymil Bluebell of Gorthleck	Miss C. Macnelly	Mis C. Macnelly	1.12.86
Ch. Jezalin Crown Jewel	B	Am. Ch. Joseter Geefax	Jezalin Top Magic	Miss T. Maddox	Miss P. Walker	5.6.87
Ch. Joseter Benita	B	Joseter Bentinck	Ringinglow Valentine	Mrs & Miss Smart	Peter Clifton	21.4.84
Ch. Rhiwelli Martha of Kerman	B	Rhiwelli Blue Diamond	Rhiwelli Mountain Ash	Mrs Fricker	Miss M. Young	21.5.86

INDEX